R. R. Chope

The Congregational Hymn and Tune Book

R. R. Chope
The Congregational Hymn and Tune Book
ISBN/EAN: 9783337813208

Printed in Europe, USA, Canada, Australia, Japan

Cover: Foto ©Thomas Meinert / pixelio.de

More available books at **www.hansebooks.com**

The Congregational Hymn & Tune Book,

CONTAINING

THREE HUNDRED DIFFERENT FOUR-PART TUNES,

WITH

THEIR HYMNS, ANCIENT AND MODERN.

BY THE

REV. R. R. CHOPE, B.A.,

ASSISTED BY

REV. J. B. DYKES, M.A.,
Mus. Doc., Precentor of Durham Cathedral;

W. T. BEST, Esq.,
Organist of St. George's Hall, Liverpool;

G. COOPER, Esq.,
Organist of Her Majesty's Chapels Royal;

REV. R. F. SMITH, M.A.,
Southwell;

E. J. HOPKINS, Esq.,
Organist of the Temple Church, London;

DR. MONK,
Organist of York Cathedral;

J. TURLE, Esq.,
Organist of Westminster Abbey;

AND OTHERS.

LONDON:
WILLIAM MACKENZIE, 22 PATERNOSTER ROW;
SIMPKIN, MARSHALL, & CO., STATIONERS' HALL COURT.

[Entered at Stationers' Hall.]

PREFACE

TO THE

ENLARGED EDITION.

More than four years ago, this Work made its first appearance, introduced by no names of high patronage, explained by no Preface, and, except in two or three instances, mentioning no authorship of either the Hymns or Tunes. It was thought that a Book designed for such extensive use in Public Worship had better be distinguished as little as possible by individual peculiarities.

But notwithstanding the unprecedented success of the Work, and the Author's unchanged conviction, that it was more suitable to such a book to avoid as far as possible all parade of names, he has been induced to make public the obligations which he is under, to those who have helped his labour for the Church's sake. One reason which has weighed greatly with him has been the appearance of other Collections, under auspices which might seem of a semi-public kind; and it might appear unjust to the present undertaking to conceal the wide-spread sympathy which it commands throughout the Church. Some guarantee, too, might be due to the Clergy and Parishes by whom the "Congregational Hymn and Tune Book" has been adopted, that the scientific correctness of the music has been secured beyond all doubt; as well as an appropriate adaptation of tunes to words, of which all might not so easily judge for themselves. It is hoped, therefore, that the appearance of the present

"Enlarged Edition," in the form which it now assumes, is sufficiently justified.

To link the best tunes to the best words, that they may at length become almost suggestive of each other, has been one distinctive object before the Author's mind throughout. The structural arrangement of each page will show how unswervingly this has been aimed at; and if it has been secured, the Author cannot forget how much is owing to his gifted fellow-helpers for the rich variety of words and music generously placed at his disposal.

Special thanks are due to the Rev. J. R. Woodford, for permission kindly given to make his Selection of Hymns the basis of the first edition of the "Congregational Hymn and Tune Book;" to the Rev. John Keble for the use of his Hymns, which are beyond praise; to the Very Rev. Dean Milman, for his soul-stirring poetry; to the Revs. Canon Wordsworth, D.D., Isaac Williams, Dr. Neale, Dr. Faber, E. Caswall, Godfrey Thring, Canon Hutton, and W. Walsham How, for their original Hymns and Translations; to the Rev. Prebendary Irons, D.D., and the Rev. J. H. Butterworth, for much valuable help in Revision, as well as for their own original Hymns and Translations; to the Revs. John Baron, Canon Eaton, G. Hervey, E. Budge, Charles Walters, A. B. Hemsworth, C. T. Billings, and G. C. Campbell, for selecting Hymns; to the Earl Nelson, the Rev. R. T. Lowe, and other Authors of Hymn-books, for liberty to select from their Works; to the Right Rev. the Lord Bishop of Oxford, for very important suggestions; to the Right Rev. the Lord Bishop of Ely, for his sterling tunes—interesting also, as written by him after he had passed his eightieth year; to the Revs. W. H. Havergal, Canon of Worcester, Dr. Maurice, Charles Walker, Esq., and H. Lahee, Esq., for permission to make selections from their Tune-books; to the Rev. Sir Frederick A. Gore Ouseley, Bart., Professor of Music in the University of Oxford; to Dr. W. Sterndale Bennett, Professor of Music in the University of Cambridge; to John Hullah, Esq., (whose labours in the field of Church Music have borne so much fruit); to the Revs. W. Mercer, S. M. Barkworth, E. T. Billings, C. J. Taylor, C. T. Bowen, T. B. Hosken, T. G. Parry, Esq., Dr. G. J. Elvey, Dr. Gauntlett, S. Reay, Esq., R. Stuart, Esq., J. A. Lloyd, Esq., A. H. Brown, Esq., S. Gee, Esq., R.A.M., W. James, Esq., Organist of Kenn, A. R. Reinagle, Esq., E. B. Fripp, Esq., W. B. Gilbert, Esq., Mus. Bac., Oxon., T. Graham, Esq., R. B. Wall, Esq., W. Cummings, Esq., J. L. Summers, Esq., W. Horsley, Esq., and Mr. W. Meadows, for kindly contributing tunes. Acknowledgments must be made to Messrs. Longman, Green, & Co., for their permission to print Miss Winkworth's Hymn, 275; to Messrs. Burns & Lambert, for the tune set to Hymn 51; to Messrs. Novello & Co., for the music set to Hymn 181; to Messrs. Masters & Co., for Mr. Redhead's tunes; to Messrs. Cocks & Co., for the arrangement of Hymn 179; to Messrs. Cramer, Beale, & Chappell, for the tune called "Waterstock," by John Goss, Esq., Organist of St. Paul's Cathedral; and lastly, though by no means in a less degree, the Author desires warmly to thank his friends whose high names he has the privilege of adding to his Title-page. Specially he feels bound to say how deeply he is indebted to the Rev. R. F. Smith of Southwell, who was the earliest with him in this work —whose unwearying labours, indeed, began with the Author's first edition. Nor can the name of James Turle, Esq., Organist of Westminster Abbey be here omitted, who by the uniform exercise of his musical skill has helped to keep the work free from grammatical errors in harmony, &c., and has added his own contributions. The Organist, too, of the Temple Church, E. J. Hopkins, Esq., with no less heartiness and goodwill examined with the Author a large quantity of original manuscript and other tunes, and gave his own tunes and some other excellent specimens of harmony. And there is one to be remembered whose name and musical writings are indeed well known, though not *so* well as they deserve to be, as his tunes in the present work will abundantly prove—the Rev. J. B. Dykes, M.A., Mus. Doc., and Precentor of Durham Cathedral: it is impossible to value too much the assistance which he has rendered the Author in this Work. After him, through a tried friend, was secured the help of a sound musician of the highest school—Herbert S. Irons, Esq., Organist of Southwell Collegiate Church, many of whose gems of harmony will be found here and in the Author's "Prayer-Book Noted." And further, to Dr. Monk, Organist of York Cathedral; to W. T. Best, Esq., Organist of St. George's Hall, Liverpool; and to Geo. Cooper, Esq., Organist of Her Majesty's Chapels Royal, great thanks are due for their careful professional help, and music kindly written at the Author's request. Finally; If justice has been done to this combined effort of so many of the highest names in the Church of England, it will be seen at a glance how much is owing to the enterprise, munificence, and skill of the Publisher.

That GOD may bless this Work to the souls of His people, is the prayer of one who can truly say, as in His Sight, that nothing has been spared, to make both the Hymns and Tunes worthy of being sung by all Congregations to the Honour and Glory of His Holy Name!

PRIZE TUNES.—Of the 857 Competitive Tunes received by the Author, Prizes have been awarded for Numbers 118, 125, 150, and 156; and Extra Prizes for Numbers 103 and 154.

R. R. C.

BROMPTON, S.W.,
NOVEMBER, 1862.

HYMNS AND TUNES.

Advent.

7s (3 of.)   HYMN 1.   Adapted from FELTON.

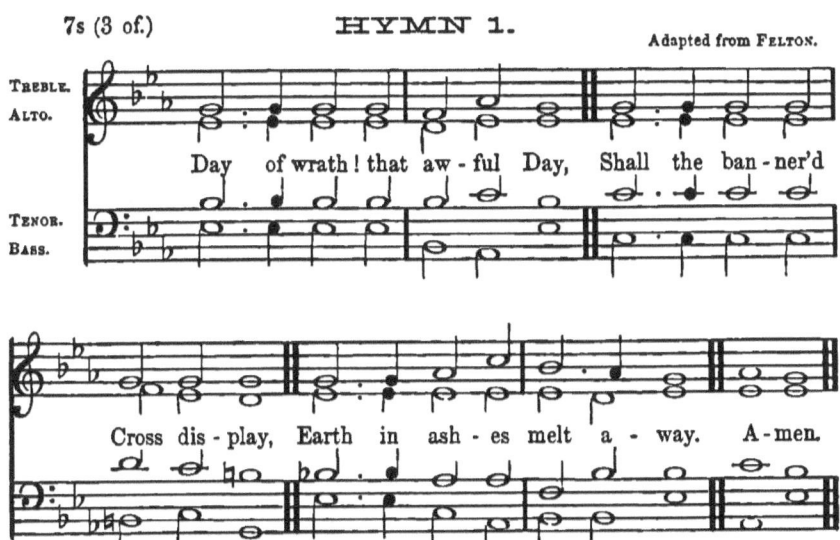

Day of wrath! that aw-ful Day, Shall the ban-ner'd Cross dis-play, Earth in ash-es melt a-way. A-men.

2 When the trumpet's thrilling tone,
Through the tombs of ages gone,
Summons all before the throne.

3 Death and time shall stand aghast,
And creation—at the blast,
Rise to answer for the past.

4 Then the volume shall be spread,
And the writing shall be read,
Which shall judge the quick and dead.

5 JUDGE of Justice! Thee I pray,
Wash Thou all my sins away,
Ere that awful reckoning Day.

6 Nought of Thee my prayers can claim,
Save in Thy free Mercy's name—
Shield me from the deathless flame.

7 KING of Dreadful Majesty,
Saving souls in mercy free,
FOUNT of Pity, save Thou me.

8 Weary seeking me wast Thou,
And for me in death didst bow,
Be Thy Toils availing now.

9 When the lost to silence driven,
To devouring flames are given,
Call me with the Blest to Heaven.

10 Day of sorrow—Day of fear,
When the risen dead draw near,
At the Judgment to appear.

Two last lines of music.

11 LORD, All-pitying JESU, Blest,
Grant us Thine Eternal Rest. Amen.

Advent

HYMN 2.

The Ad-vent of our GOD Our prayers must now em-ploy, And we must meet Him on His Road With hymns of so-lemn joy. A-men.

2 The Everlasting SON,
  A Virgin's offspring see,
A servant's form He putteth on,
  To make His people free.

3 Daughter of Sion, rise,
  And greet thy lowly KING;
Nor with unfaithful heart despise
  The mercies He will bring.

4 As JUDGE, in clouds of light
  He will come down again,
And all His scattered saints unite
  With Him in Heaven to reign.

5 Before that dreadful day,
  O, may our sins be gone!
May the "old man" be put away,
  And the "new man" put on!

6 Praise to the SAVIOUR SON,
  Who came to seek the lost;
And praise be to the FATHER done,
  And to the HOLY GHOST. Amen.

Advent.

HYMN 3.   8, 7s.   Winter. Arranged by H. S. Irons.

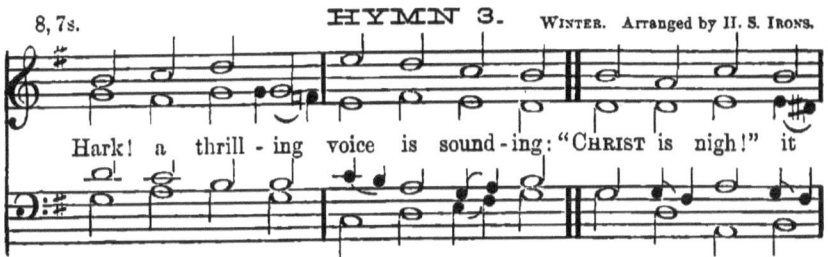
Hark! a thrill-ing voice is sound-ing: "Christ is nigh!" it

seems to say; "Cast a-way the works of dark-ness,

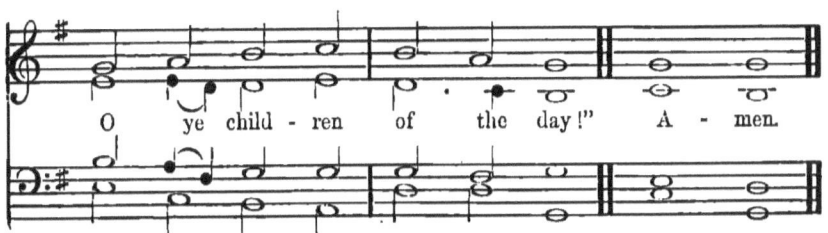
O ye child-ren of the day!" A-men.

2
Startled at the solemn warning,
  Let the earth-bound soul arise;
Christ, our Sun, all gloom dispelling,
  Shines upon the morning skies.

3
Lo! the Lamb, so long expected,
  Comes with pardon down from Heaven;
Let us haste, with tears of sorrow,
  One and all to be forgiven.

4
So when next He comes in glory,
  Wrapping all the earth in fear;
May He with His Mercy shield us;
  May He, to forgive, draw near!

5
Honour, glory, virtue, merit,
  To the Father and the Son,
With the Everlasting Spirit,
  While Eternal ages run.   Amen.

Advent.

2
In pity to our fallen race,
Thou in the fulness of Thy Grace
Didst bow the Heavens on high, and come,
Meek OFFSPRING of the Virgin's womb.

3
Majestic is Thy Glory now,
To Thee both Heaven and earth must bow;
Thee things terrestrial must own,
And things celestial, LORD, alone.

4
To Thee, O LORD, to Thee we pray,
Judge of the last tremendous Day;
Protect us through the unearthly fight,
With armour of celestial light.

5
To GOD the FATHER, GOD the SON,
And HOLY SPIRIT, THREE IN ONE,
All honour, might, and glory be,
Now and throughout Eternity.
                              Amen.

Advent.

HYMN 5.

O come, come Thou, Emman-u-el, Redeem Thy captive Israel,
Who mourns in lonely exile here, Until the Son of God appear.
Rejoice! Rejoice! Emman-u-el Shall come to thee, O Israel. Amen.

2
O come, Thou Rod of Jesse, free
Thine own from Satan's tyranny;
From depths of hell Thy people save,
And give them victory o'er the grave.
Rejoice! Rejoice! Emmanuel
Shall come to thee, O Israel!

3
O come, Thou Day-Spring, come and cheer
Our spirits by Thine Advent here;
Disperse the gloomy clouds of night,
And death's dark shadows put to flight.
Rejoice! Rejoice! Emmanuel
Shall come to thee, O Israel!

4
O come, Thou Key of David, come
And open wide our Heavenly Home;
Make plain the way that leads on high,
And close the path to misery.
Rejoice! Rejoice! Emmanuel
Shall come to thee, O Israel!

5
O come, come now, Thou Lord of Might,
Who to Thy tribes on Sinai's height,
In ancient time didst give the law
In cloud, and majesty, and awe.
Rejoice! Rejoice! Emmanuel
Shall come to thee, O Israel! Amen.

Advent.

HYMN 6.

C. M. — T. G. Parry.

Thou who didst leave Thy Father's Breast, Eternal Word Sublime! And cam'st to aid a world distressed In Thine appointed time. Amen.

2
Our hearts enlighten, Lord, we pray,
  And kindle with Thy Love;
That, dead to earthly things, we may
  Live but to things above.

3
So, when before the Judgement-seat
  The sinner hears his doom,
And when a voice, Divinely sweet,
  Shall call the righteous home;—

4
Safe from the burning, fiery flood,
  Safe from the dread abyss,
May we behold the Face of God,
  In Everlasting Bliss.

5
All glory to the Father be,
  All glory to the Son,
All glory Holy Ghost, to Thee,
  While Endless ages run. Amen.

Advent.

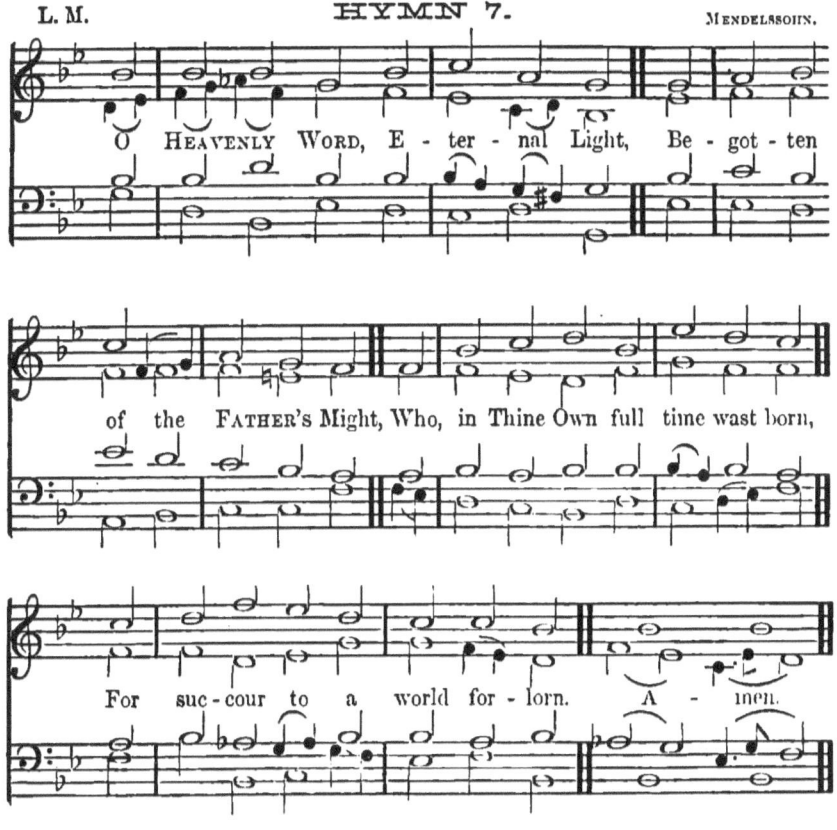

Hymn 7. L.M. Mendelssohn.

O Heavenly Word, Eternal Light, Begotten of the Father's Might, Who, in Thine Own full time wast born, For succour to a world forlorn. Amen.

2
Our saddened hearts, O Lord, illume,
Their ills with Thy true Love consume,
That we, who hear Thy Call to-day,
May cast earth's vanities away.

3
And when as Judge Thou drawest nigh,
The secrets of all hearts to try;
When sinners meet their awful doom,
And saints attain their Heavenly Home;

4
O let us not, for evil past,
Be driven from Thy Face at last;
But with the blessed Evermore
Behold and love Thee and adore.

5
To God the Father, God the Son,
And God the Spirit, Three in One,
Praise, honour, might, and glory be,
Now, and through all Eternity.   Amen.

Pre - pare, my soul, to meet Him. A - men.

2

The dead in CHRIST shall first arise
    At that last Trumpet's sounding;
Caught up to meet Him in the skies,
    With joy their LORD surrounding;
No gloomy fears their souls dismay;
His Presence sheds Eternal Day
    On those prepared to meet Him.

3

The ungodly, filled with guilty fears,
    Behold His Wrath prevailing;
In woe they rise, but all their tears
    And sighs are unavailing.
The Day of Grace is past and gone;
Trembling they stand before His Throne,
    All unprepared to meet Him.

4

GREAT JUDGE, to Thee our prayers we pour,
    In deep abasement bending;
O shield us through that last dread hour,
    Thy wondrous Love extending;
May we, in this our trial day,
With faithful hearts Thy Word obey,
    And thus prepare to meet Thee. Amen.

Advent.

HYMN 9.

8, 7s. From Meyerbeer.

2
With Truth your loins be girt around,
　Your lamps for ever burning;
That watching ye may still be found,
　Your Lord on earth returning.

3
For thus on souls that watch shall fall
　No sound from Heaven more cheering,
Than the Archangel's Trumpet-call,
　At Christ's last great Appearing.

4
Watch, then, ye Christians, watch and pray,
　Hear, how your Saviour pleaded;
Be watchful, Christians, while ye may;—
　In Heaven no watch is needed. Amen.

Advent.

HYMN 10.

The Lord will come! the earth shall quake, The hills their ancient seat forsake; And withering from the vault of night, The stars no more shall yield their light. Amen.

2
The Lord will come! but not the same
As once in lowly form He came;
A silent Lamb to slaughter led,
The Bruised, the Suffering, and the Dead.

3
The Lord will come! a dreadful Form,
Mid cloud and darkness, fire and storm!
On cherub wings, and wings of wind,
Anointed Judge of human-kind.

4
O King of Mercy, grant us power
To stand in that tremendous hour,
Before Thy Wrath when sinners flee,
Vouchsafe to gather us to Thee.

5
To Jesus, Lord of earth and Heaven,
Incarnate God, all praise be given,
To Father, Son, and Holy Ghost,
From men on earth, and Angel Host.
Amen.

Advent.

HYMN 11. — 8, 7, 8, 7, 4, 7. — J. B. Dykes.

Lo! He comes with clouds descending, Once for favoured sinners slain; Thousand thousand saints attending Swell the triumph of His Train: Alleluia! Christ appears on earth to reign. Amen.

2 Every eye shall now behold Him
   Robed in dreadful majesty;
 They who set at nought and sold Him,
   Pierced and nailed Him to the Tree,
     Deeply wailing,
   Shall the true Messiah see.

3 Those dear tokens of His Passion
   Still His dazzling Body bears;
 Cause of endless exultation
   To His ransomed worshippers;
     With what rapture
   Gaze we on those glorious scars.

4 Yea, Amen, let all adore Thee,
   High on Thine Eternal Throne;
 Saviour, take the power and glory;
   Claim the kingdom for Thine Own:
     O come quickly!
   Alleluia! Amen.   Amen.

Advent.

HYMN 12.

On Jordan's bank, the Baptist's cry
Announces that the Lord is nigh;
Come ye and hearken, for he brings
Glad tidings from the King of kings. Amen.

2
Now cleansed be every Christian breast,
And furnished for so great a Guest;
Yea, let us each our heart prepare
For Christ to come and enter there.

3
For Thou art our Salvation, Lord,
Our Refuge and our great Reward;
Without Thy Grace our souls must fade,
And wither like a flower decayed.

4
All praise and glory be to Thee,
Whose Advent set Thy people free!
Like praise be to the Father done,
And Holy Spirit, Three in One.
                  Amen.

Advent.

L. M.   HYMN 13.   H. MÜLLER, 1659.

When Christ the Lord would come on earth, His Messenger before Him went, The greatest born of mortal birth, On high prophetic mission bent. Amen.

2
Yet all that here in worship bend,
Have honour greater far than he;
He was the Bridegroom's joyful Friend,
His Body and His Spouse are we.

3
A higher race, the sons of light,
Of water and the Spirit born;
He the last star of parting night,
And we the children of the morn.

4
Boldly he spake the Heaven-taught word,
And joyed to hear the Bridegroom's Voice;
Thus may Thy Pastors teach, O Lord,
And thus Thy listening Church rejoice.

5
To Father, Son, and Holy Ghost,
The God Whom Heaven and earth adore,
Be glory from the Angel Host,
And all mankind for Evermore. Amen.

Advent.

HYMN 14.

L. M. — J. A. Lloyd.

When shades of night a-round us close, And wea-ry limbs in sleep re-pose, The faith-ful soul a-wake may be, And long-ing sigh, O Lord, to Thee. A-men.

2
Desire of Nations! Heavenly WORD!
The World's Salvation! Mighty LORD!
O hear our penitential cries,
And bid our fallen souls arise!

3
REDEEMER, come! and burst the chain
Which doth on earth Thy flock detain;
And, closed by Adam's crime of old,
To us the gates of Heaven unfold!

4
All praise, Eternal SON, to Thee,
Whose Advent doth Thy people free;
Whom, with the FATHER, we adore,
And HOLY GHOST, for Evermore. Amen.

Christmas Eve.

HYMN 15.

Angels, from the realms of glory, Wing your flight o'er all the earth, Ye who sang creation's story, Now proclaim Messiah's Birth: Come and worship! Worship Christ, the New-born King! Amen.

2 Shepherds, in the fields abiding,
   Watching o'er your flocks by night,
God with man is now residing,
   Yonder shines the Heavenly Light:
     Come and worship!
Worship Christ, the New-born King!

3 Saints, before the altar bending,
   Watching long in hope and fear:
Suddenly the Lord, descending,
   In His Temple shall appear.
     Come and worship!
Worship Christ, the New-born King!

4 Saints and Angels join in praising
   Thee, the Father, Spirit, Son,
Evermore their voices raising
   To the Eternal Three in One;
     Come and worship!
Worship Christ, the New-born King!
              Amen.

Christmas Eve.

8. 7s.   HYMN 16.   R. R. Chope.

Hark! what mean those ho-ly voic-es, Sweet-ly sound-ing

through the skies? Lo! th' An-gel-ic Host re-joic-es,

Heaven-ly Al-le-lu-ias rise. A-men.

2

"Glory in the Highest, glory,"
  Thus they chant their joyful strain;
"Glory in the Highest, glory,
  Peace on earth, good-will to men."

3

With their blessed Alleluias,
  Hear what wondrous things they tell,
How lost man has now a SAVIOUR,
  Born to conquer death and hell.

4

Born Thy people to deliver,
  JESU! from the death of sin;
Born to make us Thine for ever,—
  Still abide our souls within!

5

SON of GOD! Most Holy JESU!
  Endless glory be to Thee;
To the FATHER and the SPIRIT,
  Now and through Eternity.   Amen.

2

Very GOD of Very GOD,
LIGHT of LIGHT Eternal;
The Virgin's womb He hath not abhorred;
True GOD Everlasting,
Not made but Begotten.
O come let us adore Him!
O come let us adore Him!
O come let us adore Him, CHRIST, the LORD.

3

Sing, Chorus of Angels,
Sing, in exultation,
Thro' Heaven's wide Court be your praises poured,
To GOD in the Highest,
Be honour and glory;
O come let us adore Him!
O come let us adore Him!
O come let us worship our GOD and LORD.

4

Yea, LORD, we greet Thee,
Born this happy morning!
For ever, O CHRIST, be Thy Name adored,
True WORD of the FATHER,
Late in flesh appearing.
O come let us adore Him!
O come let us adore Him!
O come let us worship our GOD and LORD.   Amen.

Christmas.

HYMN 18.

Hark! the Herald Angels sing Glo-ry to the New-born KING. A - men.

2

CHRIST, by highest Heaven adored,
CHRIST, the Everlasting LORD,
Late in time behold Him come,
Offspring of a Virgin's womb.
Veiled in flesh the GODHEAD see;
Hail, the Incarnate DEITY!
Pleased as MAN with man to dwell,
JESUS, our EMMANUEL.
Hark! the Herald Angels sing
Glory to the New-born KING.

3

Hail, the Heaven-born PRINCE of Peace,
Hail, the SUN of Righteousness!
Light and life to all He brings,
Risen with healing in His Wings.
Now He lays His Glory by,
Born that man no more may die,
Born to raise the sons of earth,
Born to give them Second Birth.
Hark! the Herald Angels sing
Glory to the New-born KING. Amen.

Christmas.

HYMN 19.

C. M. T. Tallis. Died 1585.

While shepherds watched their flocks by night, All seat-ed on the ground, The An-gel of the Lord came down, And glo-ry shone a-round. A-men.

2
"Fear not," said he, (for mighty dread
    Had seized their troubled mind ;)
"Glad tidings of great joy I bring
    To you and all mankind.

3
"To you in David's town this day
    Is born, of David's line,
The Saviour, Who is Christ the Lord,
    And this shall be the sign :

4
"The Heavenly Babe you there shall find
    To human view displayed,
All meanly wrapped in swathing bands
    And in a manger laid."

5
Thus spake the Seraph, and forthwith
    Appeared a shining throng
Of Angels, praising God, and thus
    Addressed their joyful song :

6
"All glory be to God on High,
    And to the earth be peace ;
Good-will, henceforth, from Heaven to men,
    Begin and never cease." Amen.

Christmas.

HYMN 20.

God from on High hath heard, Let sighs and sorrows cease;
The skies unfold, and lo! Descends the gift of Peace.
Hark! on the midnight air Celestial voices swell;
The Hosts of Heaven proclaim, "God comes on earth to dwell." A-men.

2 Haste with the shepherds; see
The Mystery of Grace.
A manger bed—a Child,
Is all the eye can trace.
Is this the Eternal Son,
Who on the starry Throne,
Before the worlds began,
Ruled glorious and alone?

3 Yea, faith can pierce the cloud
Which shrouds His Glory now;
And hails Him Lord and God,
To Whom the Angels bow.
To God the Father, Son,
And Spirit, glory be;
Of Virgin-mother born,
All glory, Christ, to Thee! Amen.

Christmas.

HYMN 21.

L. M.   J. B. Dykes.

Je-su! Re-deem-er of the world! Who in the earliest dawn of light Wast from E-ter-nal a-ges born, Co-e-qual with the Father's Might. A-men.

2
Immortal Hope of all mankind!
In Whom the Father's Face we see,
Hear Thou the prayers Thy people pour
This day throughout the world to Thee.

3
Remember, O Creator Lord!
That in the Virgin's sacred womb
Thou wast conceived, and of her flesh
Our very nature didst assume.

4
This Ever-blest recurring Day
One precious truth to all makes known,—
"Christ from the Father's Throne came down,
Christ came to save us, Christ alone."

5
O Day! to which the seas and sky,
And earth and Heaven, glad welcome sing,
O Day! which healed our misery,
And brought on earth salvation's King.

6
We too, O Lord, who have been cleansed
In Thine Own Fount of Blood Divine,
Offer the tribute of sweet song
On this blest Natal-day of Thine.

7
O Jesu! Virgin-born, to Thee
Eternal praise and glory be;
Praise to the Father Infinite,
And Holy Ghost Eternally. Amen.

Christmas.

High let us swell our tuneful notes, And join the Angelic Throng, For Angels no such love have known, To raise a cheerful song. Amen.

2
Good-will to sinful men is shown,
And peace on earth is given,
For lo! the Incarnate SAVIOUR comes
With messages from Heaven.

3
Justice and grace, with sweet accord,
His rising Beams adorn;
Let Heaven and earth in concert join,
To us a CHILD is born.

4
Glory to GOD in highest strains,
In highest worlds be given;
His Will by us on earth be done,
As it is done in Heaven.   Amen.

2

Then to the watchful shepherds it was told,
Who heard the Angelic Herald's voice, "Behold,
I bring good tidings of a SAVIOUR's Birth
To you and all the nations of the earth:
This day hath GOD fulfilled His promised Word,
This day is born a SAVIOUR, CHRIST the LORD."

3

He spake; and straightway the Celestial Choir
In hymns of joy, unknown before, conspire;
The praises of redeeming love they sang,
And Heaven's whole orb with Alleluias rang:
GOD's highest Glory was their anthem still,
Peace upon earth, and unto men good-will.

4

To Bethlehem straight the enlightened shepherds run,
To see the wonders GOD had wrought for man;
Then to their flocks, still praising GOD, return,
And their glad hearts with holy rapture burn:
To all the joyful tidings they proclaim,
The first apostles of the SAVIOUR's Name.

5

Oh! may we keep and ponder in our mind
GOD's wondrous Love in saving lost mankind;
Trace we the BABE, Who hath retrieved our loss,
From the poor manger to the bitter Cross;
Tread in His Steps, assisted by His Grace,
Till man's first Heavenly state again takes place.

6

Then may we hope, the Angelic Hosts among,
To join, redeemed, a glad triumphant Throng:
He that was born upon this joyful day
Around us all His Glory shall display:
Saved by His Love, incessant we shall sing
Eternal praise to Heaven's ALMIGHTY KING. Amen.

Christmas.

O Saviour of the world forlorn! This Day to save us Thou wast born; Protect us thro' the coming night, And ever save us by Thy Might. Amen.

2 Thy Gracious Presence now bestow
  To guard us safely here below;
  Thy Mercy to our prayers accord,
  And lighten Thou our darkness, Lord!

3 O let not sleep the soul oppress,
  Nor secret foe the heart possess;
  Our flesh keep chaste, that it may be
  A holy temple unto Thee.

4 Restorer of our every sense!
  Blot out, we pray, our past offence!
  That pure and free from inward stain
  We from our beds may rise again.

5 All praise to God the Father be,
  All praise, Eternal Son, to Thee,
  Whom with the Spirit we adore
  For ever and for Evermore. Amen.

Christmas.

HYMN 25.

C. M.   From Dr. Tye, by S. Reay.

O Saviour! Whom this ho-ly morn Gave to our

world be-low; To mor-tal want and la-bour born,

And more than mor-tal woe! A-men.

2

Incarnate Word! by every grief,
  By each temptation tried,
Who lived to yield our ills relief,
  And to redeem us died!

3

If gaily clothed, and proudly fed,
  In dangerous wealth we dwell,
Remind us of Thy Manger-bed,
  And lowly Cottage-cell!

4

If pressed by poverty severe,
  In envious want we pine,
Oh! may Thy Spirit whisper near,—
  How poor a lot was Thine!

5

Through fickle fortune's various scene
  From sin preserve us free;
Like us Thou hast a Mourner been,
  May we rejoice with Thee!   Amen.

S. Stephen.

HYMN 26.

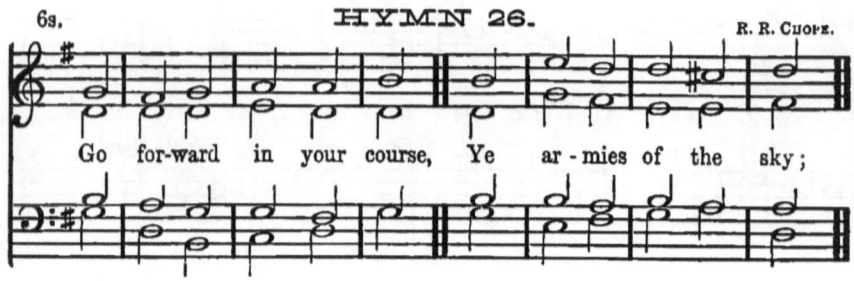

Go forward in your course, Ye armies of the sky;
Because the LORD your GOD Doth lead to victory. Amen.

2
The first who dared to die
Had blessed visions given;—
The Glory on him shone
Down from the open Heaven.

3
Look up into the skies,
Ye children of the day;
The shining of that Light
Shall never pass away.

4
Your bitter foes in vain
Their storms of malice shower,
Behold your Captain stand
At GOD's Right Hand in power.

5
Each scattering of the Church
The Word of GOD doth sow;
For every rending stroke
The holy plant doth grow.

6
Lift up the voice of prayer
Before your cruel foes;
And soon the fiercest ranks
Fresh martyrs shall disclose.

7
To GOD the FATHER, SON,
And SPIRIT, ever be
All laud and glory given
Now and Eternally.   Amen.

S. Stephen.

O God, Thy soldiers' Crown and Guard, And their exceeding great Reward! From fears and weakness set us free, Who sing Thy Martyr's victory. A-men.

2
The first to tread the appointed road
Across the deep Red Sea of blood,
He dared by death his LORD to own,
Partaker of His thorny Crown.—

3
On this Thy Martyr's triumph day,
To Thee, O KING of Saints, we pray;
Uphold us in our ghostly fight,
And shield us with Thine arm of Might.

4
Teach us from every snare to turn,
The pleasures of the world to spurn,
And for the glory of Thy Name,
With Thee to bear the Cross and shame.

5
To GOD the FATHER, GOD the SON,
And HOLY SPIRIT, THREE IN ONE,
Unceasing praise and glory be,
Now and through all Eternity.   Amen.

S. John the Evangelist.

HYMN 28.

C. M.   J. A. Lloyd.

The Life which God's Incarnate Word Lived here below with men, Three blest Evangelists record With Heaven-inspired pen. Amen.

2
John soars on eagle wing to see
　The Father's dread Abode;
And learns the awful mystery
　The Word is Very God.

3
Upon the Saviour's loving Breast
　Invited to recline,
'Twas thence he drew, in moments blest,
　Rich stores of Truth Divine.

4
There, too, with that Angelic love
　Did he his bosom fill,
Which, once enkindled from above,
　Breathes in his pages still.

5
Jesu, the Virgin's Holy Son,
　We praise Thee and adore,
Who art with God the Father One
　And Spirit Evermore. Amen.

S. John the Evangelist.

HYMN 29. C. M. W. Jones, 1799.

The loved dis-ci-ple of the Lord, To wea-ry ex-ile driven, Caught by the Spi-rit up-ward soared From earth to high-est Heaven. A-men.

2
He That was dead, and is alive,
   Then cheered his eyes again;
The Lion, strong with death to strive,
   The Lamb, for sinners slain.

3
O grant us, Lord, with Thee to die,
   With Thee from death to rise;
With Thee from this vain world to fly,
   To meet Thee in the skies.

4
Now unto Him Who vanquished death,
   Who showed the way to Heaven,
From Heaven above and earth beneath,
   Be Endless praises given. Amen.

S. John the Evangelist.

L. M. HYMN 30. H. Lawes, 1662.

O Thou! Who gav'st Thy serv-ant grace, On Thee, the Liv-ing Rock, to rest; To look on Thine In-car-nate Face, And lean on Thy pro-tect-ing Breast. A-men.

2
Grant us, O KING of Mercy, still
To feel Thy Presence from above,
And in Thy Word and in Thy Will
To hear Thy Voice, and know Thy Love;

3
And when the toils of life are done,
And earthly cares shall ended be,
To find our rest beneath Thy Throne.
And look in certain hope to Thee.

4
To Thee, O JESU, LIGHT of LIGHT,
Whom, as their KING, Thy Saints adore,
Their Strength and Refuge in the fight,
Be laud and glory Evermore.   Amen.

Holy Innocents.

2
A voice from Ramah was there sent,
A voice of weeping and lament,
When Rachel mourned her children sore,
Whom for the tyrant's sword she bore;
Triumphant is their glory now,
The first for CHRIST in death to bow.

3
Dwelling on Sion's holy hill,
The LAMB's Own Steps they follow still;
Death hath no power to hurt them more,
The hour of pain and grief is o'er;
All bright they shine in Heavenly day,
And every tear is wiped away.   Amen.

Holy Innocents.

HYMN 32. S. M. German.

Glo-ry to Thee, O Lord! Who from this world of sin, By cru-el Her-od's ruth-less sword Those pre-cious ones didst win! A-men.

2 Baptized in their own blood,—
Earth's untried perils o'er,
They passed unconsciously the flood,
And safely gained the shore.

3 Glory to Thee! for all
The ransomed infant band,
Who since that hour have heard Thy Call,
And reached the quiet land!

4 Oh! that our hearts within,
Like theirs, were pure and bright;
Oh! that as free from deeds of sin
We shrank not from Thy Sight.

5 Lord, help us every hour
Thy cleansing Grace to claim;
In life to glorify Thy Power,
In death to praise Thy Name.

6 To God the Father, Son,
And Spirit glory be;
Now whilst the years of time shall run,
And through Eternity.   Amen.

New Years' Eve.

2

In our weakness and distress,
  Rock of Strength! be thou our Stay;
In the pathless wilderness
  Be our true and living Way.

3

Who of us death's awful road
  In the coming year shall tread?
With Thy Rod and Staff, O God,
  Comfort Thou his dying bed.

4

Make us faithful, make us pure;
  Keep us Evermore Thine Own;
Help, O help us to endure;
  Fit us for the promised crown.

5

So within Thy Palace-gate,
  We shall praise, on golden strings,
Thee, the only Potentate,
  Lord of lords and King of kings.
              Amen.

New Year's Day.

Hymn 34. — P. M. — J. B. Dykes.

Days and moments quickly fly-ing Blend the liv-ing with the dead. Soon will you and I be ly-ing Each with-in our nar-row bed.

2
Soon our souls to God Who gave them,
　Swiftly will have sped away;
Able now by grace to save them—
　O, that while we can we may.

3
Jesu, Infinite Redeemer,
　Maker of this mighty frame,
Teach, O teach us to remember
　What we are and whence we came.

4
Whence we came and whither wending,
　Soon we must through darkness go,
To inherit Bliss Unending,
　Or Eternity of woe.

Circumcision.

HYMN 35. C.M. — Ravenscroft's Psalter, 1621.

Shadows are fled, a brighter ray
Dawns with the opening year;
The Law of Moses fades away,
Love reigns instead of fear. Amen.

2
The Son has left His Father's Throne,
  Our pain and grief to share;
In human form the Sinless One
  The shame of sin will bear.

3
For us to cancel every claim
  This day the Lord began;
Freely a Debtor He became
  To the whole Law for man.

4
This day that Name He first did own,
  At which the world should bow;
This day His Name in deed was shown,
  Jesus, true Saviour, now.

5
To Him Whose Precious Blood was shed
  That guilty man might live,—
To our Redeemer, and our Head,
  Blessing and praise we give. Amen.

Circumcision.

HYMN 36. S. M. MENDELSSOHN, 1847.

The year be-gins with Thee, And Thou be-ginn'st with woe, To let the world of sin-ners see That Blood for sin must flow. A - - men.

2
Oh! are we born to tears,
  Cradled in grief and care?
And seems it hard, our tender years
  Few joys unmixed may share?

3
Look here and hold thy peace!
  The GIVER of all good
E'en from the womb takes no release
  From sorrow, tears, and blood.

4
If thou would'st reap in love,
  First sow in holy fear;
So life a winter's morn may prove
  To a bright Endless year.

5
Praise to the SAVIOUR SON
  Who came to seek the lost;
Like praise be to the FATHER done,
  And to the HOLY GHOST. Amen.

Circumcision.

Hymn 37.

L. M. — Dr. Howard, 1782.

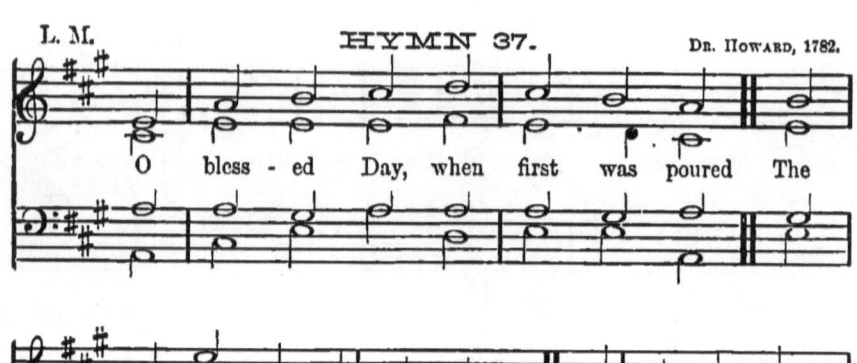

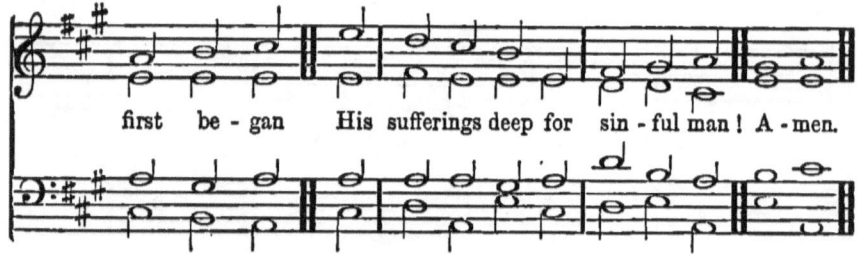

O bless-ed Day, when first was poured The Blood of our Re-deem-ing Lord! O bless-ed Day, when first be-gan His sufferings deep for sin-ful man! A-men.

2

Scarce entered on this world of woe,
His Infant Blood begins to flow:
Thus early was His Love confessed,
His mighty Sacrifice expressed.

3

From Heaven descending to fulfil
The mandate of His Father's Will,
E'en now behold the Victim lie,
The Lamb of God, ere long to die.

4

Lord, circumcise our hearts, we pray,
And take what is not Thine away;
Thy Name, Thy Likeness may they bear!
Yea, stamp Thy Holy Image there.

5

O Lord, the Virgin-born, to Thee
Eternal praise and glory be;
Whom with the Father we adore
And Holy Ghost for Evermore.   Amen.

Circumcision.

HYMN 38.

2
Crown Him, ye morning stars of light,
   Who fixed this fleeting ball;
Now hail the STRENGTH of Israel's might,
   And crown Him LORD of all.

3
Crown Him, ye Martyrs of our GOD,
   Who from His Altar call;
Extol the STEM of Jesse's Rod,
   And crown Him LORD of all.

4
Ye chosen seed of Israel's race,
   Ye ransomed from the fall,
Hail Him, Who saves you by His Grace,
   And crown Him LORD of all.

5
Ye Gentile sinners, ne'er forget
   The wormwood and the gall;
Go spread your trophies at His Feet,
   And crown Him LORD of all.

6
Thou, Who dost with the SPIRIT live,
   Thy ransomed children call!
Thy Kingdom to the FATHER give,
   And GOD be ALL IN ALL!   Amen.

Epiphany.

HYMN 39.

10, 10, 10, 4. J. B. Dykes.

"From Heaven to earth glad tídings I unfold," The Angel cries, "The Sáviour Christ is born In Bethlehem Judah, ás the Seers foretold, This hallowed Morn." Amen.

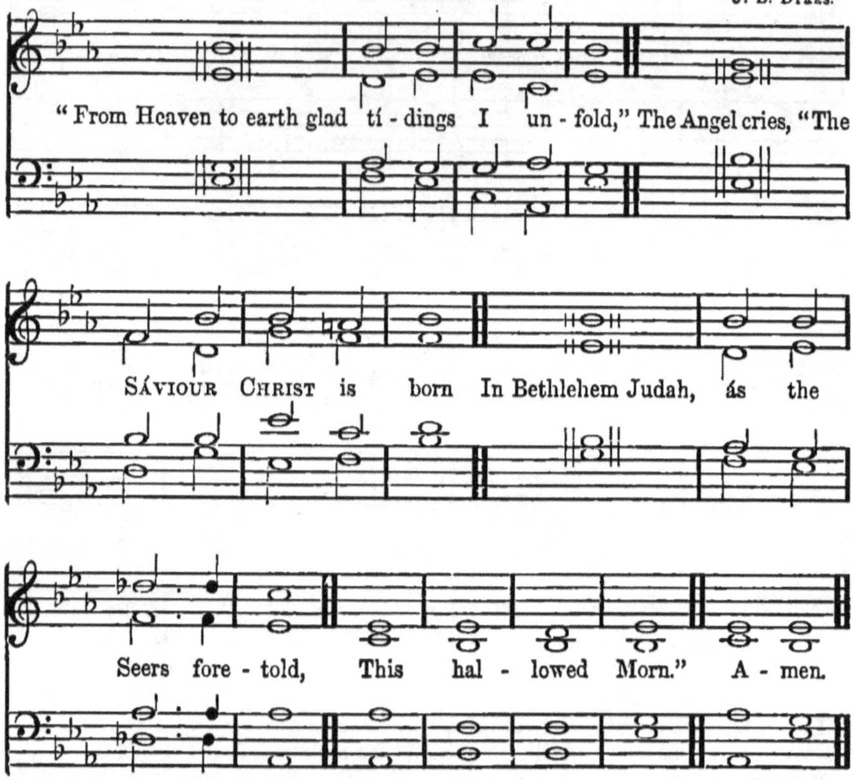

2
His Birth the joyful Chóir of Angels sing;
The Star reveals His Hóme, where Princes greet
The New-born Babe, and gifts adoring bring,
    Oblations meet;—

3
Incense to God, and Mýrrh to grace His Tomb,
For tribute to their Kíng, a golden store;
One God they hail; three with three offerings come,
    And Three adore!

4
All glory to the Óne yet Triune Lord,
To God and to His Róyal Offspring be;
Praise to the Spirit bé by all outpoured
    Eternally.   Amen.

Epiphany.

HYMN 40.

L. M.
Ancient Proper Melody.
Arranged by J. B. D.

In vain doth Herod rage and fear, When told Judea's King is near. He takes not earthly crowns away, Who gives the crowns that ne'er decay. A-men.

2
Led onward by the guiding Star,
The Wise Men seek Him from afar;
Called by its light, to LIGHT they pressed,
And, by their gifts, their GOD confessed.

3
The opening Heavens their witness gave,
When He, baptized in Jordan's wave,
Hallowed the water, by His Grace
To cleanse from sin the human race.

4
Their GOD the blushing waters own,
By mighty sign and wonder known,
When the pure stream, poured forth in wine,
Obeyed His Power and Will Divine.

5
Now unto Him, the Incarnate SON,
Whose GODHEAD to the world was shown,
With GOD the FATHER glory be,
And HOLY GHOST Eternally. Amen.

Epiphany.

Hymn 41. — S. M. Barkworth. 8, 7s.

Bethlehem! earth's noblest cities
May not with thy name compare;
Thou alone the Lord from Heaven
Didst for us Incarnate bear. Amen.

2

Fairer than the sun at morning
   Was the Star that told His Birth;
To the lands their God announcing,
   Hid beneath a form of earth.

3

By its radiant beauty guided,
   See the Eastern kings appear,
See them bend, their gifts to offer,
   Gifts of incense, gold, and myrrh,

4

Offerings of mystic meaning!
   Incense doth the God disclose,
Gold His Kingly State proclaimeth,
   Myrrh the future Tomb foreshows.

5

Holy Jesu! in Thy Brightness
   To the Gentile world displayed,
With the Father and the Spirit,
   Endless praise to Thee be paid. Amen.

Epiphany.

HYMN 42. — L.M. — W. H. HAVERGAL.

Praise GOD, Who sent His guid-ing Star To shed its hope-ful beams a-far; As once His fie-ry Pil-lar's ray Led Is-rael on their toil-some way. A-men.

2
Where all in Gentile darkness lay,
The Eastern Princes tracked its ray;
And while in faith they journeyed on,
O'er Bethlehem's lowly walls it shone.

3
First-fruits of all the Gentile race,
They sought the SAVIOUR's Resting-place;
And worshipped with their costly store
Their New-born LORD, unknown before.

4
O may we too, with offerings meet,
Be found at our REDEEMER's Feet;
With richer gifts than those of old,
Of incense rare and shining gold.

5
All glory, JESU, be to Thee,
For this Thy glad Epiphany:
Whom, with the FATHER, we adore,
And HOLY GHOST for Evermore. Amen.

Epiphany.

HYMN 43.

6, 6, 6, 6, 8, 8.   R. R. Chope.

A-rise, O Lord, and shine, In all Thy sav-ing Might, And pros-per each de-sign To spread Thy glo-rious Light: Let heal-ing streams of mer-cy flow, That all on earth Thy Truth may know. A-men.

2
O bring the nations near,
  That they may sing Thy Praise;
Let all the people hear,
  And learn Thy holy Ways.
Reign, mighty God, assert Thy Cause,
And govern by Thy righteous Laws.

3
Put forth Thy glorious Power!
  The nations then shall see,
And earth present her store
  Of Christians born to Thee:
God, our own God, His Church shall bless,
And earth be filled with righteousness.

4
To God the Father, Son,
  And Spirit Ever Blest,
Eternal Three in One,
  All worship be addrest:
Join, all on earth, rejoice and sing;
All glory give to God our King. Amen.

Epiphany.

HYMN 44.

Bright was the guiding Star that led, With mild benignant ray, The Gentiles to the lowly shed, Where the Redeemer lay. Amen.

2
But, oh! a brighter, clearer light,
　Now points to His Abode;
It shines through sin and sorrow's night,
　To guide us to our God.

3
Then haste to follow where it leads;
　Its gracious call obey!
Be rugged wilds, or flowery meads,
　The Christian's destined way.

4
O gladly tread the narrow path!
　While light and grace are given:
Who meekly follow Christ on earth,
　Shall reign with Him in Heaven.
　　　　　　　　　Amen.

2
Though by a Star Thou dost not lead
　Thy servants now below;
Yet Thy Good Spirit, when they need,
　The path of life will show.

3
O grant us then Thy Light and Grace,
　To make us pure in heart;
That we may see Thee face to Face
　Hereafter as Thou art.

4
To God the Father, God the Son,
　And God the Holy Ghost,
By men on earth all praise be done,
　And by the Heavenly Host.　Amen.

Epiphany.

HYMN 46.

C. M.   R. R. Chope.

In stature grows the Heavenly CHILD, With death before His Eyes, A LAMB unblemished meek, and mild, Prepared for sacrifice. A-men.

2
The SON of GOD His Glory hides
  With parents mean and poor,
And He, Who made the Heavens, abides
  In dwelling-place obscure.

3
Those mighty Hands that rule the sky
  No earthly toil refuse.
And He Who set the stars on High
  A lowly path pursues.

4
He Whom the Choirs of Angels praise,
  Bearing each dread decree,
On earth His Parents' will obeys
  In deep humility.

5
For this Thy Lowliness revealed,
  JESU, we Thee adore ;
And praise to GOD the FATHER yield,
  And SPIRIT, Evermore.   Amen.

Epiphany.

HYMN 47.

7s (6 of.)
O. Gibbons, 1623.
Adapted by R. R. C.

God of Mer-cy, God of Grace, Show the brightness of Thy Face;

Shine up-on us, Saviour, shine, Fill Thy Church with Light Divine;

And Thy sav-ing Health ex-tend Un-to earth's re-mot-est end. A-men.

2
Let the people praise Thee, Lord;
Let Thy Love on all be poured;
Let the nations shout and sing
Glory to their Saviour King;
At Thy Feet their tribute pay,
And Thy holy Will obey.

3
Let the people praise Thee, Lord;
Earth shall then her fruits afford;
God to man His Blessing give,
Man to God devoted live;
All below, and all above,
One in joy, and light, and love.　Amen.

Epiphany.

HYMN 48.

7s (6 of.)   Arranged by W. H. Havergal.

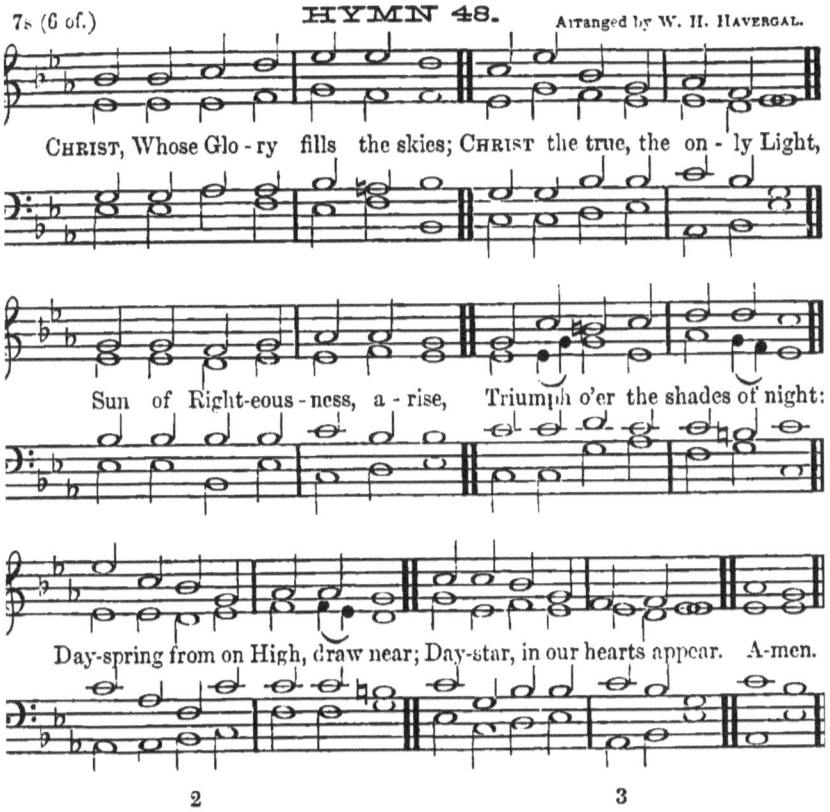

Christ, Whose Glo-ry fills the skies; Christ the true, the on-ly Light,
Sun of Right-eous-ness, a-rise, Triumph o'er the shades of night:
Day-spring from on High, draw near; Day-star, in our hearts appear. A-men.

2
Dark and cheerless is the morn,
Lord, if it be reft of Thee;
Joyless is the day's return,
Till Thy Mercy's Beams we see,
Till they pour their gladdening light
Through the darkness of our night.

3
Visit then these souls of Thine,
Pierce the gloom of sin and grief;
Fill us Lord, with Light Divine;
Scatter all our unbelief;
More and more Thyself display,
Shining to the perfect Day.

4
Father, glory be to Thee,
Glory to the Blessed Son,
Glory to the Spirit be,
Glory to the Three in One;
As it was, is now, shall be,
Filling all Eternity.   Amen.

Epiphany.

HYMN 49.

7s.   T. Graham.

Sons of men, be-hold from far, Hail the long ex-pect-ed Star! Ja-cob's Star that gilds the night Guides be-wil-dered na-ture right. A-men.

2 Mild it shines on all beneath,
   Piercing through the shades of death,
   Scattering error's wide-spread night,
   Kindling darkness into light.

3 Nations all, afar and near,
   Haste to see your God appear!
   Haste, for Him your hearts prepare,
   Meet Him manifested there!—

4 There behold the Day-spring rise,
   Pouring brightness on our eyes,
   God in His Own Light survey,
   Shining to the perfect Day!

5 Sing, ye morning stars, again!
   God descends on earth to reign!
   Deigns for man His Life to give,
   Shout, ye sons of men, and live! Amen.

Epiphany.

HYMN 50.

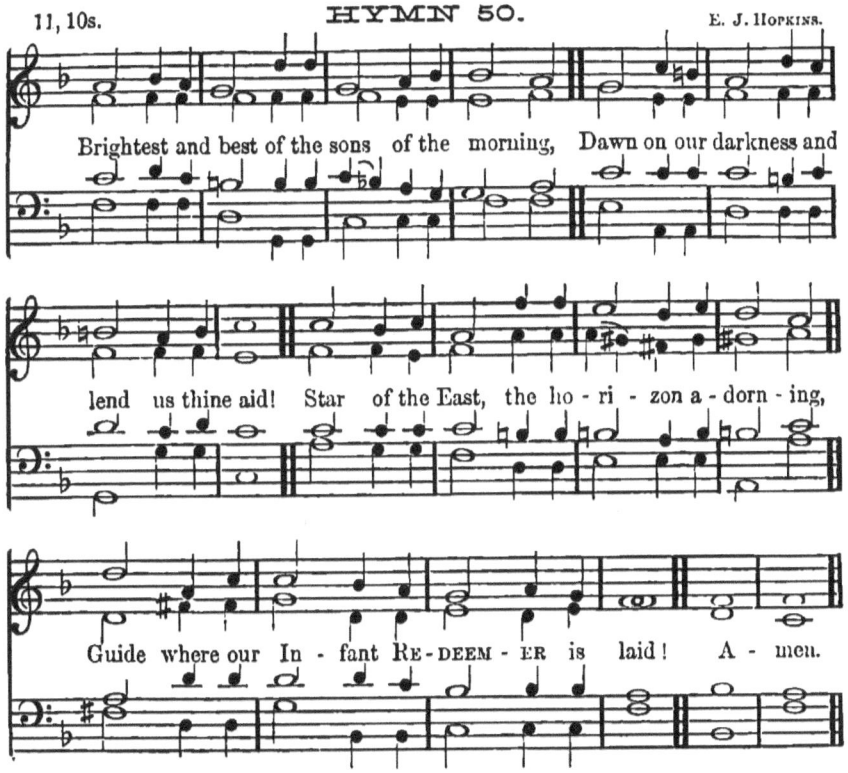

Brightest and best of the sons of the morning, Dawn on our darkness and lend us thine aid! Star of the East, the ho-ri-zon a-dorn-ing, Guide where our In-fant Re-deem-er is laid! A-men.

2
Cold on His Cradle the dew-drops are shining,
   Low lies His Head with the beast of the stall;
Angels adore Him in slumber reclining,
   Maker, and Monarch, and Saviour of all!

3
Say, shall we yield Him, in costly devotion,
   Odours of Edom and offerings Divine;
Gems of the mountain and pearls of the ocean,
   Myrrh from the forests and gold from the mine?

4
Vainly we offer each ample oblation,
   Vainly with gifts would His Favour secure;
Richer by far is the heart's adoration,
   Dearer to God are the prayers of the poor. Amen.

Epiphany.

HYMN 51. C. M. By permission of Messrs. Burns & Co.

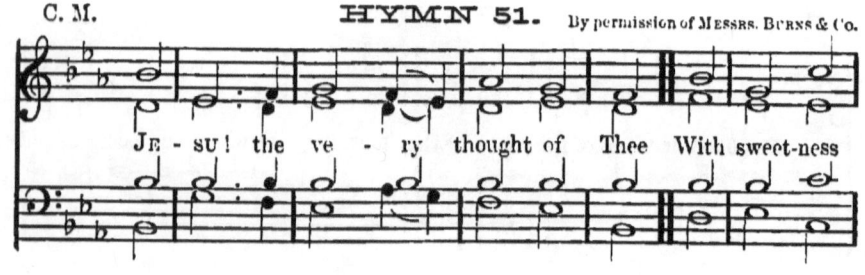
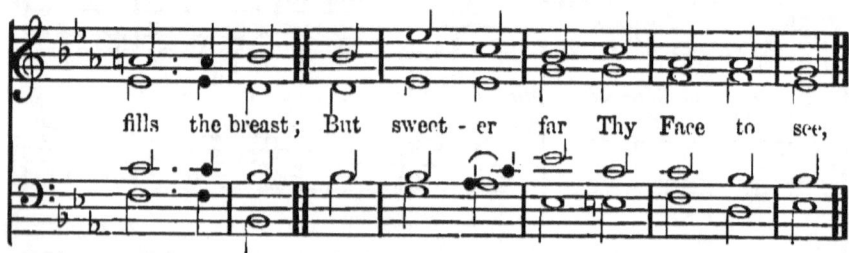

Jesu! the very thought of Thee
With sweetness fills the breast;
But sweeter far Thy Face to see,
And in Thy Presence rest. Amen.

2 No voice can sing, no heart can frame,
   Nor can the memory find
  A sweeter sound than Thy Blest Name,
   O Saviour of mankind!

3 O Hope of every contrite heart!
   O Joy of all the meek!
  To those who fall, how kind Thou art!
   How good to those who seek!

4 But what to those who find? ah! this
   Nor tongue nor pen can show;
The Love of Jesus, what it is,
   None but His loved ones know.

5 O Jesu, Light of all below!
   Thou Fount of life and fire!
Surpassing all the joys we know,
   And all we can desire!

6 Jesu, our only Joy be Thou,
   As Thou our Prize wilt be;
Jesu, be Thou our Glory now,
   Our Hope and Victory. Amen.

Part II.

1

O Thou, in Whom our love doth find
  Its rest and perfect end ;
O Jesu, Saviour of mankind,
  And their Eternal Friend!

2

Stay with us, Lord ; and with Thy Light
  Illume the soul's abyss ;
Scatter the darkness of our night,
  And fill the world with bliss.

3

May every soul Thy Love return,
  And strive to do Thy Will ;
And, keeping Thy Commandments, learn
  To love Thee better still!

4

Grant us, while here on earth we stay,
  Thy Love to feel and know ;
And when from hence we pass away,
  To us Thy Glory show.

5

And, O our Jesu, pardon us!
  Unfit to speak Thy Praise ;
Who, loving Thee, are daring thus
  Our trembling hymn to raise.   Amen.

Part III.

1

O Jesu, Lord, hear Thou the sighs
  Which unto Thee we send ;
To Thee our inmost spirit cries,
  Our being's Hope and End!

2

Come, O Thou King of boundless Might,
  Come Majesty adored !
Come and illume us with Thy Light,
  Our long-expected Lord !

3

Thy Presence with us we desire,
  Wherever we may be ;
This, Lord, is all that we require
  For our felicity.

4

Hark ! how the Heavens with praise o'er-
  O priceless gift of Blood !   [flow ;
Jesus makes glad the world below,
  And gains us peace with God.

5

To Him praise, glory without end,
  And adoration be ;
O Jesu, grant us to ascend,
  And reign in Heaven with Thee! Amen.

The Week before Septuagesima.

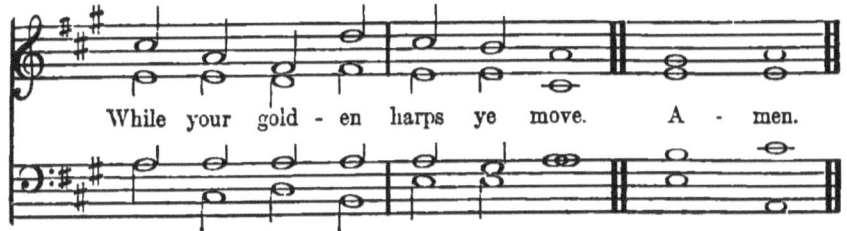

2

Alleluia! Church victorious
  Join the concert of the sky!
Alleluia! bright and glorious
  Lift, ye Saints, this strain on High!
We, poor exiles,—we, poor exiles,
  Join not yet your melody.

3

Alleluia! strains of gladness
  Suit not souls with anguish torn:
Alleluia! sounds of sadness
  Best become our state forlorn:
Our offences,—our offences
  We with bitter tears must mourn.

4

But our earnest supplication,
  HOLY GOD! we raise to Thee:
Visit us with Thy Salvation,
  Make us all Thy Joys to see.
Alleluia! Alleluia!
  Ours at length this strain shall be.
                              Amen.

Septuagesima.

HYMN 53. Arranged by W. H. Havergal.

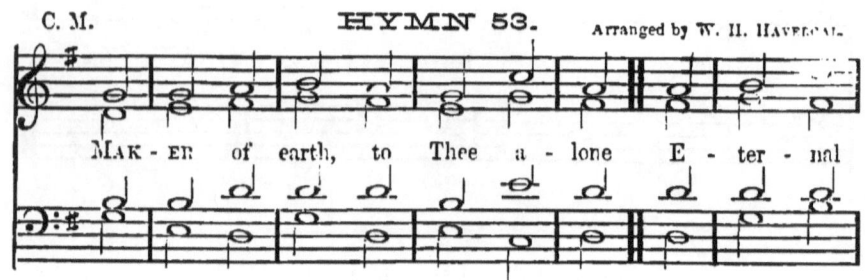

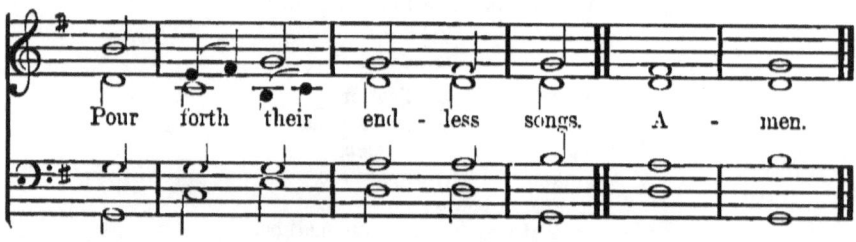

2
But we corrupt and sinful, here
  Are doomed to toil and pain;
How then can we in exile drear
  Uplift the Heavenly strain?

3
FATHER, Whose Promise binds Thee still
  To make the captive free;
Grant us to mourn the deeds of ill
  That banish us from Thee.

4
Yet while we mourn, grant us to rest
  Upon Thy Love and Care,
Till Thou restore us with the Blest
  The joys of Heaven to share.

5
O GOD the FATHER, GOD the SON,
  And GOD the HOLY GHOST,
To Thee be praise, Great THREE IN ONE,
  From Thy created Host. Amen.

Septuagesima.

HYMN 54.

6, 6, 6, 6, 4, 4, 4, 4.   J. Goss.

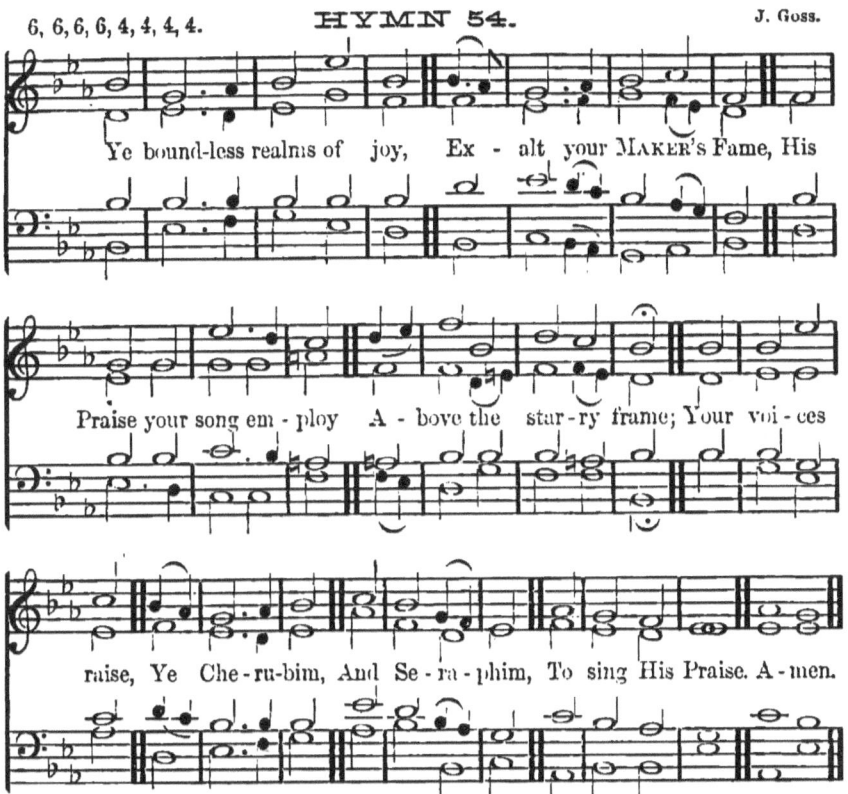

Ye boundless realms of joy, Exalt your MAKER's Fame, His Praise your song employ Above the starry frame; Your voices raise, Ye Cherubim, And Seraphim, To sing His Praise. Amen.

2 Thou moon that rulest the night,
And sun, that guidest the day;
Ye glittering stars of light,
To Him your homage pay;
His Praise declare,
Ye Heavens above,
And clouds that move
In liquid air.

3 Let them adore the LORD,
And praise His holy Name,
By Whose Almighty Word
They all from nothing came;
And all shall last,
From changes free;
His firm Decree
Stands ever fast.

4 To GOD the FATHER, SON,
And SPIRIT Ever Blest,
Eternal THREE IN ONE,
All worship be addrest;
As heretofore
It was, is now,
And shall be so
For Evermore.   Amen.

Septuagesima.

HYMN 55. — 7s. — R. R. Chope.

Source of light and life Divine, Thou didst cause the light to shine; Thou did'st give Thy Sun-beams birth O'er the new cre-a-ted earth. A-men.

2
Shade of night, and morning ray,
Took from Thee the name of day—
Now again the shades are nigh,
Listen to our suppliant cry.

3
May we ne'er by guilt oppressed
Lose the way to Endless rest;
May no thoughts impure and vain
Draw our souls to earth again.

4
Rather lift them to the skies,
Where our lasting treasure lies,
Help us in our daily strife,
Lead us in the way of life.

5
HOLY FATHER, HOLY SON,
HOLY SPIRIT, THREE IN ONE!
Praise and glory be to Thee
Now and through Eternity.   Amen.

Septuagesima.

HYMN 56.

7, 7, 7, 7, 8, 8.   J. B. Dykes.

Lord, we raise our cry to Thee, Like the blind beside the way: Make our darkened souls to see Glories of Thy perfect Day. O Lord! rebuke our sullen night, And give Thyself unto our sight! A-men.

2 Lord! we ask for brighter rays
  Than this dim and earthly sun,
  For the Light that still shall blaze
  When the stars their course have run;—
The Light that gilds Thy Blest Abode,
The Glory of the Lamb of God!

3 Lord! our souls' Blest Light, to Thee
  We poor sinners lift our prayer;
  Hear this day our Litany,—
  Hear, and in Thy Mercy spare!
Oh! Holy One! Oh! Blessed Three!
Blest be Thy Name Eternally!   Amen.

Septuagesima.

HYMN 57.

6, 6, 6, 6, 4, 4, 4, 4. J. B. DYKES.

2
O happy souls that pray
Where GOD appoints to hear!
O happy men that pay
Their constant service there!
 They praise Thee still;
 And happy they
 That love the way
 To Sion's Hill.

3
They go from strength to strength
Through this dark vale of tears;
Till each arrives at length,—
Till each in Heaven appears.
 O glorious Seat
 Of GOD our KING;
 LORD, thither bring
 Our willing feet. Amen.

Septuagesima.

HYMN 58.

L. M.   R. B. Wail.

How blest were they who walked in love With CHRIST, while yet He dwelt a-bove, First child-ren of Al-might-y Grace, First fa-thers of the faith-ful race. A-men.

2
Who can, in words of equal worth,
The wonders of their faith set forth;
Or tell of all the longing sighs
Of hope, uplifted to the skies?

3
Strangers and pilgrims here below,
They deemed the world an empty show;
To purer joys their hearts were given,
The resting-place they sought was Heaven.

4
The soul that truly cleaves to GOD
Still longs to gain that blest Abode:
SAVIOUR, forbid our souls to roam,
And fix them on our future Home.

5
To GOD the FATHER, GOD the SON,
And HOLY SPIRIT, THREE IN ONE,
Eternal praise be ever given
By all on earth, and all in Heaven. Amen.

Septuagesima.

HYMN 59.

Lord, Thy Word abideth,
And our footsteps guideth;
Who its truth believeth
Light and joy receiveth. Amen.

2 When our foes are near us,
Then Thy Word doth cheer us,
Word of consolation,
Message of salvation.

3 When the storms are o'er us,
And dark clouds before us,
Then its light directeth,
And our way protecteth.

4 Who can tell the pleasure,
Who recount the treasure,
By Thy Word imparted
To the simple-hearted ?

5 Word of mercy, giving
Succour to the living;
Word of life, supplying
Comfort to the dying !

6 O, that we discerning
Its most holy learning,
Lord, may love and fear Thee,
Evermore be near Thee ! Amen.

Septuagesima.

HYMN 60. — Sir F. A. Gore Ouseley, Bart.

8, 8, 6, 8, 8, 6.

Great Mover of all hearts, Whose Hand Doth all the se-cret springs command Of hu-man thought and will, Thou since the world was made dost bless Thy saints with fruits of ho-li-ness, Their or-der to ful-fil. A-men.

2
...ith, Hope, and Love, here weave one
 t Love alone shall then remain [chain;
 When this short day is gone:
Love, O Truth, O Endless Light!
 hen shall we see Thy Sabbath bright,
 With all our labours done?

3
We sow in dangers here and tears;
There, the glad hand the harvest bears,
 Which here in grief hath sown:
Great God Triune! the increase give,
And these Thy Gifts, by which we live,
 With Heavenly Glory crown! Amen.

Septuagesima.

HYMN 61.

C. M.   R. R. Chope.

All ye who seek a calm relief In trouble

and distress, What-ever sorrows vex the mind,

Or guilt the soul oppress: A - men.

2
Jesus, Who gave Himself for you,
  Upon the Cross to die,
Opens to you His sacred Heart,
  Oh! to that Heart draw nigh!

3
Ye hear how kindly He invites;
  Ye hear His Words so blest;
"All ye that labour, come to Me,
  And I will give you rest."

4
O Jesu! Joy of Saints on High,
  Thou Hope of sinners here;
Led onward by those loving Words,
  To Thee I lift my prayer.

5
Wash Thou my wounds in that dear Blood
  Which from Thy Side did flow;
New grace, new hope inspire; a new
  And better heart bestow.   Amen.

Lent.

HYMN 62.

C. M.   Arranged by R. F. Smith.

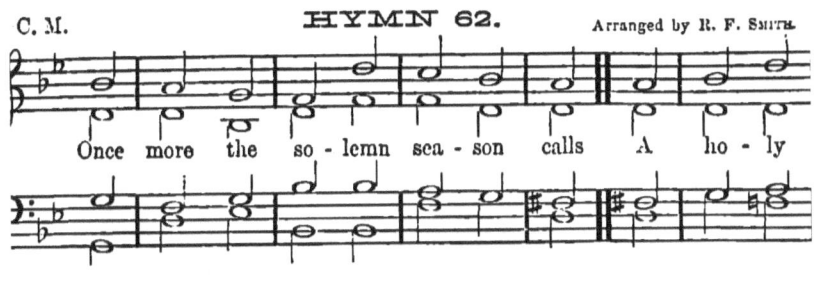
Once more the solemn season calls A holy

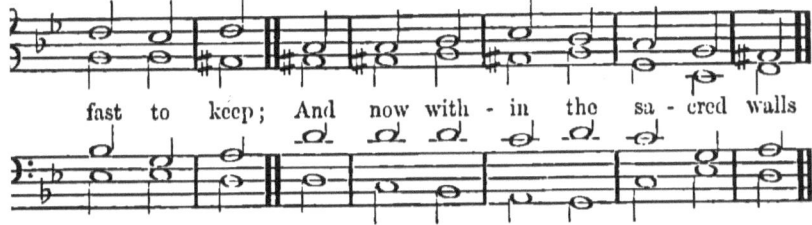
fast to keep; And now within the sacred walls

Let priest and people weep. A - men.

2
it come not thou with tears alone,
Or outward form of prayer;
it let it in thy heart be known,
That penitence is there.

3
ly breast to beat, thy clothes to rend,
God asketh not of thee;
ly stubborn soul He bids thee bend
In true humility.

4
Oh! let us, then, with heartfelt grief,
Draw near unto our God,
And pray to Him to grant relief,
And stay the uplifted rod.

5
Blest THREE IN ONE! with grief sincere,
To Thee we humbly pray,
In fruits of love and holy fear
To bless our fasting day.   Amen.

Lent.

2
Repentant unto Thee we turn,
O let not Thy fierce Anger burn;
But for the glory of Thy Name,
Thy servants spare from wrath and shame.

3
So teach us to the world to die,
Each evil lust to mortify,
That while we fast, from stain of sin
Our souls may grow all pure within.

4
O Holy FATHER, SPIRIT, SON,
Blest, Co-eternal, THREE IN ONE!
Grant that our prayers and fast may be
The lifting of our hearts to Thee. Amen.

Lent.

HYMN 64.

L. M.   S. Gee.

While now with shades of night op-prest, Our weary limbs are laid to rest, To Thee, O God, our hearts shall raise Their evening hymn of prayer and praise. A-men.

2
Controlled be every vain desire,
Each passion quenched, and lawless fire;
Let no unchastened thought rebel
To force the soul's weak citadel.

3
Let us, each one, with downcast eye,
The Altar of our God draw nigh,
And mourn our guilt, if so we may
His just Resentment turn away.

4
O awful Judge of quick and dead,
Our sins lie heavy on our head;
Too vast a weight for us to bear:—
Yet, Gracious Father, deign to spare!

5
Grant, Ever-blessed Three in One,
Grant Thou, Who art One God alone,
Our fast, through all its holy round,
May with the Spirit's Fruits be crowned.
                                                Amen.

Lent.

HYMN 65.

8, 7s.   J. B. Dykes.

Lord have mer-cy, and re-move us Quick-ly to Thy Place of rest; Where the Heavens are calm a-bove us, And as calm each saint-ed breast. A-men.

2
Holiest! hear us! by the anguish
On the Cross Thou didst endure,
Let no more our sad hearts languish
In this weary world obscure.

3
Gracious! yet if our repentance
Be not perfect and sincere,
Lord, suspend Thy fatal Sentence,
Leave us still in sadness here!

4
Leave us, Saviour! till our spirit
From each earthly taint is free;
Fit Thy Kingdom to inherit,
Fit to take its rest with Thee! Amen.

Lent.

HYMN 66.

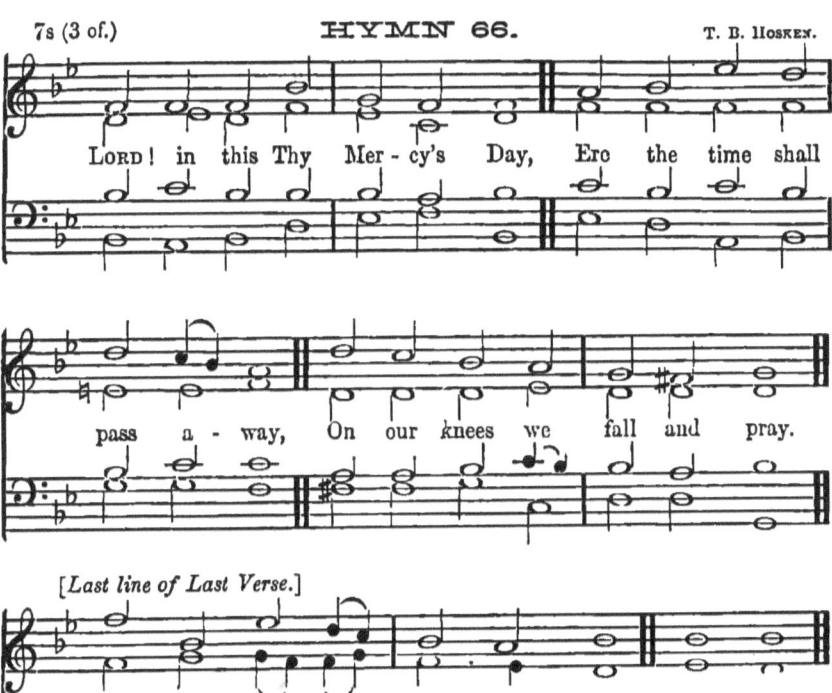

Lord! in this Thy Mercy's Day, Ere the time shall pass away, On our knees we fall and pray.

[Last line of Last Verse.]
By the pardoned round Thy Throne. A-men.

2 Holy Jesu! grant us tears,
Fill us with heart-searching fears,
Ere the hour of doom appears.

3 Lord, on us Thy Spirit pour,
Kneeling lowly at Thy Door,
Ere it close for Evermore.

4 By Thy Night of Agony,
By Thy supplicating Cry,
By Thy Willingness to die,

5 By Thy Tears of bitter woe,
For Jerusalem below,
Let us not Thy Love forego.

6 Judge and Saviour of our race,
When we see Thee face to Face,
Grant us 'neath Thy Wings a place.

7 On Thy Love we rest alone,
And that Love will then be known
By the pardoned round Thy Throne.
Amen.

Lent.

HYMN 67.

7s.   J. B. Dykes.

When our heads are bowed with woe, When our bitter tears o'er-flow, When we mourn the lost, the dear, Je-su, Son of Ma-ry, hear! A-men.

2 Thou our throbbing flesh hast worn,
  Thou our mortal griefs hast borne,
  Thou hast shed the human tear;
  Jesu, Son of Mary, hear!

3 When the solemn death-bell tolls
  For our own departing souls,
  When our final doom is near,
  Jesu, Son of Mary hear!

4 Thou hast bowed the dying Head,
  Thou the Blood of life hast shed,
  Thou hast filled a mortal bier;
  Jesu, Son of Mary, hear!

5 When the heart is sad within
  With the thought of all its sin;
  When the spirit shrinks with fear,
  Jesu, Son of Mary, hear!

6 Thou the shame, the grief, hast known,
  Though the sins were not Thine Own;
  Thou hast deigned their load to bear;
  Jesu, Son of Mary, hear!   Amen.

Lent.

HYMN 68.

S. M.   J. CHETHAM, 1736.

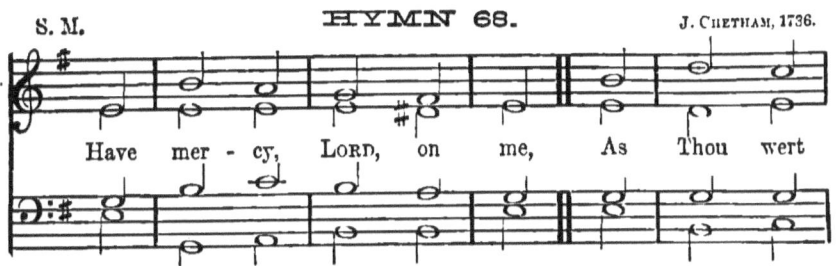

Have mer-cy, Lord, on me, As Thou wert e-ver kind, Let me, op-pressed with loads of guilt, Thy wont-ed Mer-cy find. A-men.

2

Wash off my foul offence,
And cleanse me from my sin;
For I confess my crime, and see
How great my guilt has been.

3

Withdraw not Thou Thy Help,
Nor cast me from Thy Sight;
Nor let Thy HOLY SPIRIT leave
My soul to endless night.

4

The joy Thy Favour gives
Let me again obtain;
And Thy free SPIRIT's firm Support
My fainting soul sustain.

5

JESU, Eternal SON,
To Thee all glory be,
With FATHER, SPIRIT, THREE IN ONE,
Through all Eternity.   Amen.

2

Oh! in the years, if years there be,
  That yet to me remain,
Before I cross the Eternal sea
  Not to return again;
GIVER of all! to me, O give
  Thyself in all to see;
And from henceforth by faith to live
  More worthily of Thee.

3

Thee suffering, and Thee crucified,
  Thee dead and in the grave,
Thee risen, ascended, glorified,
  Able all flesh to save;—
Thee I beseech, O SAVIOUR GOD!
  To purge my soul within;
Nor let me faint beneath the load
  Of unforgiven sin.   Amen.

Lent.

O Lord, turn not Thy Face from us Who lie in woe-ful state, La-ment-ing all our sin-ful life Be-fore Thy Mer-cy-gate. A-men.

2
That Mercy-gate which opens wide
  To those who weep for sin;
Shut not that gate, O Lord, to us,
  But let us enter in.

3
Mercy, Good Lord, mercy we ask,
  This is our humble prayer;
For mercy, Lord, is all our suit,
  O let Thy Mercy spare.

4
To Father, Son, and Holy Ghost,
  The God Whom we adore
Be glory, as it was, is now,
  And shall be Evermore.   Amen.

Lent.

HYMN 71.

C. M.
Dr. Turton,
Lord Bishop of Ely.

Lord, in the des-ert bleak and bare, Thou wroughtest still thy plan, Still waked, a-mid wild beasts, Thy Care To save un-con-scious man. A-men.

2
We thank Thee, SAVIOUR, that when all
    The Tempter's power was tried,
Thou didst not Angel-legions call,
    To chase him from Thy Side.

3
For us, Thou didst endure awhile,
    To teach us arms to wield,
Stronger than hellish force or wile,
    Thy Word, to man revealed.

4
The Scriptures in that hour prevailed,
    The Tempter's might to quell;
The flesh, the world, the Devil failed,
    The threefold force of Hell.

5
Deeply on every heart engraved
    Be this Thy Conflict, LORD!
That body, soul, and spirit saved
    May thank Thee for Thy Word.
                  Amen.

2
By Thy Birth and early Years,
By Thy human Griefs and Fears,
By Thy Fasting and Distress
In the lonely wilderness,
By Thy Victory in the hour
Of the subtle tempter's power;
JESU, look with pitying Eye,
Hear our solemn Litany.

3
By Thine Agony of grief,
By Thy Pleading for relief,
By the purple Robe of scorn,
By Thy Wounds, Thy Crown of thorn,
By Thy Cross, Thy Pangs, and Cries,
By Thy perfect Sacrifice,
JESU, look with pitying Eye,
Hear our solemn Litany.

4
By Thy deep expiring Groan,
By the sealed sepulchral stone,
By Thy Triumph o'er the grave,
By Thy Power from death to save;—
Mighty GOD, ascended LORD,
To Thy Throne in Heaven restored,
PRINCE and SAVIOUR, hear the cry
Of our solemn Litany.   Amen.

Lent.

HYMN 73.

Glo-ry be to Jesus, Who in bitter pains, Poured for us the Life-blood From His Sa-cred Veins. A-men.

2 Grace and Life Eternal
　In that Blood we find;
　Blest be His Compassion,
　Infinitely kind.

3 Blest through Endless ages
　Be the Precious Stream,
　Which from Endless torment
　Doth the world redeem!

4 There the fainting spirit
　Drinks of life her fill;
　There as in a fountain
　Laves herself at will.

5 Abel's blood for vengeance
　Pleaded to the skies;
　But the Blood of Jesus
　For our pardon cries.

6 Oft as it is sprinkled
　On our guilty hearts,
　Satan in confusion
　Terror-struck departs.

7 Oft as earth exulting
　Wafts its praise above,
　Hell with terror trembles;
　Heaven is filled with love.

8 Lift ye, then, your voices;
　Swell the mighty flood;
　Louder still and louder
　Praise the Precious Blood.　Amen.

2

Here I'll stay, for ever viewing
  Mercy's streams in streams of Blood;
Precious Drops, my soul bedewing,
  Plead and claim my peace with GOD.

3

Truly blessed is the Station
  Low before His Cross to lie,
While I see Divine Compassion
  Floating in His languid Eye.

4

LORD, in ceaseless contemplation
  Fix my thoughtful heart on Thee,
Till I taste Thy full Salvation,
  And unveiled Thy Glory see.

5

Honour, glory, virtue, merit,
  To the Blessed THREE IN ONE,
FATHER, SON, and HOLY SPIRIT,
  While Eternal ages run.   Amen.

Lent.

Hymn 75.

C. M. — Printed for R. R. C.

O Per-fect God, and Per-fect Man! 'Tis not for us to know How Thy pure Soul and Bo-dy felt Tempt-a-tion, pain, and woe. A-men.

2
Our faith is weak: O Light of Light!
  Clear Thou our clouded view;
Thou Son of Man, and Son of God!
  We give Thee honour due.

3
O Son of Man! Thyself hast proved
  Our trials and our tears;
Life's thankless toil and scant repose,
  Death's agonies and fears.

4
Incarnate God! in glory raised,
  Thou sittest on the Throne;
Thence, by Thy Pleadings and Thy Grace,
  Still succouring Thine Own.

5
Brother and Saviour, Friend and Judge!
  To Thee, O Christ, is given
To bind upon Thy Crown the names
  Most blest in earth and Heaven. Amen

Lent.

HYMN 76.

O help us, Lord! Each hour of need Thy Heavenly Suc-cour give; Help us in thought and word, and deed, Each hour on earth we live. A-men.

2
O help us when our spirits bleed
   With contrite anguish sore,
And when our hearts are cold and dead,
   O help us, Lord, the more.

3
O help us through the power of faith
   More firmly to believe;
For still the more the servant hath,
   The more shall he receive.

4
O help us, Saviour! from on High;
   We know no help but Thee;
O help us so to live and die,
   As Thine in Heaven to be.   Amen.

2

From the depth of nature's blindness,
  From the hardening power of sin,
From all malice and unkindness,
  From the pride that lurks within,
    By Thy Mercy,
    O deliver us, Good LORD.

3

When temptation sorely presses,
  In the day of Satan's power,
In our times of deep distresses,
  In each dark and trying hour;
    By Thy Mercy,
    O deliver us, Good LORD.

4

In the weary night of sickness,
  In the throes of grief and pain,
When we feel our mortal weakness,
  When all human help is vain,
    By Thy Mercy,
    O deliver us, Good LORD.

5

In the solemn hour of dying,
  In the awful Judgment-day,
May our souls, on Thee relying,
  Find Thee still our Hope and Stay;
    By Thy Mercy,
    O deliver us, Good LORD.   Amen.

2

With forbidden pleasures
  Should this vain world charm,
Or its tempting treasures
  Spread, to work me harm;
Bring to my remembrance
  Sad Gethsemane,
Or, in dark resemblance,
  Cross-crowned Calvary.

3

Should Thy Mercy send me
  Sorrow, toil, and woe;
Or should pain attend me
  On my path below;
Grant that I may never
  Fail Thy Hand to see;
Grant that I may ever
  Cast my care on Thee.

4

When my last hour cometh,
  Fraught with strife and pain;
When my dust returneth
  To the dust again;
On Thy Truth relying
  Through that mortal strife,
JESU, take me, dying,
  To Eternal Life.   Amen.

Lent.

HYMN 79. 8, 8, 6, 8, 8, 6. A. H. Brown.

Jesus! all hail, Who for my sin Didst die, and by that Death didst win Eternal Life for me; Send me Thy Grace, Good Lord, that I Unto the world and flesh may die, And hide my life with Thee. A-men.

2

Jesus! from out Thine opened Side
Thou hast the thirsty world supplied
  With Endless streams of love!
Come ye who would your sickness quell,
Draw freely from that sacred Well,
  Its Heavenly virtues prove.

3

Jesus! Thy Passion's bitter smart
Pierced like a sword Thy Mother's heart,
  As Simeon prophesied;
So fix my heart unto Thy Cross,
That I may count all gain but loss
  For Jesus Crucified!

4

Jesus! Who from the dead arose,
And straightway sought to comfort those
  Whose weak faith mourned for Thee;
Oh, may I rise from sin and earth,
And so make good that Second Birth
  Which Thou hast wrought in me.

5

Jesus! Who shalt in glory come
With Angels to the final doom,
  Men's works and wills to weigh;
Since from that doom I cannot flee,
Be pitiful, Great Lord, to me
  In that tremendous Day!   Amen.

Lent.

HYMN 80.

C. M. — E. J. Hopkins.

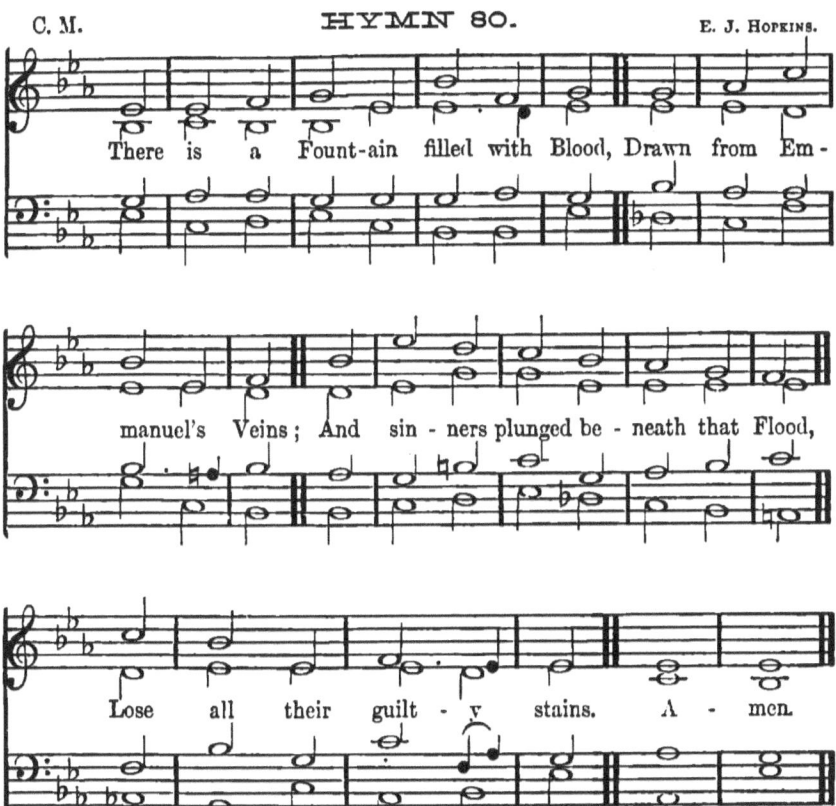

There is a Fountain filled with Blood, Drawn from Emmanuel's Veins; And sinners plunged beneath that Flood, Lose all their guilty stains. A-men.

2
The dying Thief rejoiced to see
That Fountain in his day;
And there may I, as well as he,
Wash all my sins away.

3
O Lamb of God! Thy Precious Blood
Shall never lose Its Power,
Till all the ransomed Church of God
Be saved, to sin no more.

4
E'er since by faith I saw the stream
Thy flowing Wounds supply,
Redeeming Love has been my theme,
And shall be till I die.

5
Then in a nobler, sweeter song,
I'll sing Thy Power to save,
When this poor lisping, stammering tongue
Lies silent in the grave.   Amen.

Passion Sunday.
FIFTH SUNDAY IN LENT.

HYMN 81.

L. M.   Ancient.

Forth goes the Standard of our KING, The sacred Banner gleams on high, The Cross, on which to conquer death, The LORD of Life vouchsafed to die. A-men.

2
Pierced by the spear, He yielded forth
Water and Blood a mingled Tide;
A cleansing Fount of priceless worth,
For sinners flowing from His Side.

3
O sacred, ever glorious Cross!
Than purple throne of kings more dear,
On thee what honour was conferred,
That thou Those Holy Limbs should'st bear.

4
O wondrous Cross! man's only Hope,
Through which alone we look for Heaven;
To Him Who hung on thee we come,
That every sin may be forgiven.

5
To GOD, the Eternal THREE IN ONE,
From every soul all glory be;
Crown, LORD, Thy servants, who have gained
Through Thine Own Cross the victory.

Amen.

Passion Sunday.
FIFTH SUNDAY IN LENT.

HYMN 82. Arranged by T. B. Hosken.

In our Lord's a-ton-ing Grief, Be our rest and sure re-lief; Je-su! Thou our Re-fuge be, Sweet it is to trust in Thee. A-men.

2
Crucified! we Thee adore,
Thee with all our hearts implore;
In the realms of Heavenly Light,
With Thy faithful, us unite.

3
Thee, our only Hope and Tower,
In Thy Passion's solemn hour,
Now we pray; our sins efface,
And increase Thy Gifts of Grace.

4
Christ! by faithless hands betrayed
Christ! for us a Captive made,
Christ! upon the bitter Tree
Slain for man, all praise to Thee! Amen.

Palm Sunday.
SUNDAY NEXT BEFORE EASTER.

Hymn 83. 10s. Goudimel, 1562. Arranged by J. B. D.

Glo-ry and praise to Thee, Re-deem-er Blest! By loud Ho-san-nas on Thy Road con-fessed! Hail! Is-rael's King! Hail! Da-vid's Son a-dored, Who com-est In the Name of Is-rael's Lord! A-men.

2

Thee once with palms the Jews went forth to meet,
Thee now with prayers and holy hymns we greet.
Glory and praise to Thee, Incarnate WORD,
Who comest in the Name of Israel's LORD!

3

Thee, on Thy Way to die, they crowned with praise!
To Thee, enthroned on High, our song we raise.
Glory and praise to Thee, Incarnate WORD,
Who comest in the Name of Israel's LORD!

4

Thee their frail homage pleased, O Gracious KING,
Ours too accept, the best that we can bring.
Glory and praise to Thee, Incarnate WORD,
Who comest in the Name of Israel's LORD!

5

Thy Praise in Heaven the Host Angelic sings,
On earth mankind with all created things.
Glory and praise to Thee by all adored,
Who comest in the Name of Israel's LORD! Amen.

Palm Sunday.

SUNDAY NEXT BEFORE EASTER.

L.M.   HYMN 84.   J. B. Dykes.

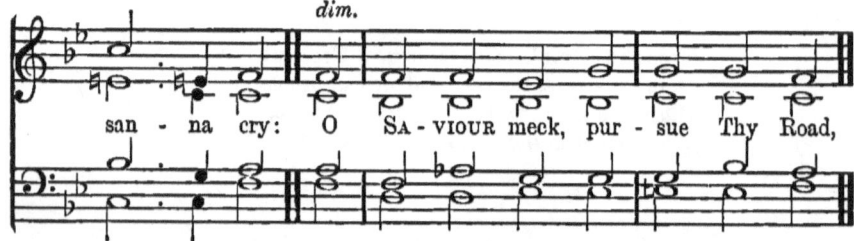

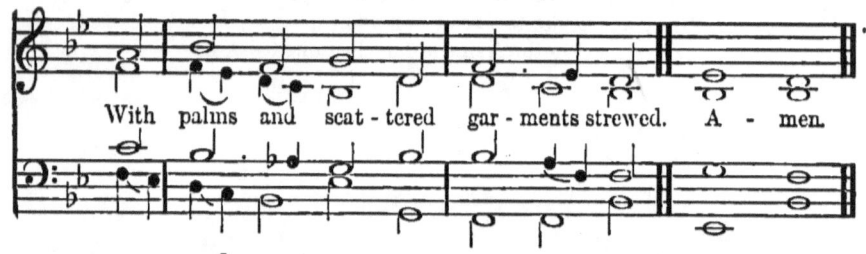

2
Ride on! ride on in majesty!
In lowly pomp ride on to die!
O Christ, Thy Triumphs now begin
O'er captive death and conquered sin.

3
Ride on! ride on in majesty!
The Angel Armies of the sky
Look down with sad and wondering eyes,
To see the approaching sacrifice.

4
Ride on! ride on in majesty!
The last and fiercest strife is nigh:
The Father on His sapphire Throne,
Expects His Own Anointed One.

5
Ride on! ride on in majesty!
In lowly pomp ride on to die!
Bow Thy meek Head to mortal pain,
Then take, O God, Thy Power and reign.

6
Reign on! reign on in majesty!
Reign on in triumph, Lord Most High!
We hymn Thee on Thy Throne of Love,
Almighty King, in realms above. Amen.

Hymns on the Passion.

L. M.   HYMN 85.   J. Milton 1621.

We sing the praise of Him Who died, Of Him Who died upon the Cross; The sinner's Hope let man deride, For this we count the world but loss. A-men.

2
Inscribed upon the Cross we see
In shining letters, "God is Love,"
He bears our sins upon the Tree,
He brings us mercy from above.

3
The Cross! it takes our guilt away;
It holds the fainting spirit up;
It cheers with hope the gloomy day,
And sweetens every bitter cup.

4
It makes the coward spirit brave,
And nerves the feeble arm for fight;
It takes its terror from the grave,
And gilds the bed of death with light.

5
The balm of life, the cure of woe,
The measure and the pledge of love,
The sinner's refuge here below,
The Angels' theme in Heaven above.

6
To Christ, Who won for sinners grace
By bitter grief and anguish sore,
Be praise from all the ransomed race
For ever and for Evermore.   Amen.

Hymns on the Passion.

C.M.   HYMN 86.   Ravenscroft's Psalter, 1621.

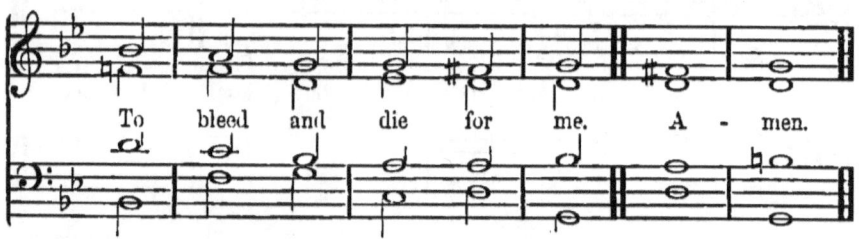

Be-hold the Saviour of man-kind Nailed to the shame-ful tree! How vast the love that Him in-clined To bleed and die for me. A-men.

2
Hark, how He groans! while nature shakes,
   And earth's strong pillars bend;
The Temple's veil in sunder breaks;
   The solid marbles rend.

3
'Tis done! into His Father's Hands
   His tortured Spirit flies;
His Soul has rent her mortal bands,
   He bows His Head, and dies.

4
And soon He'll break death's envious chain,
   And in full glory shine:
O Lamb of God! was ever pain,
   Was ever Love like Thine?   Amen.

Hymns on the Passion.

HYMN 87.

7s. R. Redhead.

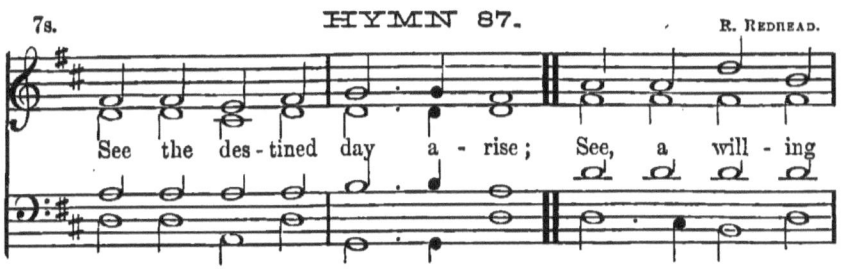
See the des-tined day a-rise; See, a will-ing

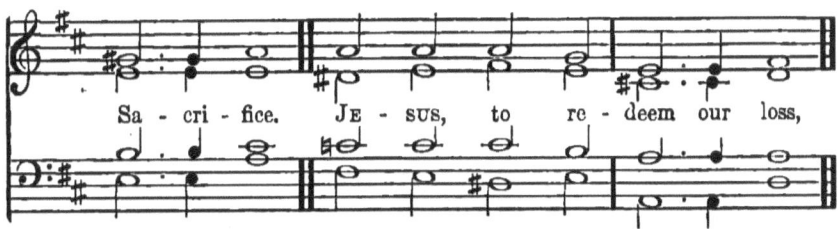
Sa-cri-fice. Je-sus, to re-deem our loss,

Hangs up-on the shame-ful Cross. A-men.

2
Jesu, who but Thou had borne,
Lifted on that Tree of scorn,
Every pang and bitter throe,
Finishing Thy Life of woe?

3
Who but Thou had dared to drain,
Steeped in gall, the Cup of pain;
And with tender Body bear
Thorns, and nails, and piercing spear?

4
Thence the cleansing Water flowed,
Mingled from thy Side with Blood,
Sign to all attesting eyes
Of the finished Sacrifice.

5
Holy Jesu, grant us Grace,
In that Sacrifice to place
All our trust for life renewed,
Pardoned sin, and promised good. Amen.

Hymns on the Passion.

8, 8, 7, 8, 8, 7.   HYMN 88.   Ancient. Arranged by R. F. Smith.

By the Cross sad Vigil keeping, Stood the Mother

mourning, weeping, Where He hung, the dying Lord;

For her soul, of joy bereaved, Bowed with anguish,

deeply grieved, Felt the sharp and piercing sword. Amen.

2

Oh! how sad and sore distressed
Now was she, that Mother Blessed,
   Of the High Eternal ONE!
Pierced by woe, with heart's prostration,
Mother meek, the bitter Passion
   Saw she of her Glorious SON.

3

Who on CHRIST's fond Mother gazing,
Touched with tenderest woe amazing,
   Born of woman, would not weep?
Who, on CHRIST's fond Mother thinking,
Such a cup of sorrow drinking,
   Would not share her sorrows deep?

4

For His people's sins rejected,
She her SON saw unprotected,
   Wear a crown with thorns entwined;
Saw Him then from judgment taken,
And in death by all forsaken,
   Till His Spirit He resigned.

5

JESU, may such deep devotion
Stir in us the same emotion,
   Fount of Love, REDEEMER Kind!
That our hearts, fresh ardour proving,
Thee, our GOD and SAVIOUR, loving,
   May with Thee acceptance find. Amen.

Hymns on the Passion.

7, 6s (8 of.)   HYMN 89.   Arranged by J. S. Bach, 1750.

2

Lo! now Thy Strength and Vigour
　Are failing in the strife,
And death with cruel rigour
　Bereaveth Thee of Life;
O agony and dying!
　O love to sinners free!
Jesu, all Grace supplying,
　Turn, turn Thy Face on me.

3

O Jesu! by Thy Passion,
　Hear now my suppliant cry,
Who ever in compassion
　To contrite souls art nigh.
Beneath Thy Cross abiding,
　The weary seeketh rest,
And in Thy Love confiding,
　Implores Thy Presence blest.

4

O Saviour, Undefiled,
　Remain with us, we pray,
Who, for our sins reviled,
　Didst take their guilt away.
And when our strength all faileth
　In death's dark hour of pain,
Do Thou, Whose Death availeth,
　Revive our soul again.　　　Amen.

Hymns on the Passion.

HYMN 90.

S. M.   J. B. Dykes.

O'er-whelmed in depths of woe, Upon the Tree of scorn Hangs the Re-deem-er of mankind, With rack-ing an-guish torn. A - men.

2
See! how the nails those Hands
And Feet so tender rend;
See! down his Face, and Neck, and Breast,
His sacred Blood descend.

3
Hark! with what awful Cry
His Spirit takes its flight;
That Cry, it pierced His Mother's heart,
And whelmed her soul in night.

4
Earth hears, and to its base
Rocks wildly to and fro;
Tombs burst; seas, rivers, mountains [quake;
The veil is rent in two.

5
The sun withdraws his light;
The mid-day Heavens grow pale;
The moon, the stars, the universe,
Their Maker's Death bewail.

6
Shall man alone be mute?
Has he no griefs or fears?
Come, old and young! come, all mankind!
And bathe those Feet in tears!

7
Come, fall before His Cross,
Who shed for us His Blood;
Who died the Victim of pure love,
To make us sons of God.

8
Jesu! all praise to Thee,
Our Joy and Endless Rest!
Be Thou our Guide while pilgrims here,
Our Crown amid the Blest.   Amen.

Hymns on the Passion.

HYMN 91.

L. M. — J. B. Dykes.

O come and mourn with me a-while, And tarry here the Cross beside; O come together let us mourn; Jesus, our Lord, is crucified. A-men.

2
Have we no tears to shed for Him,
While soldiers scoff and Jews deride?
Ah! look how patiently He hangs;
Jesus, our Lord, is crucified!

3
How fast His Hands and Feet are nailed;
His blessed Tongue with thirst is tied;
His failing Eyes are blind with Blood;
Jesus, our Lord, is crucified!

4
Seven times He spake, seven words of love,
And all three hours His Silence cried
For mercy on the souls of men;
Jesus, our Lord, is crucified!

5
Come, take thy stand beneath the Cross,
And let the Blood from out that Side
Fall gently on thee drop by drop;
Jesus, our Lord, is crucified!

6
A broken heart, a fount of tears,
Ask, and they will not be denied;
A broken heart love's cradle is;
Jesus, our Lord, is crucified!

7
O Love of God! O sin of man!
In this dread act your strength is tried;
And victory remains with love;
For He, our Love, is crucified.   Amen.

Hymns on the Passion.

L. M.   HYMN 92.   Scotch Psalter, 1635.

Whilst on the Cross, Thy lat-est Breath Thou draw-est in the pains of death, Teach us, O Christ, our eyes to raise, And fix on Thee our stead-fast gaze. A-men.

2

Thou, by Thy Cross, Thy Saints dost mould;
Thou, by Thy Cross, Thy Love hast told;
Thou, by Thy Cross, hast healing given,
Thou, by Thy Cross, hast opened Heaven.

3

So, from Thy Cross, as from a throne,
Thou dost command the world alone;
Uplifted on the accursed Tree,
Thou drawest all men unto Thee.

4

Hail, Jesu! Thou, Whose Graces shower
Upon our lives all cleansing power;—
We stand beneath Thy Cross, we would
Be sprinkled with Thy Precious Blood.

5

To Thee, Who gav'st Thine Only Son;
To Thee, Who hast the Victory won;
To Thee, with Son and Father, be
Glory and praise Eternally.   Amen.

Hymns on the Passion.

HYMN 93. L. M. R. R. Chope.

Ye that pass by, behold the MAN! The MAN of griefs, condemned for you! The LAMB slain ere the world began, Weeping, to Calvary pursue. Amen.

2
See! how His Back the scourges tear,
Unto the bloody pillar bound!
The ploughers make long furrows there,
Till all His Body is one wound.

3
In scorn they robe Him, crown, adore;
In spite they rend His Robe away:
They crush Him with that burden sore,
They drag Him up the accursed way.

4
Behold His Temples crowned with thorn,
His bleeding hands spread out so wide!
His streaming Feet transfixed and torn,
The Fountain gushing from His Side!

5
Beneath our load He faints and dies—
We filled His Soul with pangs unknown;
We caused those mortal groans and cries;
We slew the FATHER's Only SON.

6
Yet we through Him may humbly bring
Our thankful praise to GOD Most High;—
To Him, our PROPHET, PRIEST, and KING,
Who came on earth for us to die.   Amen.

Hymns on the Passion.

HYMN 94.

7s (6 of.) By permission of W. Horsley.

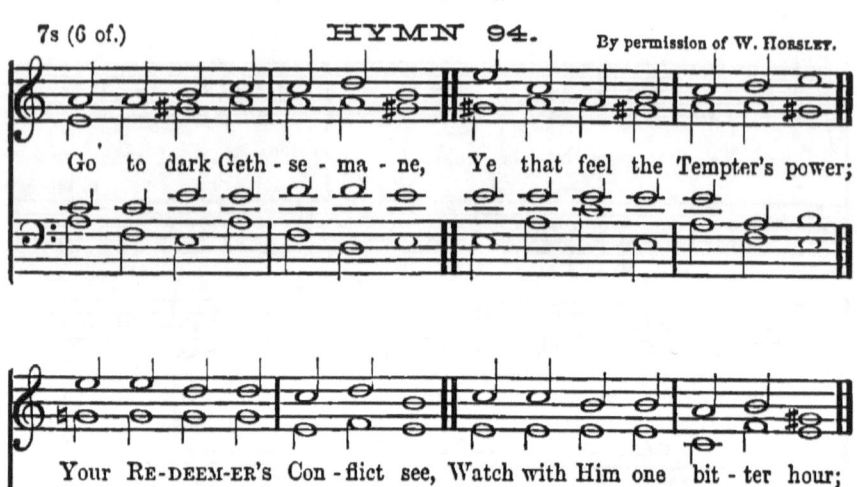

Go to dark Gethsemane, Ye that feel the Tempter's power; Your Redeemer's Conflict see, Watch with Him one bitter hour; Turn not from His Griefs away, Learn of Him to watch and pray. A-men.

2
See Him at the judgment-hall,
Beaten, bound, reviled, arraigned!
See Him meekly bearing all!
Love to man His Soul sustained!
Shun not suffering, shame, or loss,
Learn of CHRIST to bear the Cross.

3
Calvary's mournful mountain view;
There the LORD of Glory see
Made a Sacrifice for you,
Dying on the accursed Tree:
"It is finished," hear Him cry;—
Learn of JESUS CHRIST to die. Amen.

Hymns on the Passion.

L. M. HYMN 95. Arranged by R. F. Smith.

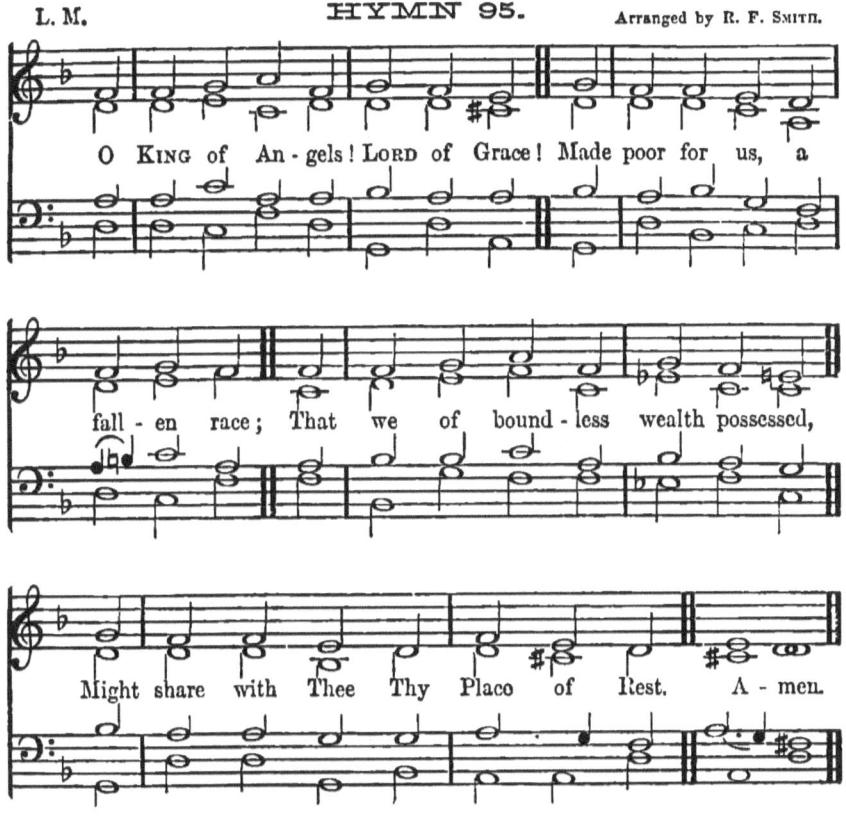

O King of Angels! Lord of Grace! Made poor for us, a fallen race; That we of boundless wealth possessed, Might share with Thee Thy Place of Rest. A-men.

2
Thou didst the bitter scorn sustain,
The deep indignity and pain;
And dying hast on us bestowed
The gift of Endless life with God.

3
While still on this low earth we move,
Remember us with ceaseless love;
And grant us like the Thief to see
The joys of Paradise with Thee.

4
To God the Father, God the Son,
And Holy Spirit, Three in One,
By Hell, and Earth, and Highest Heaven,
Be fear, and praise, and homage given.
                          Amen.

Hymns on the Passion.

L. M.   HYMN 96.   Adapted by R. R. Chope.

When I survey the wondrous Cross On which the Prince of Glory died, My richest gain I count but loss, And pour contempt on all my pride. A-men.

2
Forbid it, Lord, that I should boast,
Save in the death of Christ, my God;
All the vain things that charm me most,
I sacrifice them to His Blood.

3
See from His Head, His Hands, His Feet,
Sorrow and love flow mingled down;
Did e'er such love and sorrow meet,
Or thorns compose so rich a crown!

4
Were the whole realm of nature mine,
That were a present far too small;
Love so amazing, so Divine,
Demands my life, my soul, my all.

5
To Him Who gave His Son to die,
To Him Whose Dying bids me live,
To Him, the Spirit Blest, will I
My heart, my life, my spirit give. Amen.

Easter Eve.

HYMN 97.

4, 4, 7, 7, 6.   J. S. Bach, 1750.

So rest, my REST! Thou e-ver blest! Thy Grave with sin-ners mak-ing: By Thy pre-cious Death from sin My dead soul a-wak-ing. A-men.

2 Here hast Thou lain
　After much pain,
LIFE of my life, reposing:
Round Thee now a rock-hewn grave,
　ROCK OF AGES, closing.

3 BREATH of all breath!
　I know, from death
Thou wilt my dust awaken;
Wherefore should I dread the grave,
　Or my faith be shaken?

4 O may the tomb
　Be but a room
Where I lie down on roses;
Who by death hath conquered death,
　Sweetly there reposes.

5 The body dies
　(Nought else) and lies
In dust, until victorious
From the grave, it shall arise
　Beautiful and glorious.

6 Meantime I will,
　My SAVIOUR, still
Deep in my bosom lay Thee,
Musing on Thy Death; in death
　Be with me, I pray Thee.　　Amen.

Easter Eve.

HYMN 98.

8, 7, 8, 7, 7, 7.   J. B. Dykes.

All is o'er, the pain, the sor-row, Hu-man taunts and fiend-ish spite; Death shall be de-spoiled to-mor-row Of the prey he grasps to-night. Yet once more to seal his doom, Christ must sleep with-in the tomb. A-men.

2

Fierce and deadly was the anguish
Which on yonder Cross He bore;
How did Soul and Body languish,
Till the toil of death was o'er!
But that toil, so fierce and dread,
Bruised and crushed the serpent's head.

3

Close and still the cell that holds Him,
While in brief repose He lies;
Deep the slumber that enfolds Him,
Veiled awhile from mortal eyes:
Slumber such as needs must be
After hard-won victory.

4

All night long, with plaintive voicing,
Chant His Requiem soft and low;
Loftier strains of loud rejoicing
From to-morrow's harps shall flow:
"Death and Hell at length are slain—
CHRIST hath triumphed, CHRIST doth
    reign."   '   Amen.

Easter Eve.

HYMN 99.

Resting from His Work to-day In the tomb our Saviour lay; Still He sleeps, from Head to Feet Shrouded in the winding-sheet, In the rocky tomb alone, Hidden by the sealed stone. Amen.

2 Late at even there was seen
Watching long the Magdalene;
Early, ere the break of day,
Sorrowful she took her way
To the holy garden glade,
Where her buried Lord was laid.

3 So with Thee, till life shall end,
I would solemn vigil spend;
Let me hew Thee, Lord, a shrine
In this stony heart of mine;
Where, in pure embalmed cell,
None but Thou may ever dwell!

4 Myrrh and spices will I bring,
True affection's offering;
Close the door from sight and sound
Of the busy world around;
And in patient watch remain,
Till my Lord appear again. Amen.

Easter.

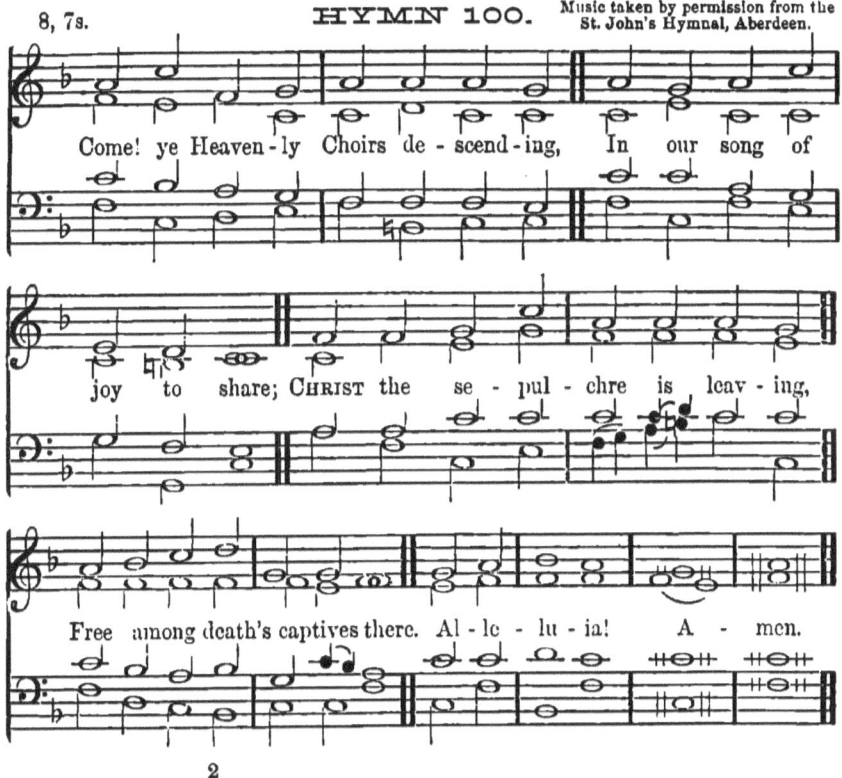

HYMN 100. 8, 7s.
Music taken by permission from the St. John's Hymnal, Aberdeen.

Come! ye Heavenly Choirs descending,
In our song of joy to share;
CHRIST the sepulchre is leaving,
Free among death's captives there. Alleluia! Amen.

2
Vain the soldiers' watching round Him,
  Through the hours of darkness lone;
Vain the care which sought to hold Him,
  Deep within the sealed stone.

3
If He will, with seals unbroken,
  He can leave the guarded tomb,
Who, our perfect manhood bearing,
  Issued from the Virgin's womb.

4
On the Cross of anguish lifted,
  He shuns not the death of pain;
But a mightier sign vouchsafeth,
  Rising into life again.

5
LORD, with Thee in daily dying,
  May we die, and with Thee rise,
And, on earth ourselves denying,
  Seek the treasure of the skies.

6
Glory to the Eternal FATHER,
  To the SPIRIT, and the SON,
Who, the LEADER of His faithful,
  Hath in death the triumph won,
          Alleluia! Amen.

Easter.

HYMN 101.

7s. Arranged by H. S. Irons.

2

Hymns of praise then let us sing, Alleluia!
Unto CHRIST, our Heavenly KING, Alleluia!
Who endured the Cross and Grave, Alleluia!
Sinners to redeem and save.   Alleluia!

3

But the pain which He endured, Alleluia!
Our salvation hath procured, Alleluia!
Now above the sky He's KING, Alleluia!
Where the Angels ever sing.   Alleluia!
                                        Amen.

Easter.

HYMN 102.

8, 8, 8, 4. E. J. Hopkins.

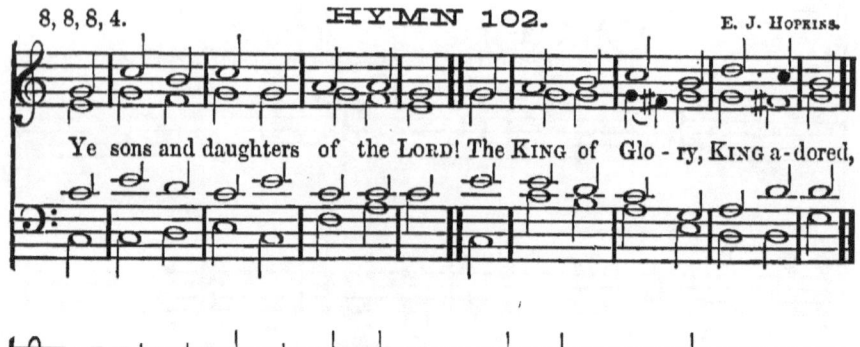

Ye sons and daughters of the Lord! The King of Glory, King a-dored,

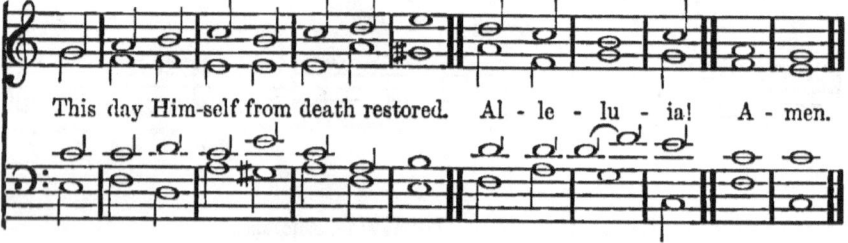

This day Him-self from death restored. Al - le - lu - ia! A - men.

2
On Sunday morn at break of day,
The faithful women went their way
To see the Tomb where Jesus lay.
           Alleluia!

3
Then straightway one in white they see,
Who saith, "Ye seek the Lord; but He
Is risen, and gone to Galilee."
           Alleluia!

4
That night the Apostles met in fear,
But Christ did in the midst appear,—
"My peace," He said, "be on all here!"
           Alleluia!

5
When Thomas first these tidings heard,
He doubted if it were the Lord,
Until He came and spake this word;
           Alleluia!

6
"Behold my Side, O Thomas! see
My Hands, my Feet, I show to thee,
Nor faithless, but believing be."
           Alleluia!

7
When Thomas saw that wounded Side,
The truth no longer he denied;
"Thou art my Lord and God!" he cried.
           Alleluia!

8
How blest are they who have not seen,
And yet whose faith hath constant been!
For they Eternal life shall win.
           Alleluia!

9
On this most holy Day of days,
To God your hearts and voices raise
In laud, and jubilee, and praise!
           Alleluia! Amen

Easter.

HYMN 103.

7, 8, 7, 8, 4.   J. B. Dykes.

Je-sus lives! No long-er now Can Thy ter-rors,
Death, ap-pal us; Je-sus lives! By this we know,
Thou, O Grave, canst not en-thral us. Al - le - lu - ia. A-men.

2
Jesus lives! henceforth is death
But the gate of Life Immortal;
This shall calm our trembling breath,
When we pass its gloomy portal.
   Alleluia!

3
Jesus lives! for us He died:
Then, alone to Jesus living,
Pure in heart may we abide,
Glory to our Saviour giving.
   Alleluia!

4
Jesus lives! our hearts know well
Nought from us His Love shall sever;
Life, nor death, nor powers of Hell
Tear us from His Keeping ever.
   Alleluia!

5
Jesus lives! to Him the Throne
Over all the world is given:
May we go where He is gone,
Rest and reign with Him in Heaven.
   Alleluia! Amen.

Easter.

HYMN 104. C.M. Arranged by W. H. Havergal.

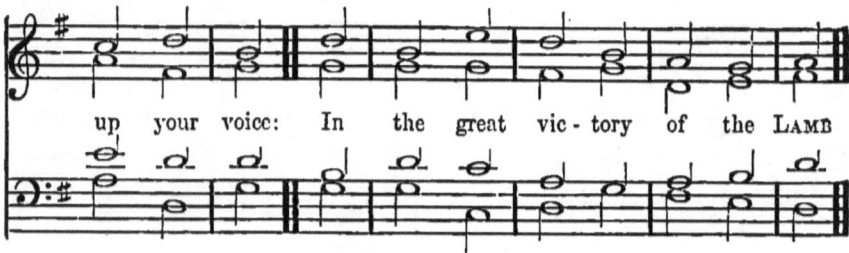

O come, and with the early morn Rise and lift up your voice: In the great victory of the Lamb Let all the world rejoice. Alleluia! Amen.

2
He, by His Own most Precious Blood,
  Hath washed our sins away.
The veil is rent, the courts of Heaven
  Their Endless joys display.

3
The seed entrusted to the ground
  Dies not, nor fruitless lies,
From Jesu's Slumber in the dust
  What glorious harvests rise!

4
Through Him shall all the sleeping dead
  Burst forth again to life,
To share with Him the crowns of light,
  Who shared with Him the strife.

5
Praise, therefore, to the Father be,
  And to the Eternal Son,
Who, quickened by the Spirit, hath
  O'er Death the triumph won.
          Alleluia! Amen.

Easter.

HYMN 105.

7s. Arranged by T. B. Hosken.

At the Lamb's high Feast we sing, Praise to our vic-to-rious King, Who hath washed us in the Tide, Flow-ing from His Wound-ed Side. Al-le-lu-ia! A-men.

2
Praise we Him, Whose Love Divine
Gives His sacred Blood for wine,
Gives His Body for the Feast,
Christ the Victim,—Christ the Priest.

3
Where the Paschal Blood is poured,
Death's dark angel sheathes his sword;
Israel's hosts triumphant go
Through the wave that drowns the foe.

4
Christ, our Paschal Lamb, is slain,
Holy Victim without stain;
Death and Hell defeated lie,
Heaven unfolds its gates on High.

5
From the power of sin, set free
Those new-born, O Lord, in Thee.
Easter triumph, Easter joy—
Sin alone can this destroy.

6
Hymns of glory and of praise,
Father, unto Thee we raise;
Risen Lord, all praise to Thee,
With the Spirit ever be.
Alleluia! Amen.

Easter.

HYMN 106. — L.M. — E. B. Fripp.

O Jesu! Lord of Heaven-ly Grace, Redeemer of our guilty race, What wondrous Love prevailed in Thee, The Bearer of our sins to be. Alleluia! Amen.

2
Unloosed is Satan's heavy chain,
The power of death is snapped in twain;
Victorious He has left the tomb
Who deigned to bless the Virgin's womb.

3
Lord, let Thy Mercy then prevail,
To heal the losses we bewail;
The light vouchsafe us of Thy Face,
Support us with Thy Gifts of Grace.

4
Be Thou our Guide unto the skies,
Be Thou the Mark before our eyes,
Our present Joy to dry our tears,
Our future Prize for endless years.
       Alleluia! Amen.

Easter.

HYMN 107.

C. M.   Dr. Howard, 1782.

Christ is be-come our Pas-chal Lamb, For us con-

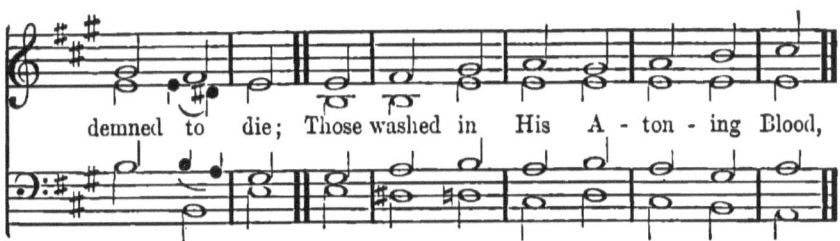

demned to die; Those washed in His A-ton-ing Blood,

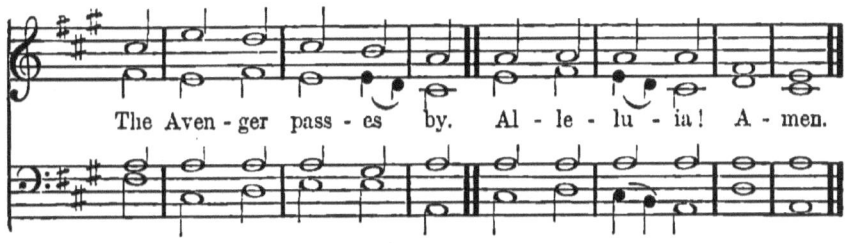

The Aven-ger pass-es by. Al-le-lu-ia! A-men.

2
Hail! Sacred Victim, by Whose Death
  Death hath been overcome;
Who by Thy Burial hast dispersed
  The darkness of the tomb.

3
He That was dead now lives again;
  The prison doors are riven;
Triumphant o'er our ghostly foe,
  He opes the gates of Heaven.

4
O grant us, Lord, with Thee to die,
  With Thee again to rise!
To spurn the things of earth, and seek
  The treasures of the Skies.

5
To Father, Son, and Holy Ghost,
  The God Whom we adore,
Be glory, as it was, is now,
  And shall be Evermore. Alleluia! Amen.

Easter.

HYMN 108.

6, 6, 6, 6, 8, 8. R. R. CHOPE.

The hap-py morn is come! Tri-umph-ant o'er the grave The LORD hath left the tomb, Om-ni-po-tent to save: Cap-tiv-i-ty is cap-tive led; For JESUS liv-eth, and was dead. Al-le-lu-ia! A-men.

2 Who now accuseth them
 For whom their Surety died?
 Who now shall those condemn
 Whom GOD hath justified?
 Captivity is captive led;
 For JESUS liveth, and was dead.

3 CHRIST hath the ransom paid;
 The glorious work is done;
 On Him our help is laid,
 By Him our victory won:
 Captivity is captive led;
 For JESUS liveth, and was dead.

4 To GOD, the risen SON,
 FATHER, and SPIRIT Blest,
 Eternal THREE IN ONE,
 All worship be addrest.
 Captivity is captive led;
 For JESUS liveth, and was dead.
  Alleluia! Amen.

Easter.

HYMN 109.

8, 7, 8, 7, 7, 7.   W. Meadows.

Come, ye sad and fearful hearted,
  With glad smile and radiant brow;
Lent's long shadows have departed,
  All His Woes are over now,—
And the Passion that He bore,
Sin and pain, can vex no more.

3 He is risen! He is risen!
  He has opened Heaven's Gate!
We are free from sin's dark prison,
  Risen to a holier state;
And a brighter Easter Beam
On our longing eyes shall stream!
              Amen

2
Placed according to Thy Will,
May we all our work fulfil;
Helpers to each other prove;
Never from our office move;
Use the grace on each bestowed;
Learn and do the Will of God.

3
Ever, Lord, Thy Blessing give,
That our souls to Thee may live;
Fill us with the FATHER'S Love;
Never from our souls remove;
Dwell in us that we may be
Thine to all Eternity.   Amen.

Easter.

HYMN 111.

C. M. — A. R. REINAGLE.

Now morn-ing lifts her dew-y veil, With new-born bless-ings crowned; O, haste we then her light to hail In Courts of ho-ly ground. A-men.

2
But CHRIST, triumphant o'er the Grave,
   Shines more Divinely bright;
O, sing we then His Power to save,
   And walk we in His Light!

3
When from the darkest shades of night
   Sprang forth the world so fair,
Arrayed in brilliant robes of light,
   What Power Divine was there!

4
When He, who gave His guiltless SON
   A guilty world to spare,
Restored to life the HOLY ONE,
   What Love Divine was there!

5
When fresh from the CREATOR'S Hand,
   The earth in beauty stood,
All decked with light at His Command,
   He saw, and called it good.

6
But still more lovely in His Sight
   The Church now stands renewed,
Since He, the LAMB, hath made it white
   In His Atoning Blood.

7
O, Holy, Blessed THREE IN ONE,
   May Thy pure Light be given,
That we the paths of death may shun,
   And keep the way to Heaven.   Amen.

Easter.

HYMN 112.

S. M.   R. R. Chope.

Saviour, abide with us; The day is now far gone: We would obtain a blessing thus, By coming to Thy Throne. Amen.

2
We have not searched that land,
That happy land, as yet,
Where holy Angels round Thee stand,
Where suns can never set.

3
Our sun is sinking now,
Our day is almost o'er;
O Sun of Righteousness, do Thou
Shine on us Evermore!

4
Praise Christ, the Only Son!
Praise to the Father give!
Praise to the Spirit! One alone
In Whom alone we live.   Amen.

Easter.

HYMN 113. C. M. — GIBBONS. Arranged by J. TURLE.

My God! the Spring of all my joys, The Life of my de-lights, The Glo-ry of my bright-est days, And Com-fort of my nights. A-men.

2
In darkest shades if He appear,
  My dawning is begun!
He is my soul's sweet Morning Star,
  And He my rising Sun.

3
The opening Heavens around me shine
  With beams of sacred bliss,
While JESUS shows His Heart is mine,
  And whispers, "I am His!"

4
My soul would leave this heavy clay
  At that transporting Word,
Pursue with joy the shining way
  To meet my dearest LORD.

5
Fearless of Hell and ghastly death,
  I'd break through every foe;
The wings of love, and arms of faith,
  Should bear me conqueror through.

6
Now let the FATHER, and the SON,
  And SPIRIT be adored,
Where there are works to make Him known,
  Or Saints to love the LORD.   Amen.

Easter.

Hymn 114.

C.M. — Este's Psalter, 1599.

Be-hold the glo-ries of the Lamb, A-midst His Father's Throne! Pre-pare new honours for His Name, And songs be-fore un-known. A-men.

2
Let Elders worship at His Feet,
  The Church adore around,
With vials full of odours sweet,
  And harps of sweetest sound.

3
Those odours are the prayers of Saints,
  And these the hymns they raise;
Jesus is kind to our complaints,
  He loves to hear our praise.

4
Now to the Lamb That once was slain
  Be Endless blessings paid;
Salvation, Glory, Joy remain
  For ever on Thy Head.

5
Thou hast redeemed our souls with Blood,
  Hast set the prisoners free;
Hast made us kings and priests to God,
  And we shall reign with Thee.

6
The worlds of nature and of Grace
  Are put beneath Thy Power;
Then shorten these delaying days,
  And bring the promised hour. Amen.

Easter.

HYMN 115.

3, 7s. R. R. Chope.

Praise the LORD! ye Heavens a-dore Him; Praise Him, Angels, in the height; Sun and moon, re-joice be-fore Him; Praise Him, all ye stars and light. A-men.

2
Praise the LORD! for He hath spoken,
  Worlds His Mighty Voice obeyed;
Laws which never shall be broken,
  For their guidance He hath made.

3
Praise the LORD! for He is glorious;
  Never shall His Promise fail;
Christ hath made His Saints victorious;
  Sin and death shall not prevail.

4
Praise the GOD of our salvation;
  Hosts on High, His Power proclaim;
Heaven and earth, and all Creation,
  Laud and magnify His Name.

5
Worship, honour, glory, blessing,
  LORD, we offer to Thy Name;
Young and old, Thy Praise expressing,
  Join the SAVIOUR to proclaim.

6
As Thy Saints in Heaven adore Thee,
  We would bow before Thy Throne;
As Thine Angels serve before Thee,
  So on earth Thy Will be done! Amen.

Rogation Days.

Hymn 116.

C.M.   Arranged by Dr. Monk.

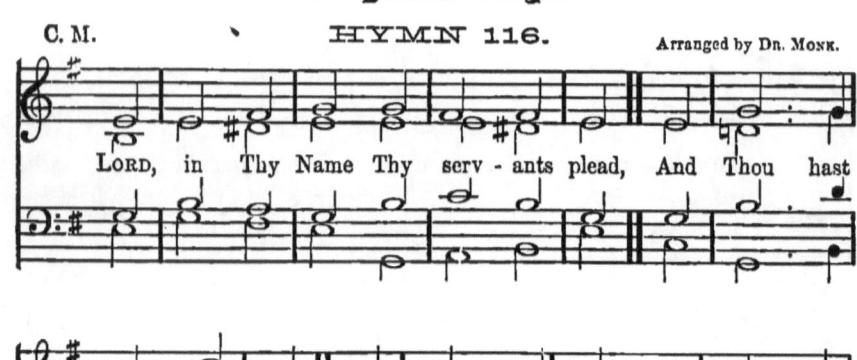

Lord, in Thy Name Thy serv-ants plead, And Thou hast

sworn to hear; Thine is the har-vest, Thine the

seed, The fresh and fad-ing year. A-men.

2
Our hope, when autumn winds blew wild,
  We trusted, Lord, with Thee;
And still, now spring has on us smiled,
  We wait on Thy Decree.

3
The former and the latter rain,
  The summer sun and air,
The green ear, and the golden grain,
  All Thine, are ours by prayer.

4
Thine too by right, and ours by grace,
  The wondrous growth unseen,
The hopes that soothe, the fears that brace,
  The love that shines serene.

5
So grant the precious things brought forth
  By sun and moon below,
That Thee in Thy new Heaven and Earth
  We never may forego.

6
To Father, Son, and Holy Ghost,
  The God Whom we adore,
Be glory, as it was, is now,
  And shall be Evermore.   Amen.

Ascension.

HYMN 117. C. M. RAVENSCROFT'S PSALTER, 1621.

O Saviour, now at God's Right Hand, High Priest with-in the veil! For us be-fore the Al-tar stand, For us with God pre-vail. A-men.

2

All our temptations, LORD, were Thine;
But Thou hast Power on High;
To Thee for Grace and Strength Divine
We lift our suppliant cry.

3

For lo! O GOD, in triumph raised,
Eternal is Thy Throne!
ONE with the FATHER, Thou art praised,
And with the SPIRIT ONE.   Amen.

Ascension.

HYMN 118. — 7s. — S. Reay.

Hail the day that sees Him rise, Alleluia!
To His Throne above the skies; Alleluia!
Christ, the Lamb for sinners given, Alleluia!
Enters now the Highest Heaven. Alleluia! Amen.

2

There for Him high triumph waits; Alleluia!
Lift your heads, Eternal gates; Alleluia!
He hath conquered death and sin, Alleluia!
Take the KING of Glory in. Alleluia!

3

Lo, the Heaven its LORD receives, Alleluia!
Yet He loves the earth He leaves; Alleluia!
Though returning to His Throne, Alleluia!
Still He calls mankind His Own. Alleluia!

4

See, He lifts His Hands above; Alleluia!
See, He shows the prints of love; Alleluia!
Hark! His gracious Lips bestow, Alleluia!
Blessings on His Church below. Alleluia!

5

Still for us He intercedes, Alleluia!
His prevailing Death He pleads, Alleluia!
Near Himself prepares our place, Alleluia!
He the First-fruits of our race. Alleluia!

6

LORD, though parted from our sight, Alleluia!
Far above the starry height; Alleluia!
Grant our hearts may thither rise, Alleluia!
Seeking Thee above the skies. Alleluia! Amen.

Ascension.

HYMN 119. C. M.   Adapted by R. R. Chope.

2
Who is the KING of Glory? Who?
  The LORD for strength renowned;
In battle mighty, o'er His foes
  Eternal Victor crowned.

3
Lift up your heads, ye gates! unfold
  In state to entertain
The KING of Glory; see, He comes
  With all His shining Train!

4
Who is the KING of Glory? Who?
  The LORD of Hosts renowned;
Of Glory He alone is KING,
  Who is with Glory crowned.

5
To FATHER, SON, and HOLY GHOST
  Immortal Glory be,
Who was, and is, and shall be still
  To all Eternity.   Amen.

Ascension.

HYMN 120.

C. M. — Arranged by Dn. Monk.

O Thou Eternal King Most High! Who didst the world redeem; And conquering Death and Hell, receive A dignity supreme. Amen.

2
Thou, through the starry orbs, this day
  Didst to Thy Throne ascend;
Thenceforth to reign in sovereign power
  And glory without end.

3
There, seated in Thy Majesty,
  To Thee submissive bow
The Heaven of Heavens, the spacious earth,
  The depths of Hell below.

4
There, waiting for the faithful souls,
  Be Thou to us, O Lord,
Our peerless Joy while here we stay,
  In Heaven our great Reward.

5
Renew our strength, our sins forgive,
  Our miseries efface,
And lift our souls on high to Thee,
  By Thy Celestial Grace.

6
Glory to Jesus, Who returns
  Triumphantly to Heaven;
Praise to the Father Evermore,
  And Holy Ghost be given.   Amen.

Ascension.

2
Thou art gone where now is given
  What no mortal might could gain;
On the Eternal Throne of Heaven,
  In Thy FATHER's Power to reign.

3
There Thy Kingdoms all adore Thee,
  Heaven above and earth below,
While the depths of Hell before Thee
  Trembling and defeated bow.

4
We, O LORD! with hearts adoring,
  Follow Thee above the sky;
Hear our prayers Thy Grace imploring,
  Lift our souls to Thee on High.

5
That when Thou again in glory
  On the clouds of Heaven shalt shine,
We Thy Flock may stand before Thee,
  Owned for Evermore as Thine.

6
Hail! all hail! in Thee confiding,
  JESU! Thee shall all adore,
In Thy FATHER's Might abiding
  With ONE SPIRIT Evermore. Amen.

Ascension.

HYMN 122.

7s. R. R. Chope.

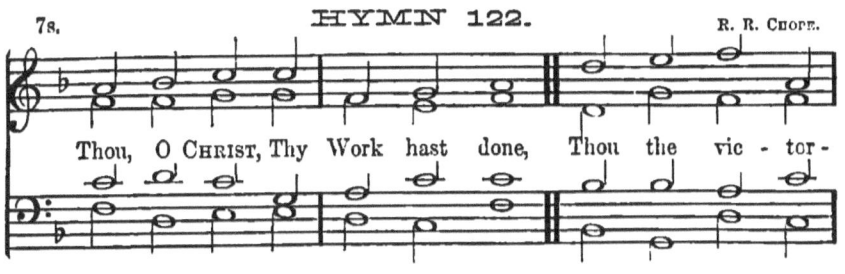

Thou, O Christ, Thy Work hast done, Thou the vic-tor-

y hast won; End-less Glo-ry, once laid by,

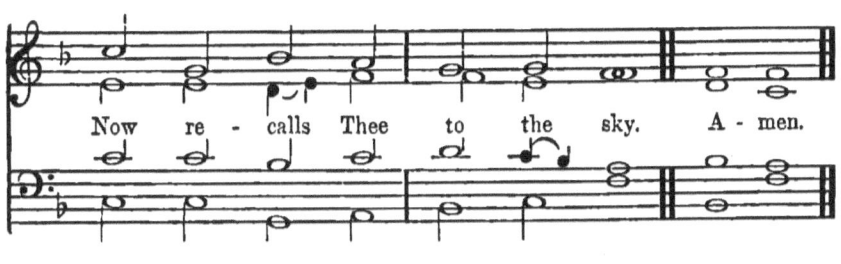

Now re-calls Thee to the sky. A-men.

2
Now unfold the Eternal Gates,
Where the Host of Angels waits;
Seated on the FATHER's Throne,
Thee both GOD and MAN we own.

3
There vouchsafe to intercede,
And for us Thy Merits plead;
Grace and glory thence bestow
On the Church, Thy Spouse below.

4
JESU! praise to Thee be given,
Now returned in peace to Heaven;
Holy FATHER, praise to Thee,
With the SPIRIT Ever be.   Amen.

Ascension.

HYMN 123. L. M. R. B. Wall.

Where high the Heavenly Tem-ple stands, The House of God not made with hands, A Great High Priest our na-ture wears, The Guard-ian of man-kind ap-pears. A-men.

2
He Who for men their Surety stood,
And poured on earth His precious Blood,
Pursues in Heaven His mighty Plan,
The Saviour and the Friend of man.

3
Though now ascended up above,
He views our griefs with pitying love;
And still remembers, in the skies,
His Tears, His Prayers, and Agonies.

4
In every pang that rends the heart
The Man of Sorrows bears a part;
Touched with the feeling of our grief,
He to the sufferer sends relief.

5
With boldness, then, before His Throne,
Let us make all our sorrows known;
And ask the aid of Heavenly Power
To help us in the evil hour.

6
Praise we the Father; praise the Son,
Our woes and weakness Who hath known;
Let equal praise, to Spirit Blest,
By men and Angels be addrest.   Amen.

Ascension.

HYMN 124. 7s. Arranged by J. B. Dykes.

Rul-er of the Hosts of Light, Death hath yield-ed to Thy Might; And Thy Blood hath marked a road Lead-ing to Thine Own A-bode. A-men.

2
From Thy Dwelling-place above,
From Thy FATHER's Throne of Love,
Still remember, SAVIOUR kind!
Those whom Thou hast left behind.

3
Thou art seated on the Throne,
By Thy Death and Sorrows won;
Now Thy Work of Mercy crown,
Send Thy HOLY SPIRIT down.

4
Praise the SON, enthroned on High
In the FATHER's Majesty,
And the HOLY GHOST adore,
THREE IN ONE for Evermore.   Amen.

Whitsuntide.

HYMN 125.

L. M. P.   R. Stuart.

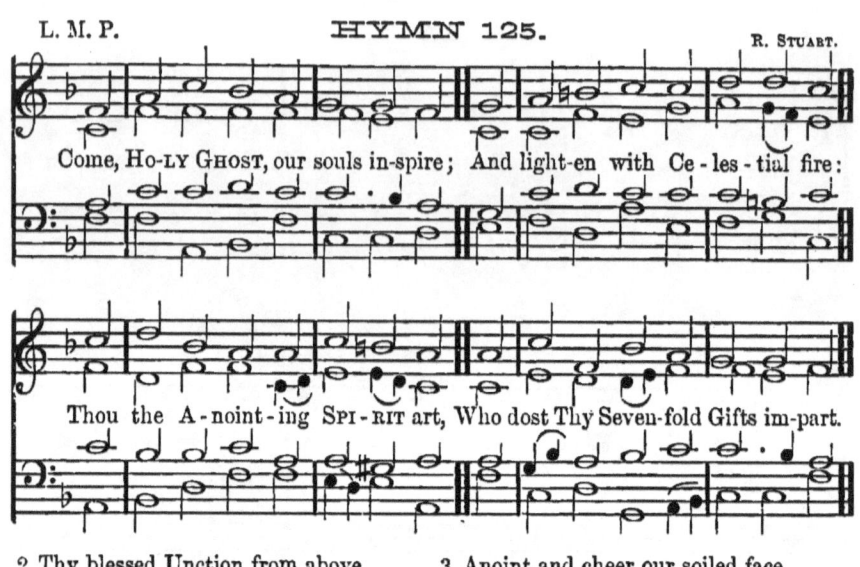

Come, Ho-ly Ghost, our souls in-spire; And light-en with Ce - les - tial fire:
Thou the A - noint-ing Spi - rit art, Who dost Thy Seven-fold Gifts im-part.

2 Thy blessed Unction from above
Is comfort, life, and fire of love;
Enable with perpetual light
The dulness of our blinded sight.

3 Anoint and cheer our soiled face
With the abundance of Thy Grace:
Keep far our foes, give peace at home;
Where Thou art Guide, no ill can come.

4 Teach us to know the Father, Son,
And Thee, of Both, to be but One;
That, through the ages all along,

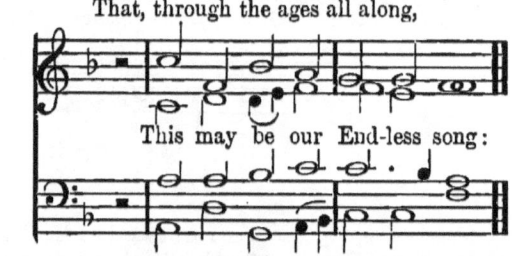

This may be our End-less song:

Praise to Thine E-ter-nal Me-rit, Father, Son, and Holy Spirit.   A - men.

Whitsuntide.

HYMN 126.

7s (6 of.) — S. Reay.

Ho-ly Spi-rit! Lord of Light! From Thy clear Ce-les-tial Height,
Thy pure beaming Radiance give; Come, Thou Father of the poor!
Come, with treasures which endure! Come, Thou Light of all that live! A-men.

2
Thou, of all consolers Best,
Visiting the troubled breast,
Dost refreshing peace bestow;
Thou in toil art Comfort sweet;
Pleasant Coolness in the heat;
Solace in the midst of woe.

3
Light Immortal! Light Divine!
Visit Thou these hearts of Thine,
And our inmost being fill:
If Thou take Thy Grace away,
Nothing pure in man will stay;
All his good is turned to ill.

4
Heal our wounds—our strength renew;
On our dryness pour Thy Dew;
Wash the stains of guilt away:
Bend the stubborn heart and will;
Melt the frozen, warm the chill;
Guide the steps that go astray.

5
Thou, on those who Evermore
Thee confess and Thee adore,
In Thy Sevenfold Gifts descend:
Give them comfort when they die;
Give them life with Thee on High;
Give them joys which never end. Amen.

Whitsuntide.

HYMN 127. — MATTHEW HUSSEY, 1762. C.M.

When God of old came down from Heaven, In power and wrath He came; Before His Feet the clouds were riven, Half darkness and half flame. Amen.

2
But when He came the second time,
 He came in power and love;
Softer than gale at morning prime
 Hovered His Holy Dove.

3
The fires that rushed on Sinai down
 In sudden torrents dread,
Now gently light a glorious crown,
 On every Sainted head.

4
And as on Israel's awe-struck ear
 The Voice exceeding loud,
The Trump that Angels quake to hear,
 Thrilled from the deep, dark cloud;

5
So, when the Spirit of our God
 Came down His flock to find,
A Voice from Heaven was heard abroad,
 A rushing, mighty Wind.

6
It fills the Church of God; It fills
 The sinful world around;
Only in stubborn hearts and wills
 No place for It is found.

7
Come Lord, come Wisdom, Love, and Power,
 Open our ears to hear;
Let us not miss the accepted hour;
 Save, Lord, by love or fear. Amen.

Whitsuntide.

HYMN 128.

S. M.   S. Gee.

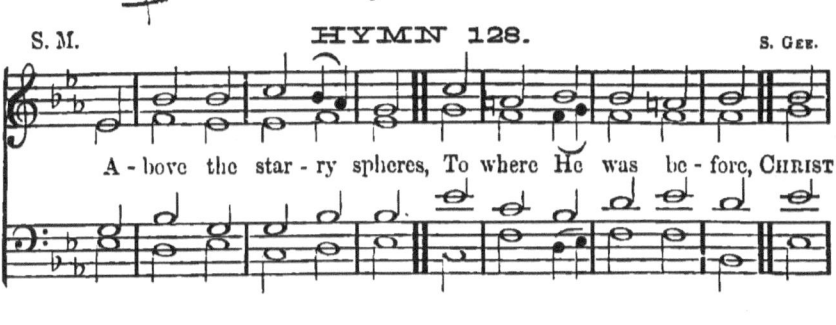

A-bove the star-ry spheres, To where He was be-fore, Christ had gone up, soon from on High, The Father's Gift to pour: A-men.

2
And now had fully come,
On mystic circle borne
Of seven times seven revolving days,
The Pentecostal morn:

3
When, as the Apostles knelt
At the third hour in prayer,
A sudden rushing sound proclaimed
The God of glory near.

4
Forthwith a Tongue of Fire
Alights on every brow;
Each heart receives the Father's Light,
The Word's enkindling Glow;

5
The Holy Ghost on all
Is mightily outpoured,
Who straight in divers tongues declare
The Wonders of the Lord.

6
While strangers of all climes
Flock round from far and near,
And their own tongue, wherever born,
All with amazement hear.

7
But Judah, faithless still,
Denies the Hand Divine,
And, mocking, jeers the Saints of Christ,
As full of new-made wine.

8
Till Peter, in the midst,
By Joel's ancient word
Rebukes their unbelief, and wins
Three thousand to the Lord.

9
The Father and the Son
And Spirit we adore;
O may the Spirit's Gifts be poured
On us for Evermore.   Amen.

Whitsuntide.

L. M. HYMN 129. R. B. Wall

Spi-rit of God, That moved of old Up-on the wa-ters' dark-ened face, Come, when our faith-less hearts are cold,

And stir them with Thine in-ward Grace. A-men.

2
Thou That art Power and Peace combined,
All highest Strength, all purest Love,
The Rushing of the mighty Wind,
The Brooding of the gentle Dove;

3
Come, give us still Thy powerful Aid,
And urge us on, and keep us Thine;
Nor leave the hearts, that once were made
Fit temples for Thy Grace Divine:

4
Nor let us quench Thy Sevenfold Light;
But still with softest Breathings stir
Our wayward souls—and lead us right,
O Holy Ghost, the Comforter!

Amen.

Whitsuntide.

HYMN 130.

L. M. T. Graham.

Spi - rit of Mer - cy, Truth, and Love, O shed Thine Influence from a - bove; And still from age to age con - vey The Wonders of this Sa - cred Day. A - men.

2
In every clime, by every tongue,
Be God's surpassing Glory sung:
Let all the listening earth be taught
The deeds our Great REDEEMER wrought.

3
Unfailing Comfort, Heavenly Guide,
Still o'er Thy Holy Church preside;
Still let mankind Thy Blessings prove,
SPIRIT of Mercy, Truth, and Love.

4
O HOLY FATHER, HOLY SON,
AND HOLY SPIRIT, THREE IN ONE,
Thy Grace devoutly we implore,
Thy Name be praised for Evermore.
                  Amen.

Whitsuntide.

Hymn 131.

L. M.   J. B. Dykes.

Cre-at-or! Spi-rit! Lord of Grace! Make Thou our hearts Thy Dwelling-place, And with Thy Might Ce-les-tial aid The souls of men which Thou hast made. A-men.

2
O Finger of the Hand Divine,
The Seven-fold Gifts of Grace are Thine;
And touched by Thee the lips proclaim
All praise to God's Most Holy Name.

3
Do Thou Thy Heavenly Light impart,
And give Thy Love to every heart;
Turn all our weakness into might,
O Thou the Source of Life and Light.

4
Protect us from the assailing foe,
And peace, the fruit of love, bestow;
Upheld by Thee, our Strength and Guide
No evil can our steps betide.

5
Spirit of Faith, on us bestow,
The Father and the Son to know;
That with Them we may worship Thee,
Eternal One, Eternal Three.

6
To God the Father let us sing;
To God the Son, our risen King,
And equally with Them adore,
The Spirit—God for Evermore. Amen.

Trinity Sunday.

HYMN 132. — R. F. Smith.

Holy, Holy, Ho-ly! Lord God Almighty, Ear-ly in the morning our song shall rise to Thee; Ho-ly, Ho-ly, Ho-ly, Mer-ci-ful and Might-y, God in Three Per-sons, Blessed Tri-ni-ty. A-men.

2
Holy, Holy, Holy! all the Saints adore Thee,
Casting down their golden crowns around the glassy sea,
Cherubim and Seraphim, falling down before Thee,
Which wert, and art, and Evermore shalt [be.

3
Holy, Holy, Holy! though the darkness hide Thee,
Though the eye of sinful man Thy Glory may not see,
Only Thou art Holy; there is none beside Thee
Perfect in power, in love, and purity.

4
Holy, Holy, Holy! Lord God Almighty,
All Thy Works shall praise Thy Name, in earth, and sky, and sea:
Holy, Holy, Holy! Merciful and Mighty,
God in Three Persons, Blessed Trinity. Amen.

Trinity Sunday.

L. M.   HYMN 133.   Dr. Rogers, 1600.

Fa-ther of all, to Thee we raise The tri-bute

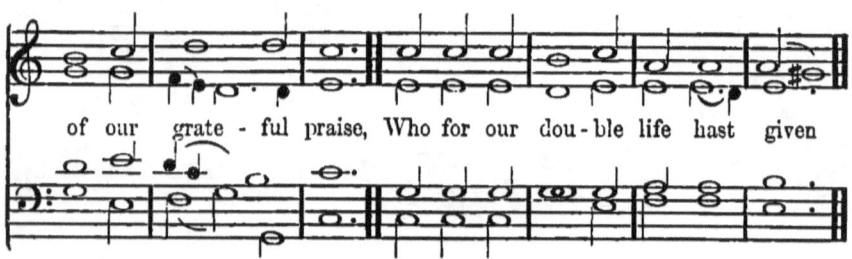

of our grate-ful praise, Who for our dou-ble life hast given

Bread from the earth, and Bread from Heaven. A-men.

2
Thou too, O Jesu! be adored,
The Only Son, the Almighty Lord,
Who our Salvation to become
Didst not abhor the Virgin's womb.

3
And Thou, Who didst vouchsafe to rest
Upon the Virgin Mother Blest,
Eternal Spirit! laud and praise,
With heart and voice to Thee we raise.

4
Three Persons but One God! Whose Grace
Preserves and saves our human race,
With hearts rejoicing, Lord, in Thee,
We hymn this mighty Mystery.

5
To God the Father, God the Son,
And God the Spirit, Three in One,
Laud, Honour, Glory, Majesty,
Now and henceforth for Ever be. Amen.

Trinity Sunday.

HYMN 134.

J. B. Dykes.

8s (3 of.)

O God of Life, Whose Power benign Doth o'er the world in mercy shine, Accept our praise, for we are Thine. A-men.

2
O Father, all-creating Lord,
Be Thou by every tongue implored,
Be Thou by every heart adored.

3
O Son of God, for sinners slain,
We bless Thee, Lord, Whose dying Pain
For us did Endless life regain.

4
O Holy Ghost, Whose guardian Care
Doth us for Heavenly joys prepare,
May we in Thy Communion share.

5
O Holy Blessed Trinity,
With faith we sinners bow to Thee;
In Heaven and earth exalted be.   Amen.

Sundays after Trinity.

HYMN 135.

7, 7, 7, 5.   German Chorale.

Three in One, and One in Three, Rul-er of the

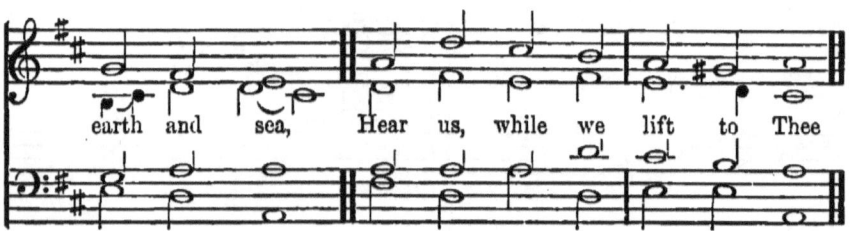

earth and sea, Hear us, while we lift to Thee

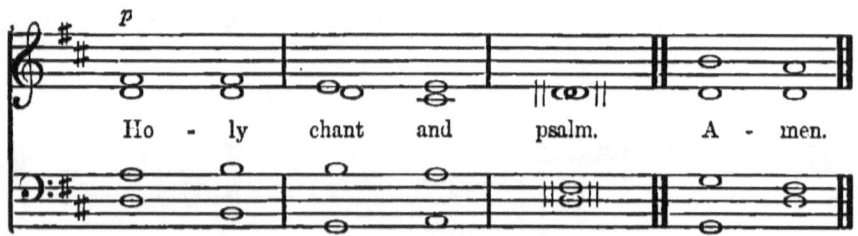

Ho - ly chant and psalm. A - men.

2
Light of Light! with morning, shine:
Lift on us Thy Light Divine;
And let charity benign
   Breathe on us her balm.

3
Light of Light! when falls the even,
Let it close on sin forgiven;
Fold us in the peace of Heaven,
   Shed a holy calm.

4
Three in One and One in Three,
Dimly here we worship Thee;
With the Saints hereafter we
   Hope to bear the palm. Amen.

Sundays after Trinity.

2
ALMIGHTY SON, Incarnate WORD,
Our PROPHET, PRIEST, REDEEMER, LORD!
Before Thy Throne we sinners bend,
To us Thy saving Grace extend.

3
Eternal SPIRIT! by Whose Breath
The soul is raised from sin and death;
Before Thy Throne we sinners bend,
To us Thy quickening Power extend.

4
THRICE HOLY! FATHER, SPIRIT, SON!
Mysterious GODHEAD, THREE IN ONE!
Before Thy Throne we sinners bend,
Grace, Pardon, Life, to all extend. Amen.

Sundays after Trinity.

HYMN 137.

C. M. — Scotch Psalter, 1565.

Have mer-cy on us, God Most High, Who lift our hearts to Thee; Have mer-cy on us worms of earth, Most Ho-ly Tri-ni-ty. A-men.

2
Most Ancient of all Mysteries!
   Before Thy Throne we lie;
Have mercy now, Most Merciful,
   Most HOLY TRINITY!

3
When Heaven and earth were yet unmade,
   When time was yet unknown,
Thou, in Thy Bliss and Majesty,
   Didst live and love alone.

4
How wonderful Creation is,
   The work that Thou didst bless;
And oh! what then must Thou be like,
   Eternal Loveliness?

5
Most Ancient of all Mysteries!
   Still at Thy Throne we lie;
Have mercy now, Most Merciful,
   Most HOLY TRINITY!   Amen.

Sundays after Trinity.

HYMN 138.

L. M. S. REAY.

This day the Light, of Heavenly birth, First streamed up-on the

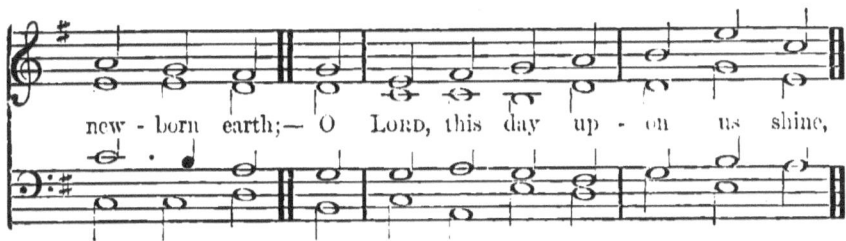

new-born earth;— O LORD, this day up-on us shine,

And fill our souls with Light Di-vine. A-men.

2
This day the SAVIOUR left the grave,
And rose Omnipotent to save;—
O JESU, may we raised be
From death of sin, to Life in Thee.

3
This day the HOLY SPIRIT came
With fiery Tongues of cloven Flame;—
O SPIRIT, fill our hearts this day
With Grace to hear, and Grace to pray.

4
O Day of Light, and Life, and Grace!
From earthly toils sweet Resting-place!
Thy hallowed hours, best gift of Love,
Give we again to GOD above!   Amen.

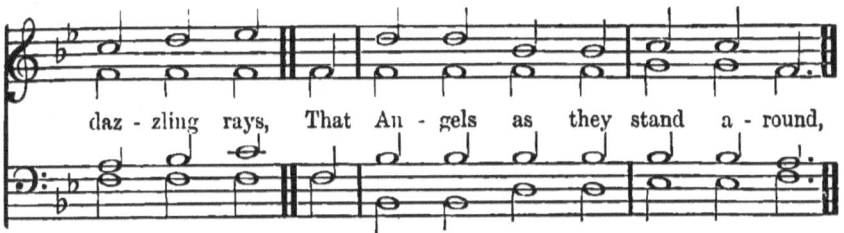
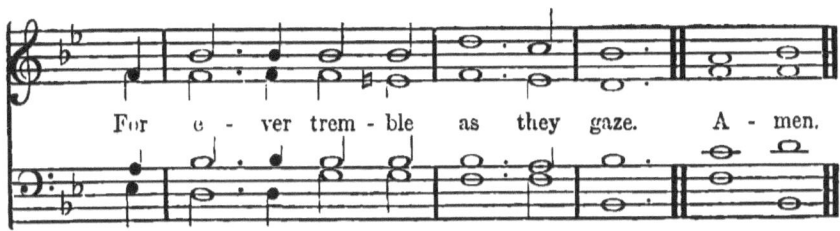

2

FATHER, may we Thy Laws fulfil!
Blest SON, may we Thy Precepts learn!
And Thou, O SPIRIT! guide our will,
Our feet unto Thy Pathway turn.
Yea, FATHER, may Thy Will be done,
May we Thy hallowed Name adore,
Together with Thy Blessed SON,
And HOLY SPIRIT Evermore.   Amen.

Sundays after Trinity.

HYMN 140.

8. 6. 8. 4.   Arranged by J. TURLE.

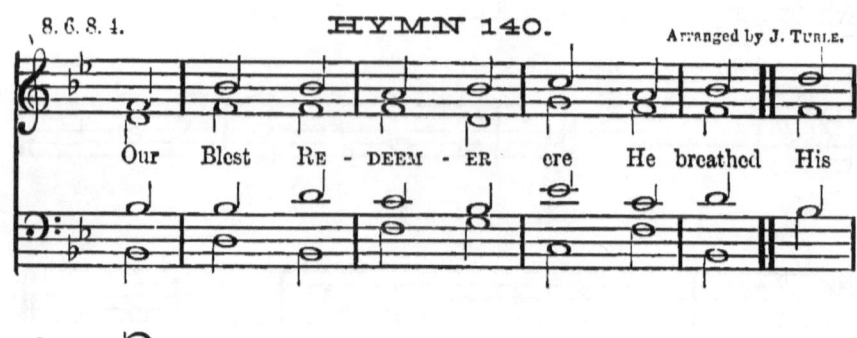

Our Blest RE-DEEM-ER ere He breathed His
ten-der last Fare-well, A Guide a COM-FORT-
ER bequeathed With us to dwell. A-men.

2
He came sweet influence to impart,
　A gracious, willing Guest,
While He can find one humble heart,
　Wherein to rest.

3
And His that gentle Voice we hear,
　Soft as the breath of even,
That checks each thought, that calms each [fear,
　And speaks of Heaven.

4
And every virtue we possess,
　And every conquest won,
And every thought of holiness,
　Are His alone!

5
SPIRIT of Purity and Grace,
　Our weakness, pitying, see:
O make our hearts Thy Dwelling-place,
　And worthier Thee.

6
Now Praise the FATHER, praise the SON,
　BLEST SPIRIT, praise to Thee,
All praise to GOD, the THREE IN ONE,
　The ONE IN THREE.   Amen.

Sundays after Trinity.

HYMN 141.

S. M. — Arranged by Dr. Monk.

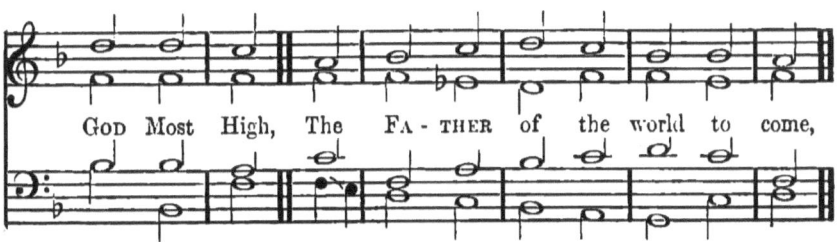
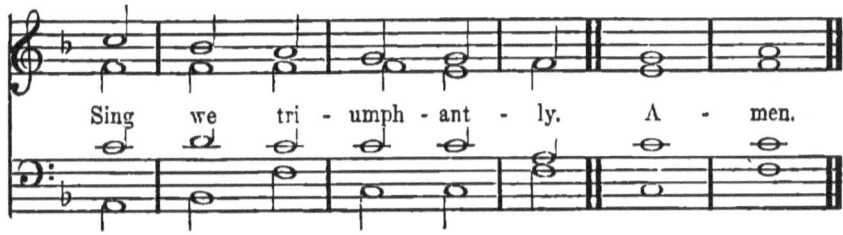

To Christ, the Prince of Peace, And Son of God Most High, The Father of the world to come, Sing we triumphantly. Amen.

2
Deep in His Heart for us
The wound of love He bore,
That love which still He kindles in
The hearts that Him adore.

3
O Jesu, Victim Blest,
What else but love Divine
Could Thee constrain to open thus
That sacred Heart of Thine?

4
O Fount of Endless Life,
O Spring of water clear!
O Flame Celestial, cleansing all
Who unto Thee draw near!

5
Hide me in Thy dear Heart,
For thither do I fly;
There seek Thy Grace through life, in death
Thine Immortality.

6
Praise to the Father be;
Praise to His Only Son;
Praise to the Blessed Comforter,
While Endless ages run! Amen.

Sundays after Trinity.

HYMN 142. — C. M. — COURTEVILLE, 1680.

O Thou, Who art gone up, on High A mansion to prepare, Hear Thou, from Heaven, Thy servants' cry, That we may meet Thee there. A-men.

2
Make us to those delights aspire,
　Which spring from love to Thee,
Which pass the carnal heart's desire,
　Which faith alone can see.

3
Where GOD shall His true children own,
　In Him for ever blest;
And He the toils of all shall crown,
　And be Himself their Rest.

4
Thy Grace alone to Thee can lead,
　And place us near Thy Throne;
To help us therefore in our need,
　Send down Thy HOLY ONE.

5
All praise to Thee at GOD's Right Hand;
　All praise be ever done,
In every age, in every land,
　To Thee, Dread THREE IN ONE. Amen.

Sundays after Trinity.

HYMN 143.

C. M.   Arranged by S. Reay.

O God of Hosts, the Mighty Lord, How lovely

is the place, Where Thou, enthroned in glory, shew'st

The Brightness of Thy Face. Amen.

2
My longing soul faints with desire
  To view Thy blest Abode;
My panting heart and flesh cry out
  For Thee, the Living God.

3
For in Thy Courts one single day
  'Tis better to attend,
Than, Lord, in any place besides
  A thousand days to spend.

4
O Lord of Hosts, my King and God,
  How highly blest are they,
Who in Thy Temple always dwell,
  And there Thy Praise display!

5
To Father, Son, and Holy Ghost,
  The God Whom we adore,
Be glory, as it was, is now,
  And shall be Evermore.   Amen.

Sundays after Trinity.

C.M.   HYMN 144.   Ravenscroft's Psalter, 1621.

O Christ, our Hope, our heart's Desire, Redemption's

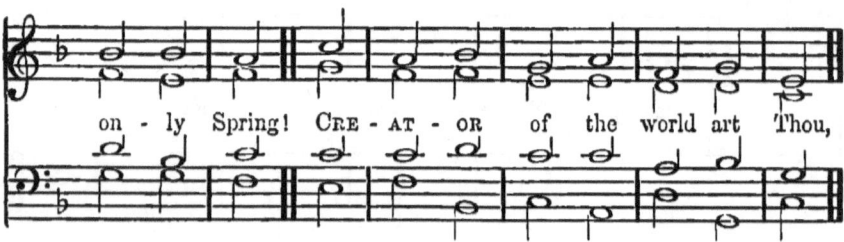

only Spring! Creator of the world art Thou,

Its Saviour and its King. A — — men.

2

How vast the mercy and the love
    Which laid our sins on Thee,
And led Thee to a cruel death,
    To set Thy people free.

3

But now the bonds of death are burst,
    The ransom has been paid,
And Thou art on Thy Father's Throne,
    In robes of light arrayed.

4

Oh! may Thy mighty Love prevail,
    Our sinful souls to spare!
Oh! may we come before Thy Throne,
    And find acceptance there!

5

O Christ, be Thou our present Joy,
    Our future great Reward;
Our only glory may it be,
    To glory in the Lord.   Amen.

Sundays after Trinity.

HYMN 145. Dr. Gauntlett. Inserted by permission of the Proprietors of the Church Hymn and Tune Book.

Jerusalem! blest City. Name of Celestial sound, With living stones upbuilded, With Angel Armies crowned. Amen.

2
Thou art the golden mansion,
　Where Saints for ever sing,
The seat of God's Own chosen,
　The Palace of our King.

3
There God for ever dwelleth,
　Himself of all the Crown;
The Lamb a Light there shineth,
　And never goeth down.

4
Nought to that City cometh
　Its people to molest;
They praise their God for ever,
　Nor day nor night they rest.

5
To Christ, the Sun that lightens
　His Church, above, below,
The Father, and the Spirit,
　Let praise for ever flow.　Amen.

Sundays after Trinity.

HYMN 146.

8s (6 of.) — Arranged by J. S. Bach, 1750.

We saw Thee not when Thou did'st come To this poor world of sin and death, Nor e'er be-held Thy Cot-tage-home In that de-spis-éd Na-za-reth; But we believe THY Footsteps trod Its streets and plains, Thou SON of GOD. A-men.

2

We did not see Thee lifted high
Amid that wild and savage crew,
Nor heard Thy meek imploring Cry,
"Forgive, they know not what they do;"
Yet we believe the deed was done,
Which shook the earth and veiled the sun.

3

We stood not by the empty tomb
Where late Thy Sacred Body lay,
Nor sat within that Upper Room,
Nor met Thee in the open way;
But we believe that Angels said,
"Why seek the living 'midst the dead?"

4

We did not mark the chosen few,
When Thou didst through the clouds ascend,
First lift to Heaven their wondering view,
Then to the earth all prostrate bend;
Yet we believe that mortal eyes
Beheld Thee journey to the skies.

5

And now that Thou dost reign on High,
And thence Thy waiting people bless,
No ray of glory from the sky
Doth shine upon our wilderness;
But we believe Thy faithful Word,
And trust in our Redeeming LORD.   Amen.

Sundays after Trinity.

HYMN 147. L.M. Adapted by R. F. Smith.

Exiled afar from their blest home, Condemned 'mid darkness long to roam; Unskilled to find the Heavenly way, The race of man had gone astray. Amen.

2
But lo! to point their steps aright,
Self-banished comes the KING of Light;
Content the joys of Heaven to lack,
That He may bring His banished back.

3
Them that were lost He safely guides,
Strength for the journey He provides;
Himself the Way the wanderer needs,
Himself the End to which He leads.

4
O Thou the Truth, Eternal GOD!
Once veiled in mortal flesh and blood,
Give us pure hearts, O CHRIST, that we
In Thy Light Endless light may see.

5
To GOD the FATHER, GOD the SON,
And HOLY SPIRIT, THREE IN ONE,
All laud and praise be ever given,
By all on earth and all in Heaven. Amen.

Sundays after Trinity.

HYMN 148. Dr. GAUNTLETT. Inserted by permission of the proprietors of the Church Hymn and Tune Book.

Brief life is here our por - tion, Brief sor - row, short - lived care: The life that knows no end - ing, The tear - less life is There. A - men.

2
O gracious retribution,
  Short toil, eternal rest;
For mortals and for sinners
  A mansion with the Blest.

3
Awhile we fight the battle,
  And then we wear the crown
Of full and Everlasting
  And passionless renown.

4
And now we watch and struggle,
  And now we live in hope,
And Sion in her anguish
  With Babylon must cope;

5
But He Whom now we trust in
  Shall then be seen and known;
And they that see and know Him
  Shall have Him for their own.

6
The morning shall awaken,
  The shadows shall decay,
And each true-hearted servant
  Shall shine as doth the day:

7
There GOD, our KING and PORTION,
  In fulness of His Grace,
Shall we behold for Ever,
  And worship face to Face. Amen.

sick - ness, And love, and life, and rest. A - men.

2

O one, O only Mansion!
  O Paradise of Joy!
Where tears are ever banished,
  And smiles have no alloy;
The LAMB is all thy splendour;
  The Crucified thy praise;
His Laud and Benediction
  Thy ransomed people raise.

3

With jasper glow thy bulwarks,
  Thy streets with emeralds blaze;
The sardis and the topaz
  Unite in thee their rays;
Thine ageless walls are bounded
  With amethyst unpriced;
The Saints build up its fabric,
  The Corner-stone is CHRIST.

4

Thou hast no shore, fair Ocean!
  Thou hast no time, bright Day!
Dear Fountain of refreshment
  To pilgrims far away!
Upon the ROCK OF AGES
  Ascends thy holy tower;
Thine is the victor's laurel,
  And thine the golden dower.

5

O sweet and blessed Country,
  The Home of GOD'S Elect!
O sweet and blessed Country,
  That eager hearts expect!
JESU! in mercy bring us
  To that dear land of rest;
Who art, with GOD the FATHER,
  And SPIRIT, Ever Blest!   Amen.

Sundays after Trinity.

HYMN 150. 7, 6s. J. B. Dykes.

Jerusalem the golden! With milk and honey blest; Beneath Thy contemplation Sink heart and voice oppressed. A-men.

2 I know not, oh! I know not
   What joys await us there;
  What radiancy of glory,
   What bliss beyond compare.

3 They stand, those halls of Sion,
   All jubilant with song,
  And bright with many an Angel,
   And all the Martyr Throng:

4 The Prince is ever in them,
   His Light is always seen;
  The pastures of the blessed
   Are decked in glorious sheen.

5 There is the Throne of David;
   And bliss without alloy,
  The shout of them that triumph,
   The song of festal joy;

6 And they, who with their Leader
   Have conquered in the fight,
  For Ever and for Ever
   Are dressed in robes of white.

7 Jesu! in mercy bring us
   To that dear land of rest;
  Who art, with God the Father,
   And Spirit, Ever Blest. Amen.

Sundays after Trinity.

HYMN 151.   L. M.   OLD HUNDREDTH.

All people that on earth do dwell, Sing to the LORD with cheer-ful voice; Him serve with fear, His Praise forth tell, Come ye be-fore Him and re-joice. A-men.

2
The LORD ye know is GOD indeed;
Without our aid He did us make;
We are His flock, He doth us feed,
And for His sheep He doth us take.

3
O enter then His Gates with praise,
Approach with joy His Courts unto;
Praise, laud, and bless His Name always,
For it is seemly so to do.

4
For why? the LORD our GOD is good,
His Mercy is for ever sure;
His Truth at all times firmly stood,
And shall from age to age endure.

5
To FATHER, SON, and HOLY GHOST,
The GOD Whom Heaven and earth adore,
From men and from the Angel Host
Be praise and glory Evermore.   Amen.

And ex-alt them to the skies. A-men.

2

That which CHRIST so hardly wrought,
That which He so dearly bought,
Let not thankless hearts again,
Sin and folly, render vain.
Rather, gladly for His Name
Let us bear the Cross and shame;
Joyfully for Him to die
Is not death, but victory.

3

JESU! Health and Life of all,
Hear us when to Thee we call;
To our prayers propitious be,
As we make our boast in Thee.
To the FATHER and the SON
Laud and praise be ever done;
Glory to the HOLY GHOST,
Ever from the Heavenly Host.   Amen.

Sundays after Trinity.

HYMN 153.

6, 4, 6, 4, 6, 6, 4.
R. R. Chope.

Nearer, my God, to Thee, Nearer to Thee, E'en though it be a Cross That raiseth me; Still all my song shall be, Nearer, my God, to Thee, Nearer to Thee! A - men.

2
Though, like a wanderer,
　　The sun gone down,
Darkness comes over me,
　　My rest a stone;
Yet in my dreams I'd be
Nearer, my God, to Thee,
　　Nearer to Thee!

3
There let my way appear
　　Steps unto Heaven;
All that Thou sendest me
　　In mercy given;
Angels to beckon me
Nearer, my God, to Thee,
　　Nearer to Thee!

4
Then, with my waking thoughts
　　Bright with Thy Praise,
Out of my stony griefs
　　Bethel I'll raise;
So by my woes to be
Nearer, my God, to Thee,
　　Nearer to Thee!　　Amen.

Sundays after Trinity.

HYMN 154.

7s (8 of.)   J. A. LLOYD.

Je-su, Lover of my soul, Let me to Thy Bosom fly,
While the gathering waters roll, While the tempest still is high:
Hide me, O my SAVIOUR, hide, Till the storm of life be past;
Safe into the haven guide, O receive my soul at last. Amen.

2 Other refuge have I none;
  Hangs my helpless soul on Thee;
  Leave, oh! leave me not alone,
  Still support and comfort me.
  All my trust on Thee is stayed,
  All my cares to Thee I bring;
  Cover my defenceless head
  With the shadow of Thy Wing.

3 Plenteous grace with Thee is found,
  Grace to cleanse from every sin;
  Let the healing streams abound,
  Make and keep me pure within;
  Thou of Life the Fountain art,
  Freely let me take of Thee;
  Spring Thou up within my heart,
  Rise to all Eternity.   Amen.

Sundays after Trinity.

HYMN 155.

Jesus came, the Heavens adoring, Came with peace from realms on High;
Jesus came for man's redemption, Lowly came on earth to die;
Alleluia! Alleluia! Came in deep humility. Amen.

2
Jesus comes again in mercy,
  When our hearts are bowed with care;
Jesus comes again in answer
  To our earnest, heartfelt prayer;
Alleluia! Alleluia!
  Comes to save us from despair.

3
Jesus comes to souls rejoicing,
  Bringing news of sins forgiven;
Jesus comes in sounds of gladness,
  Lifting up our souls to Heaven;
Alleluia! Alleluia!
  Now the gate of death is riven.

4
Jesus comes in joy and sorrow,
  Shares alike our hopes and fears;
Jesus comes, whate'er befalls us,
  Glads our hearts, and dries our tears,
Alleluia! Alleluia!
  Cheering e'en our failing years.

5
Jesus comes on clouds triumphant,
  When the Heavens shall pass away;
Jesus comes again in glory;—
  Let us then our homage pay,
Alleluia! Alleluia!
  Sing we "till the break of day." Amen.

Sundays after Trinity.

HYMN 156.

Rock of Ages, cleft for me, Let me hide myself in Thee; Let the Water and the Blood, From Thy wounded Side which flowed, Be of sin the double cure, Save from wrath and make me pure. A-men.

2 Merit I have none to bring,
Simply to Thy Cross I cling;
Could my tears for ever flow,
Could my zeal no languor know,
All for sin could not atone,
Thou must save and Thou alone.

3 While I draw this fleeting breath,
When mine eyelids close in death,
When I rise to worlds unknown,
See Thee on Thy Judgment-Throne,
Rock of Ages, cleft for me,
Let me hide myself in Thee.   Amen.

Sundays after Trinity.

HYMN 157.

6, 6, 6, 4.   W. T. Best.

O Death, thou art no more, Our fears, thy hopes are dead;

Where all have gone be-fore, Thy-self hast fled. A-men.

2

O Death, thou art no more,
For CHRIST, the lost to save,
Hath opened wide the door,
   And left the grave,—

3

In dying, thee hath slain,
In living, life hath given,
And, rending Hell in twain,
   Hath opened Heaven.

4

Then, Christian, cease to weep,
Nor drop in vain a tear,
A little while of sleep,
   And morn draws near;

5

The morn that knows no night,
The morn of cloudless day,
When glorious Saints in light
   Their homage pay.

6

Weep not! the gate of life
Henceforth is dreaded death;
The end of living strife
   Our dying breath.

7

Weep not! the victory's won;
Away with doubts and fears,
CHRIST, when our work is done,
   Will dry our tears.   Amen.

Sundays after Trinity.

2
Beneath the shadow of Thy Throne
　Thy Saints have dwelt secure;
Sufficient is Thine Arm alone,
　And our defence is sure.

3
Before the hills in order stood,
　Or earth received her frame,
From Everlasting Thou art GOD,
　To Endless years the same.

4
A thousand ages in Thy Sight
　Are like an evening gone;
Short as the watch that ends the night
　Before the rising sun.

5
Time, like an ever-rolling stream,
　Bears all its sons away;
They fly forgotten, as a dream
　Dies at the opening day.

6
O GOD, our Help in ages past,
　Our Hope for years to come,
Be Thou our Guard while troubles last,
　And our Eternal Home.　　Amen.

Sundays after Trinity.

HYMN 159.

8, 8, 8, 8, 7. J. B. Dykes.

Ho-san-na to the Liv-ing Lord, Ho-san-na to the In-car-nate Word, To Christ, Cre-at-or, Sav-iour, King, Let eve-ry voice Ho-san-na sing, Ho-san-na in the High-est. A-men.

2 O Saviour! with protecting care,
Abide in this Thy House of Prayer,
Where we Thy parting Promise claim,
Assembled in Thy sacred Name.
    Hosanna in the Highest!

3 But chiefest, in our cleansed breast,
Eternal! let Thy Spirit rest,
And make our secret soul to be
A temple pure, and worthy Thee.
    Hosanna in the Highest!

4 To God the Father, God the Son,
And God the Spirit, Three in One,
Be honour, praise, and glory given,
By all on earth and all in Heaven.
    Hosanna in the Highest!   Amen.

Sundays after Trinity.

HYMN 160. — RAVENSCROFT'S PSALTER, 1621. C.M.

My God, how wonderful Thou art, Thy Majesty how bright, How beautiful Thy Mercy-seat, In depths of burning light. Amen.

2
How dread are Thine Eternal Years,
　O Everlasting Lord;
By prostrate spirits day and night
　Incessantly adored.

3
How beautiful, how beautiful
　The sight of Thee must be,
Thine Endless Wisdom, boundless Power,
　And awful purity.

4
O how I fear Thee, Living God,
　With deepest, tenderest fears,
And worship Thee with trembling hope
　And penitential tears.

5
Yet I may love Thee too, O Lord,
　Almighty as Thou art,
For Thou hast stooped to ask of me
　The love of my poor heart.

6
Oh, then, this worse than worthless heart
　In pity deign to take,
And make it love Thee, for Thyself,
　And for Thy Glory's sake.

7
No earthly father loves like Thee,
　No mother, e'er so mild,
Bears and forbears as Thou hast done
　With me Thy sinful child.

8
Father of Jesus, Love's Reward,
　What rapture will it be,
Prostrate before Thy Throne to lie,
　And ever gaze on Thee.　　Amen.

Sundays after Trinity.

HYMN 161.

7, 7, 7, 5.   W. B. Gilbert.

Lord of Mer-cy and of Might! Of man-

kind the Life and Light; Mak-er, Teach-er,

In-fi-nite! Je-su, hear and save. A-men.

2
Who, when sin's tremendous doom
Gave Creation to the tomb,
Didst not scorn the Virgin's womb,
   Jesu, hear and save!

3
Mighty Monarch! Saviour Mild!
Humbled to a mortal Child,
Captive, beaten, bound, reviled,
   Jesu, hear and save!

4
Throned above Celestial things,
Borne aloft on Angels' wings,
Lord of lords, and King of kings,
   Jesu, hear and save!

5
Soon to visit earth again,
Judge of Angels and of men,
Hear us now, and hear us then,
   Jesu, hear and save!   Amen.

Sundays after Trinity.

C. M.   HYMN 162.   John Selby, 1702.

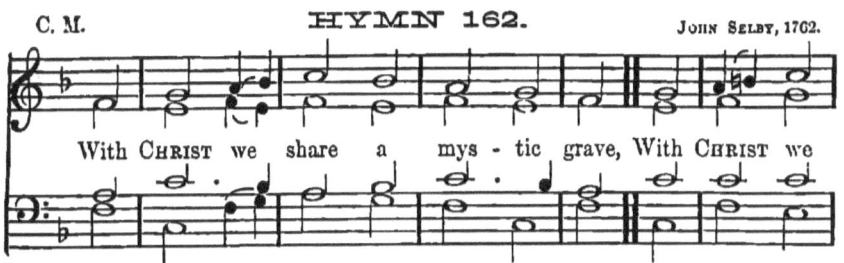

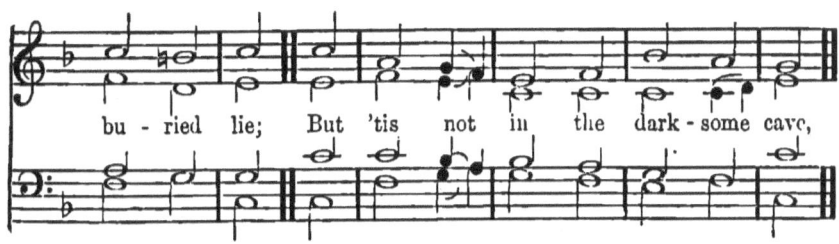

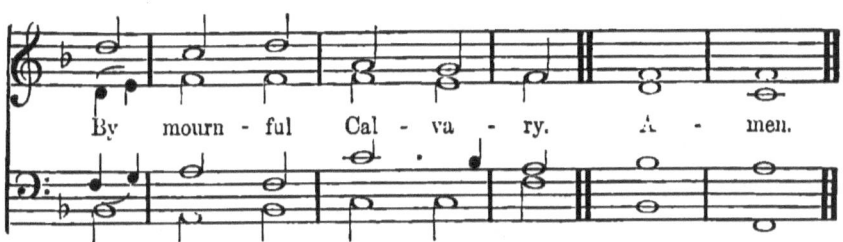

With Christ we share a mystic grave, With Christ we buried lie; But 'tis not in the darksome cave, By mournful Calvary. Amen.

2
The pure and bright Baptismal Flood
  Entombs our nature's stain;
New creatures from the cleansing wave,
  With Christ we rise again.

3
Happy, if through this world of strife,
  And sin, and selfish care,
This robe of new-born righteousness
  We undefiled wear.

4
Happy, if through the gate of death,
  Glorious at last and free,
We to our joyful rising pass,
  O Risen Lord, with Thee!

5
And now to Thy Thrice Holy Name,
  The God Whom we adore,
To Father, Son, and Holy Ghost,
  Be glory Evermore.   Amen.

Sundays after Trinity.

HYMN 163.

P. M.   J. B. Dykes.

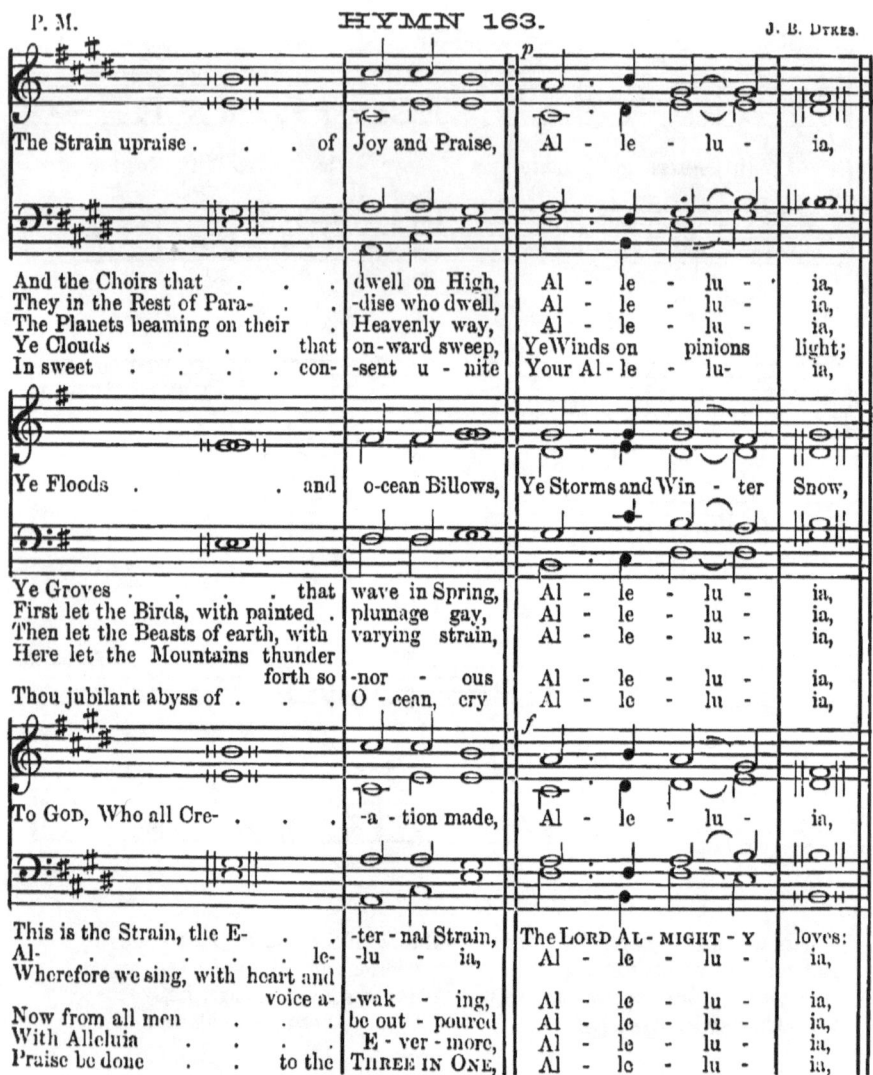

The Strain upraise . . . of Joy and Praise,   Al - le - lu - ia,

And the Choirs that . . . dwell on High,   Al - le - lu - ia,
They in the Rest of Para- . . -dise who dwell,   Al - le - lu - ia,
The Planets beaming on their . Heavenly way,   Al - le - lu - ia,
Ye Clouds . . . . that on-ward sweep, Ye Winds on pinions light;
In sweet . . . . con- -sent u - nite Your Al - le - lu - ia,

Ye Floods . . . and o-cean Billows, Ye Storms and Win - ter Snow,

Ye Groves . . . . that wave in Spring,   Al - le - lu - ia,
First let the Birds, with painted . plumage gay,   Al - le - lu - ia,
Then let the Beasts of earth, with varying strain,   Al - le - lu - ia,
Here let the Mountains thunder forth so -nor - ous   Al - le - lu - ia,
Thou jubilant abyss of . . . O - cean, cry   Al - le - lu - ia,

To God, Who all Cre- . . -a - tion made,   Al - le - lu - ia,

This is the Strain, the E- . . -ter - nal Strain, The Lord Al - might - y loves:
Al- . . . . . le- -lu - ia,   Al - le - lu - ia,
Wherefore we sing, with heart and voice a- -wak - ing,   Al - le - lu - ia,
Now from all men . . . be out - poured   Al - le - lu - ia,
With Alleluia . . . E - ver - more,   Al - le - lu - ia,
Praise be done . . to the Three in One,   Al - le - lu - ia.

Music proper, in Hymnal Noted.

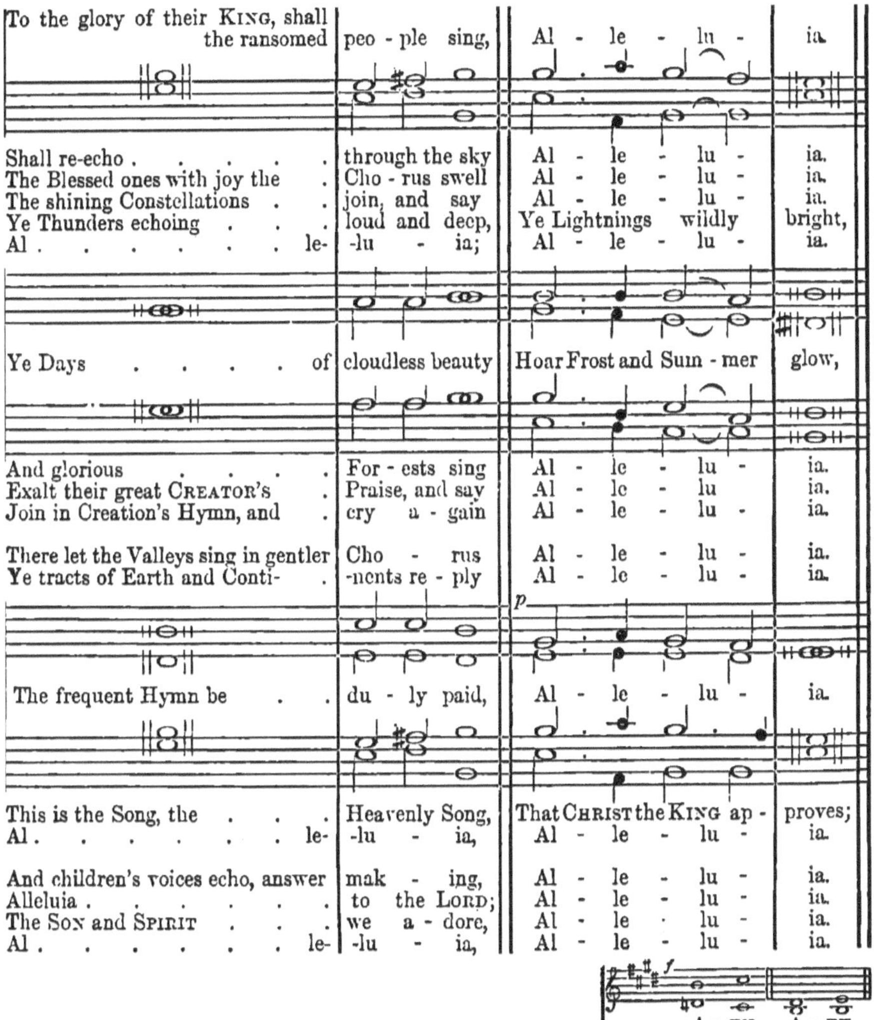

To the glory of their KING, shall the ransomed	peo - ple sing,	Al - le - lu -	ia.

Shall re-echo	through the sky	Al - le - lu -	ia.
The Blessed ones with joy the .	Cho - rus swell	Al - le - lu -	ia.
The shining Constellations . .	join, and say	Al - le - lu -	ia.
Ye Thunders echoing . . .	loud and deep,	Ye Lightnings wildly	bright,
Al . . . . . . le-	-lu - ia;	Al - le - lu -	ia.

Ye Days . . . . of	cloudless beauty	Hoar Frost and Sum - mer	glow,

And glorious	For - ests sing	Al - le - lu -	ia.
Exalt their great CREATOR'S .	Praise, and say	Al - le - lu -	ia.
Join in Creation's Hymn, and	cry a - gain	Al - le - lu -	ia.

There let the Valleys sing in gentler	Cho - rus	Al - le - lu -	ia.
Ye tracts of Earth and Conti-	-nents re - ply	Al - le - lu -	ia.

The frequent Hymn be . .	du - ly paid,	Al - le - lu -	ia.

This is the Song, the . . .	Heavenly Song,	That CHRIST the KING ap -	proves;
Al . . . . . . le-	-lu - ia,	Al - le - lu -	ia.

And children's voices echo, answer	mak - ing,	Al - le - lu -	ia.
Alleluia	to the LORD;	Al - le - lu -	ia.
The SON and SPIRIT . . .	we a - dore,	Al - le - lu -	ia.
Al . . . . . . le-	-lu - ia,	Al - le - lu -	ia.

A - men. A - men.

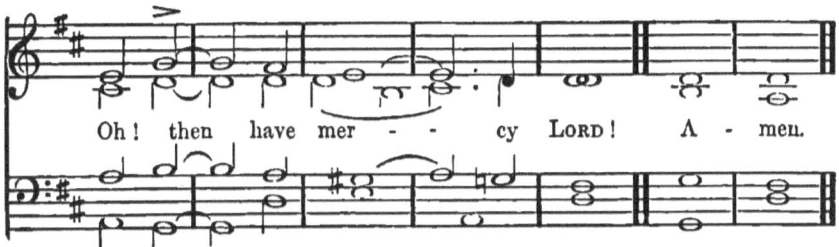

2

Lord! have mercy whén we lie
On the réstless bed and sigh,
Sigh for death, yet féar it still,
From the thóught of former ill;
When all other hope is gone;
When our course is almost done;
When the dim advancing gloom
Tells us that the hour is come,
Oh! then have mercy, Lord!

3

Lord! have mercy whén we know
First how váin this world below;
When the earliest gléam is given
Of Thy bríght but distant Heaven!
When our darkened thoughts oppress,
Doubts perplex and fears distress,
And our saddened spirits dwell
On the open gates of Hell,
Oh! then have mercy, Lord!   Amen.

Sundays after Trinity.

HYMN 165.

C. M. RAVENSCROFT'S P'SALTER, 1621.

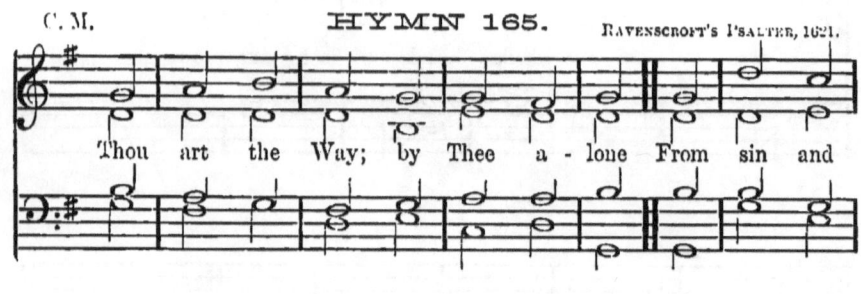

Thou art the Way; by Thee alone From sin and death we flee: And he who would the Fa-ther seek Must seek Him, Lord, by Thee. A-men.

2
Thou art the Truth, Thy Word alone
  True wisdom can impart;
Thou only canst inform the mind,
  And purify the heart.

3
Thou art the Life; the empty tomb
  Proclaims Thy conquering Arm;
And those who put their trust in Thee
  Nor death nor Hell shall harm

4
Thou art the Way, the Truth, the Life,
  Grant us that Way to know,
That Truth to keep, that Life to win,
  Whose Joys Eternal flow. Amen.

Sundays after Trinity.

HYMN 166.

8, 8, 8, 4. R. R. Chope.

My God, my Father, while I stray Far from my home in life's rough way, O teach me from my heart to say, "Thy Will be done." A-men.

2
Though dark my path, and sad my lot,
Let me be still and murmur not,
Or breathe the prayer Divinely taught,
"Thy Will be done."

3
What though in lonely grief I sigh
For friends beloved no longer nigh,
Submissive would I still reply,
"Thy Will be done."

4
If Thou shouldst call me to resign
What most I prize, it ne'er was mine;
I only yield Thee what is Thine;
"Thy Will be done."

5
Let but my fainting heart be blest
With Thy sweet Spirit for its Guest,
My God, to Thee I leave the rest;
"Thy Will be done."

6
Renew my will from day to day,
Blend it with Thine, and take away
All that now makes it hard to say,
"Thy Will be done."

Sundays after Trinity.

HYMN 167.

L. M. — Dr. Turton, Lord Bishop of Ely.

O Christ, the Light of Heaven-ly day, The shades of dark-ness chase a-way: Those who in paths of dan-ger roam Bring to Thy Fold, their hap-py home. A-men.

2
Oh! that the deaf may hear Thy Voice,
The dumb to speak of Thee rejoice;
The thankless heart its silence break,
And, taught by Thee, confession make.

3
O Lord, give sight unto the blind,
And join us all in heart and mind;
O gather the dispersed to Thee,
The wavering, Lord, from doubt set free.

4
Those who in error wander wide,
Let Thy bright Beams of Mercy guide;
Whom sin hath bruised and wounded, heal;
To all "the Hope of Glory" seal.

5
So they who sing Thy Praise above,
With us shall join in bonds of love;
And Thee for all Thy Grace adore
On earth,—in Heaven,—for Evermore.
　　　　　　　　　　Amen.

Sundays after Trinity.

HYMN 168.

C. M. — Scotch Psalter, 1635.

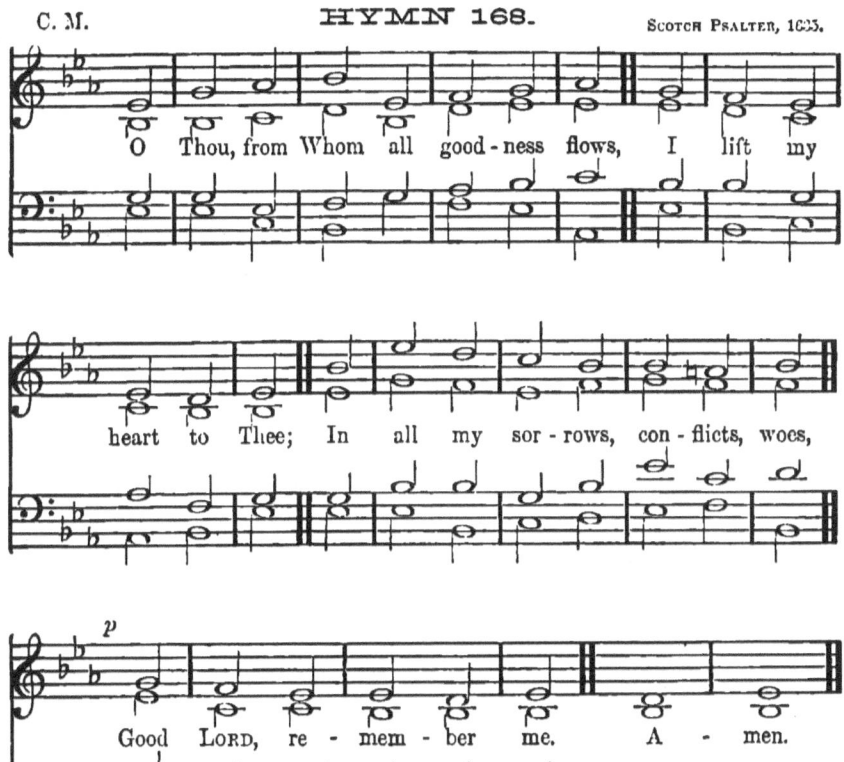

O Thou, from Whom all goodness flows, I lift my heart to Thee; In all my sorrows, conflicts, woes, Good Lord, remember me. Amen.

2
When on my aching, burdened heart,
  My sins lie heavily,
Thy Pardon grant, Thy Peace impart;
  Good Lord, remember me!

3
When trials sore obstruct my way,
  And ills I cannot flee,
Then let my strength be as my day;
  Good Lord, remember me!

4
If worn with pain, disease, and grief,
  This body frail should be,
Grant patience, rest, and sure relief;
  Good Lord, remember me!

5
And oh! when in the hour of death
  I wait Thy just Decree,
Jesu, receive my parting breath;
  Good Lord, remember me!   Amen.

Sundays after Trinity.

HYMN 169. — 8, 7s. — Gnadau's Choralbuch.

Jesus calls us o'er the tumult Of our life's tempestuous sea, Day by day His sweet Voice soundeth, Saying, "Christian, follow Me." Amen.

2
Jesus calls us—from the worship
 Of the vain world's golden store,
From each idol that would keep us,—
 Saying, "Christian, love Me more!"

3
In our joys and in our sorrows,
 Days of toil and hours of ease,
Still He calls 'midst cares and pleasures,
 "Christian, love Me more than these!"

4
Jesus calls us—by Thy Mercies,
 Saviour! may we hear Thy Call;
Give our hearts to Thy Obedience,
 Serve and love Thee best of all. Amen.

Sundays after Trinity.

HYMN 170.

Jesus! Name of wondrous love! Name all other names above, Unto which must every knee Bow in deep humility. Amen.

2
Jesus! Name decreed of old;
To the maiden Mother told,
Kneeling in her lowly cell,
By the Angel Gabriel.

3
Jesus! Name of priceless worth
To the fallen sons of earth,
For the promise that it gave,—
"Jesus shall His people save."

4
Jesus! Name of mercy mild,
Given to the Holy Child,
When the cup of human woe
First He tasted here below.

5
Jesus! Only Name that's given
Under all the mighty Heaven,
Whereby man, to sin enslaved,
Bursts his fetters, and is saved.

6
Jesus! Name of wondrous love!
Human Name of God above!
Pleading only this, we flee,
Helpless, O our God, to Thee. Amen.

Sundays after Trinity.

HYMN 171. L. M. — Dr. Turton, Lord Bishop of Ely.

O Christ! who dost prepare a place
For us around Thy Throne of Grace,
We pray Thee lift our hearts above,
And draw them with the cords of love. Amen.

2
Source of all Good! Thou, Gracious Lord,
Art our exceeding great Reward;
How short is all our present pain!
How boundless our Eternal gain!

3
With open face and joyful heart
We then shall see Thee as Thou art:
Our love to Thee shall ever glow,
Our praise to Thee for ever flow.

4
Send down Thy Holy Ghost, to be
The Guide to bring our souls to Thee;
Thy never-failing Grace to prove,
A pledge of Thine Eternal Love.

5
O future Judge! Eternal Lord!
Thy Name be hallowed and adored:
To God the Father, King of Heaven,
And Holy Ghost, like praise be given.
Amen.

Sundays after Trinity.

HYMN 172.

C. M.   W. B. Gilbert.

E-ter-nal God! we look to Thee, To Thee for help we fly; Thine Eye a-lone our wants can see, Thy Hand a-lone sup-ply. A-men.

2
Lord! let Thy Fear within us dwell,
   Thy Love our footsteps guide:
That Love will all vain love expel;
   That Fear all fear beside.

3
Not what we wish, but what we want,
   Oh, let Thy Grace supply:
The good unasked in mercy grant;
   The ill, though asked, deny.

4
To God the Father, God the Son,
   And God the Holy Ghost,
All glory be from Saints on earth,
   And from the Heavenly Host. Amen.

Sundays after Trinity.

S. M.   HYMN 173.   Dr. Howard, 1762.

Cre - at - or of man - kind! Thy pro - mised

Help we claim, That so our life Thou may'st not

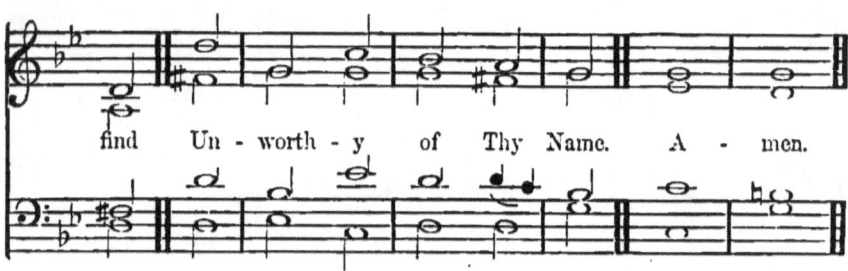

find Un - worth - y of Thy Name. A - men.

2

If Thou Thy Grace deny,
  In vain for Thee we strive;
In Thee alone to sin we die,
  In Thee alone we live.

3

Our goings, Lord, uphold,
  Till this dark vale be passed,
And in Thy Love and Fear made bold,
  We reach our rest at last.

4

O happy, peaceful rest,
  Prepared for Saints above!
Where they, with Endless quiet blest,
  Drink of Thy Streams of Love.

5

O Trinity Divine!
  To Thee our hearts we raise!
May we Thy ransomed people join,
  And share their songs of praise. Amen.

Sundays after Trinity.

HYMN 174.

C. M.   J. B. Dykes.

Je-ru-sa-lem, my hap-py home, Name ever dear to me; When shall my la-bours have an end? Thy joys, when shall I see? A-men.

2
When shall these eyes Thy Heaven-built walls
  And pearly gates behold?
Thy bulwarks, with salvation strong,
  And street of shining gold?

3
Apostles, Martyrs, Prophets, there
  Around my Saviour stand;
And all I love in Christ below
  Will join the glorious band.

4
Jerusalem, my happy home,
  When shall I come to thee?
When shall my labours have an end?
  Thy joys when shall I see?

5
O Christ, do thou my soul prepare
  For that bright Home of love;
That I may see Thee and adore
  With all Thy Saints above.   Amen.

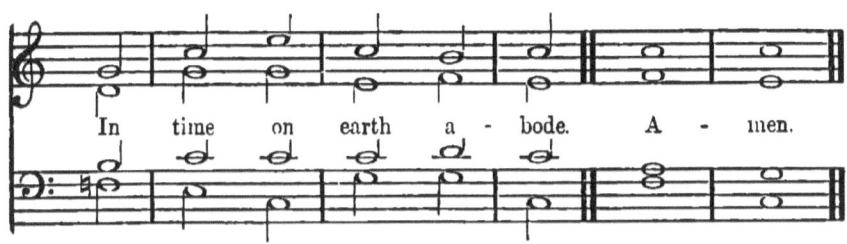

2
JESUS is GOD! Let sorrow come,
  And pain, and every ill;
All are worth while, for all are means
  His glory to fulfil;
Worth while a thousand years of life
  To speak one little word,
If only by our Faith we own
  The Godhead of our LORD!

3
JESUS is GOD! Oh, could I now
  But compass land and sea,
To teach and tell this single truth,
  How happy should I be!
Oh, had I but an angel's voice,
  I would proclaim so loud,—
JESUS, the Good, the Beautiful,
  Is Everlasting GOD!

4
JESUS is GOD! If on the earth
  This blessed faith decays,
More tender must our love become,
  More plentiful our praise.
We are not Angels, but we may
  Down in earth's corners kneel,
And multiply sweet acts of love,
  And murmur what we feel.   Amen.

2
See! the springs of living waters,
  Springing from Eternal Love,
Well supply thy sons and daughters,
  And all fear of want remove.
Who can faint while such a river
  May the spirit's thirst assuage?
Grace which, like the LORD the Giver,
  Never fails from age to age.

3
SAVIOUR, if of Zion's City
  I through Grace a member am,
Let the world deride or pity,
  I will glory in Thy Name.
Fading is the worldling's pleasure,
  All his boasted pomp and show;
Solid joys and lasting treasure
  None but Zion's children know. Amen.

Sundays after Trinity.

HYMN 177.

L. M. — Dr. Gauntlett

A-round the Throne of God a band Of bright and glo-rious An-gels stand; Sweet harps with-in their hands they hold, And on their heads are crowns of gold. A-men.

2
Some wait around Him, ready still
To sing His Praise and do His Will;
And some, when He commands them, go
To guard His servants here below.

3
Lord, give Thine Angels every day
Command to guard us on our way,
And bid them every evening keep
Their watch around us while we sleep.

4
So shall no wicked thing draw near
To do us harm or cause us fear,
And we shall dwell, when life is past,
With Angels round Thy Throne at last.

5
Praise God, from Whom all blessings flow;
Praise Him, all creatures here below;
Praise Him above, Angelic Host;
Praise Father, Son, and Holy Ghost.
      Amen.

Sundays after Trinity.

HYMN 178.

6, 6, 6, 6, 4, 4, 4, 4.   S. Reay.

Ye Ho-ly Angels bright, Who wait at God's Right Hand, Or through the realms of light Fly at your Lord's Command, Assist our song, For else the theme, Too high doth seem, For mor-tal tongue. A-men.

2
Ye blessed souls at rest,
Who ran this earthly race,
And now, from sin released,
Behold the Saviour's Face,
  God's Praises sound,
  As in His Light,
  With sweet delight,
  Ye do abound.

3
Ye saints who toil below,
Adore your Heavenly King,
And onward as ye go
Some joyful anthem sing;
  Take what He gives,
  And praise Him still,
  Through good or ill,
  Who ever lives!

4
My soul, bear thou thy part,
Triumph in God above,
And with a well-tuned heart
Sing thou the songs of love!
  Let all thy days,
  Till life shall end
  Whate'er He send,
  Be filled with praise!   Amen.

Sundays after Trinity.

HYMN 179. C.M. M. Vulpius, 1609.

O Thou Almighty Source of Love, Ruling the world alone, In Substance One, in Persons Three, Upon the Eternal Throne. Amen.

2
For Thy dear Mercy's sake receive
  The prayers to Thee we pour,
And purify our hearts, to taste
  Thy Goodness more and more.

3
Our flesh and spirit here below,
  Lord, in Thy fire refine;
Break down our self-indulgent will,
  Gird us with Strength Divine.

4
So may we all, who here are met
  Thy Holy Name to bless,
One day in our Eternal Home,
  Thine Endless Joys possess.

5
Father of Mercies, hear our cry;
  Hear us, Co-equal Son;
Who reignest with the Holy Ghost,
  While ceaseless ages run. Amen.

Sundays after Trinity.

HYMN 180. — Arranged by J. TURLE. — 7s.

Oft in danger, oft in woe,
Onward, Christians, onward go;
Fight the fight, maintain the strife,
Strengthened with the Bread of Life. Amen.

2
Let not sorrow dim your eye,
Soon shall every tear be dry;
Let not fear your course impede,
Great your strength, if great your need.

3
Let your drooping hearts be glad;
March, in Heavenly armour clad;
Fight, nor think the battle long,
Soon shall victory wake your song.

4
Onward then in battle move;
More than conquerors ye shall prove;
Though opposed by many a foe,
Christian soldiers, onward go!

5
Hymns of glory and of praise,
FATHER, unto Thee we raise:
HOLY JESU, praise to Thee,
With the SPIRIT, ever be.   Amen.

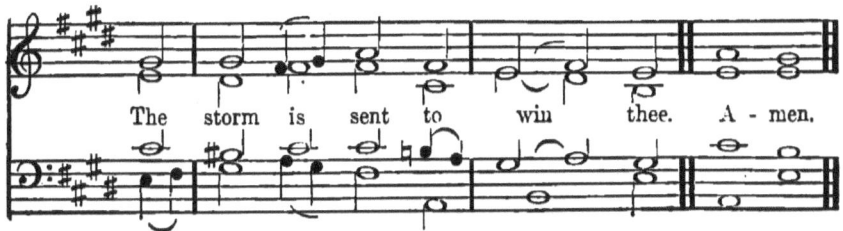

The storm is sent to win thee. A-men.

2
All things within, without, around,
  Must prove unsatisfying:—
And comes there not from all a sound,
  The echo of our sighing,
Telling that earth may never be
Our Home of Immortality,
  Or Rest for souls undying?

3
FATHER, I hear Thy warning Voice
  'Midst fears the soul appalling;
No sunny days of earthly joys
  Could stay the shadows' falling:
Sun-lighted times are types of Heaven,—
Dark nights to calm the heart are given,
  Man to his GOD recalling!

4
"Lift thyself up!" O weary heart,
  And claim thy high election:
Strength for thy Cross will He impart
  Who tasted earth's rejection.
"Joint-heirs with CHRIST," on "things above,"
The joys of GOD's Eternal Love,
  Must set their whole affection.

5
"Lift up thy heart!" His Church's chant
  Tells of the joy before us!
Such bliss as Heavenly Love can grant
  His Promises assure us.
Sing, all our souls with full accord,
"We lift them up to Thee," O LORD,
  In Eucharistic chorus!

6
"Lift Thou my heart," O GOD, to Thee.
  Thou Joy of all creation!
Almighty, Gracious TRINITY,
  Receive my whole oblation!
"O might I come e'en to Thy Seat!"
My FATHER, SAVIOUR, PARACLETE!
  The GOD of my Salvation!   Amen.

Sundays after Trinity.

HYMN 182.

7s. C. T. BOWEN.

Thou Who cam-est from a-bove, Bring-ing light, and shedding love, Gracious SPIRIT! Love Divine, Let Thy Light around us shine. A-men.

2
Thou Who once didst change our state,
Making us regenerate,
Help us Evermore to be
Faithful subjects unto Thee.

3
Where Thou art not, none can do
What is holy, just, and true;
They whose hearts Thy Wisdom leads,
Think good thoughts and do good deeds.

4
We have often grieved Thee sore;
Never let us grieve Thee more:
Thou the feeble canst protect;
Thou the wandering canst direct.

5
We are dark,—be Thou our Light;
We are blind,—be Thou our Sight:
Be our Comfort in distress;
Guide us through the wilderness.

6
Praise the Blessed THREE IN ONE;
Praise the FATHER and the SON;
To the HOLY GHOST arise
Praise from all beneath the skies. Amen.

Sundays after Trinity.

HYMN 183.

Lord of Power, and Lord of Might! God and Father of us all; Lord of day, and Lord of night, Listen to our solemn call. Listen, whilst to Thee we raise Songs of prayer, and songs of praise. A-men.

2
Light and love and life are Thine,
Great CREATOR of all good,
Fill our souls with Light Divine;
Give us with our daily food
Blessings from Thy Heavenly Store,
Blessings rich for Evermore.

3
Graft within our heart of hearts
Love undying for Thy Name,
Bid us e'er the day departs

Spread afar our MAKER's Fame:
Young and old together bless,
Clothe our souls with righteousness.

4
Full of love and full of peace
May our life on earth be blest,
When our trials here shall cease,
And at last we sink to rest,
Fountain of Eternal Love!
Call us to our Home above.   Amen.

Sundays after Trinity.

HYMN 184.

C.M.
Rinel, 1573.
Arranged by H. S. Irons.

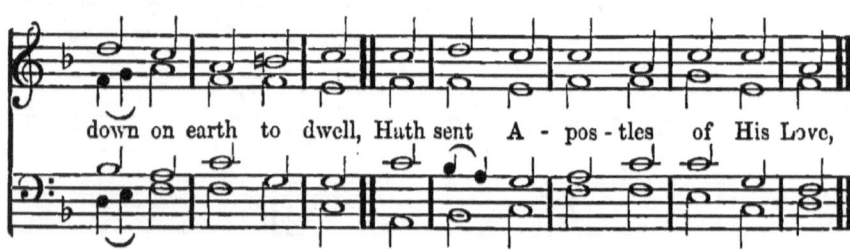
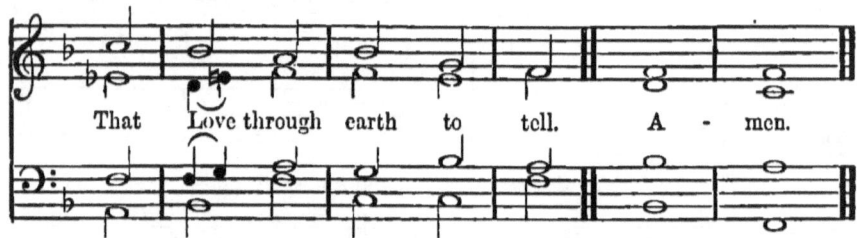

He, Whom the Father from above Sent down on earth to dwell, Hath sent A-pos-tles of His Love, That Love through earth to tell. A-men.

2
Christ they proclaim, and all around
  Sink back the gates of Hell,
As at the mystic trumpet's sound
  The heathen towers fell.

3
O Christ! Thou King Most Merciful!
  Our inmost hearts possess;
So may our songs of thankful praise
  Thy Name for ever bless!

4
Keep us, O Jesu, from the death
  Of sin; and deign to be
The Everlasting Crown and Joy
  Of all New-born in Thee.

5
Praise to the Father, and the Son,
  Who from the dead arose!
Praise to the Blessed Paraclete,
  While age on ages flows.   Amen.

Sundays after Trinity.

HYMN 185.

C. M.   A. H. Brown.

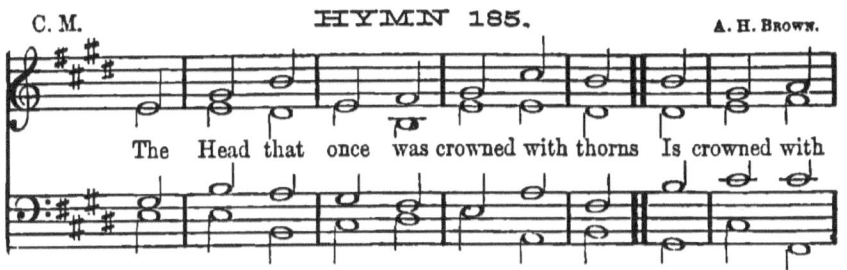

The Head that once was crowned with thorns Is crowned with

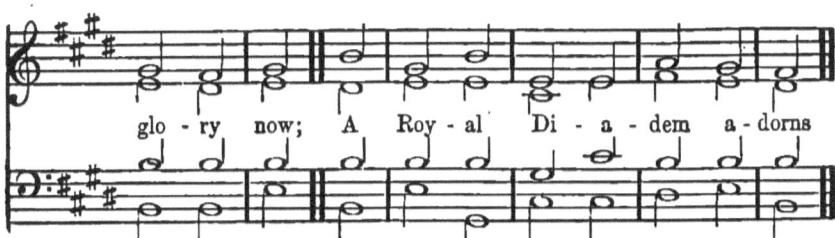

glo-ry now; A Roy-al Di-a-dem a-dorns

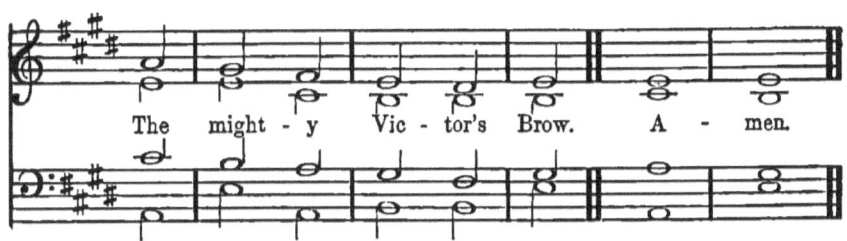

The might-y Vic-tor's Brow. A-men.

2
The highest place that Heaven affords
  Is His,—is His by right,
The KING of kings, and LORD of lords,
  And Heaven's Eternal LIGHT.

3
The Joy of all that dwell above,
  The Joy of all below,
To whom He manifests His Love,
  And grants His Name to know:

4
To them the Cross with all its shame,
  With all its grace is given;
Their name an Everlasting name,
  Their joy the joy of Heaven.

5
JESU! in deep humility
  For us Thou didst atone;
Grant us among Thy Saints to be
  In glory like Thine Own.   Amen.

Sundays after Trinity.

HYMN 186. — L. M. — Dr. Turton, Lord Bishop of Ely.

When I look back on all my sins, As memory wakes her busy train, To fear and fail my heart begins, And sadness sinks my hope again. Amen.

2
O Jesu! save me from the foe,
Who hunts, with cruel wrath, my soul;
Give sin that shame the vanquished know,
And o'er his head destruction roll!

3
But oh! to those that seek Thy Face,
And love Salvation's holy ways,
Send Thy winged Messenger of Grace,
And give the joyful songs of praise.

4
Though with the needy and the poor,
I know the path Thy sons have trod,
Yet will I plead at Mercy's door;—
There wilt Thou hear me, O my God!

5
To Father, Son, and Holy Ghost,
The God Whom Heaven and earth adore,
From men and from the Angel Host
Be praise and glory Evermore.   Amen.

Sundays after Trinity.

HYMN 187.

8, 8, 8, 3. J. B. Dykes.

Fierce raged the tem-pest o'er the deep, Watch did Thine anx-ious serv-ants keep, But Thou wast wrapt in guile-less sleep, Calm and still. A-men.

2
"Save, Lord, we perish," was their cry,
Oh, save us in our agony!
Thy Word above the storm rose high,
"Peace, be still."

3
The wild winds hushed, the angry deep
Sank like a little child to sleep,
The sullen billows ceased to leap
At Thy Will.

4
So when our life is clouded o'er,
And storm-winds drift us from the shore,
Say, lest we sink to rise no more,
"Peace, be still." Amen.

Sundays after Trinity.

HYMN 188.

Jesu, meek and gentle! Son of God Most High!

Pitying, Loving Saviour! Hear thy children's cry. A-men.

2
Pardon our offences,
 Loose our captive chains,
Break down every idol
 Which our soul contains.

3
Give us holy freedom,
 Fill our hearts with love;
Draw us, Holy Jesus!
 To the realms above.

4
Lead us on our journey
 Be Thyself the Way,
Through terrestrial darkness
 To Celestial day.

5
Jesu! meek and gentle!
 Son of God Most High!
Pitying, Loving Saviour!
 Hear Thy children's cry. Amen.

Sundays after Trinity.

HYMN 189.

7s. Arranged by W. H. Haverngal.

Songs of praise the An-gels sang, Heaven with Al-le-lu-ias rang, When Cre-a-tion was be-gun, When God spake and it was done. A-men.

2
Songs of praise awoke the morn
When the PRINCE of Peace was born;
Songs of praise arose when He
Captive led captivity.

3
Heaven and earth must pass away,
Songs of praise shall crown that day;
GOD will make new Heaven and Earth,
Songs of praise shall hail their birth.

4
And shall man alone be dumb
Till that glorious Kingdom come?

No; the Church delights to raise
Psalms, and hymns, and songs of praise.

5
Saints below, with heart and voice,
Still in songs of praise rejoice;
Learning here, by faith and love,
Songs of praise to sing above.

6
Hymns of glory, songs of praise,
FATHER, unto Thee we raise,
JESU, glory unto Thee,
With the SPIRIT, ever be. Amen.

Sundays after Trinity.

HYMN 190.

C.M. — Arranged by S. Reay.

The Saints on earth, and those above But one com-

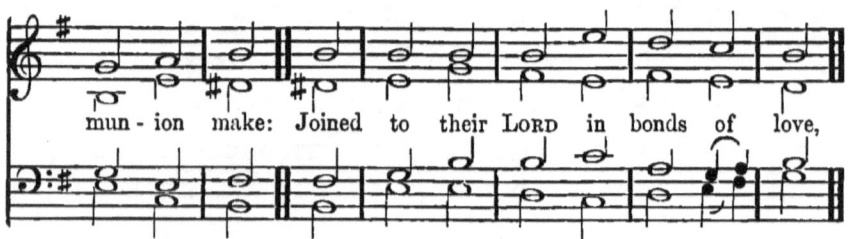

mun-ion make: Joined to their Lord in bonds of love,

All of His Grace par-take. A-men.

2
One Family, we dwell in Him,
  One Church, above, beneath,
Though now divided by the stream,
  The narrow stream of death.

3
One Army of the Living God,
  To His Command we bow;
Part of the host have crossed the flood,
  And part are crossing now.

4
E'en now to their Eternal Home
  There pass some spirits blest;
While others to the margin come,
  Waiting their call to rest.

5
Jesu, be Thou our constant Guide;
  Then, when the word is given,
Bid Jordan's narrow stream divide,
  And bring us safe to Heaven. Amen.

Sundays after Trinity.

HYMN 191.

7s. R. F. Smith.

Let us with a glad-some mind Praise the Lord, for

He is kind; For His Mer-cies aye en-dure

E - ver faith - ful, e - ver sure. A - men.

2

He, with all-commanding might,
Filled the new-made world with light;
For His mercies aye endure,
Ever faithful, ever sure.

3

All things living He doth feed;
His full Hand supplies their need,
For His mercies aye endure,
Ever faithful, ever sure.

4

He hath with a piteous eye
Looked upon our misery;
For His Mercies aye endure,
Ever faithful, ever sure. Amen.

Sundays after Trinity.

HYMN 192. 8, 7s. Arranged by E. J. H. Prins.

Lamb of God, That in the Bo-som Of the Father dwellest high, Deign to vi-sit hum-ble sin-ners From Thy Rest a-bove the sky. A-men.

2
Love Divine, all love excelling,
   Joy of Heaven, to earth come down;
Fix in us Thy humble Dwelling,
   All Thy faithful Mercies crown.

3
Jesu, Thou art all Compassion,
   Pure unbounded Love Thou art;
Visit us with Thy Salvation,
   Enter every longing heart.

4
Come, Almighty, to deliver
   May we all Thy Life receive;
Graciously return, and never,
   Never more Thy Temple leave!

5
Thee we would be ever blessing,
   Serve Thee as Thine Hosts above,
Still adore Thee without ceasing,
   Glory in Thy perfect Love.   Amen.

Sundays after Trinity.

HYMN 193.

C. M. Arranged by W. T. Best.

"Wherefore so heavy, O my soul,"—Thus to myself I said;—"Wherefore so heavy, O my soul, And so disquieted. Amen.

2
Hope thou in God; He still shall be
 Thy Glory and thy Praise;
His saving Grace shall comfort thee
 Through Everlasting days.

3
His Goodness made thee what thou art,
 And yet will thee redeem;
Be thou courageous in thy heart,
 And put thy trust in Him.

4
All praise, all glory be ascribed
 To God, the One in Three,
Who bids us cast our care on Him,
 To Him for comfort flee.   Amen.

Sundays after Trinity.

HYMN 194.

L. M. — G. Cooper.

Lord Jesu! when we stand afar,
And gaze upon Thy Holy Cross,
In love of Thee, and scorn of self,
O may we count the world as loss! Amen.

2
When we behold Thy bleeding Wounds,
And the rough way that Thou hast trod,
Make us to hate the load of sin
That lay so heavy on our God.

3
O Holy Lord, uplifted high,
With outstretched Arms, in mortal woe,
Embracing in Thy wondrous Love
The sinful world that lies below;—

4
Give us an ever-living faith
To gaze beyond the things we see;
And in the mystery of Thy Death
Draw us and all men unto Thee.   Amen.

Sundays after Trinity.

HYMN 195. C.M. Dendy, 1886.

How sweet the Name of Jesus sounds In a believer's ear! It soothes his sorrows, heals his wounds, And drives away his fear. Amen.

2
It makes the wounded spirit whole,
   And calms the troubled breast;
'Tis manna to the hungry soul,
   And to the weary rest.

3
Dear Name! the rock on which I build,
   My shield and hiding-place,
My never-failing store-house, filled
   With boundless gifts of grace.

4
Jesus! my Shepherd, Husband, Friend,
   My Prophet, Priest, and King,
My Lord, my Life, my Way, mine End,
   Accept the praise I bring.

5
Weak is the effort of my heart,
   And cold my warmest thought;
But when I see Thee as Thou art,
   I'll praise Thee as I ought.

6
Till then I would Thy Love proclaim
   With every fleeting breath;
And may the music of Thy Name
   Refresh my soul in death.   Amen.

Sundays after Trinity.

5, 5, 5, 5, 6, 5, 6, 5.   HYMN 196.   Ravenscroft's Psalter, 1621.

O worship the KING, All glorious above;
O grateful-ly sing His Power and His Love;
Our Shield and Defender, The Ancient of Days,
Pavilioned in splendour, And girded with praise. Amen.

2 O tell of His Might,
  O sing of His Grace,
Whose Robe is the light,
  Whose Canopy space;
The storm-clouds He maketh
  His Chariots of wrath,
And darkly He taketh
  Through Heaven His Path.

3 Frail children of dust,
  And feeble as frail,
In Thee do we trust,
  Nor find Thee to fail.

Thy Mercies how tender,
  How firm to the end!
Our MAKER, Defender,
  REDEEMER, and Friend.

4 O measureless Might,
  Ineffable Love!
While Angels delight
  To hymn Thee above,
Thy ransomed Creation,
  Though feeble their lays,
With true adoration
  Shall sing to Thy Praise.   Amen.

Sundays after Trinity.

HYMN 197.

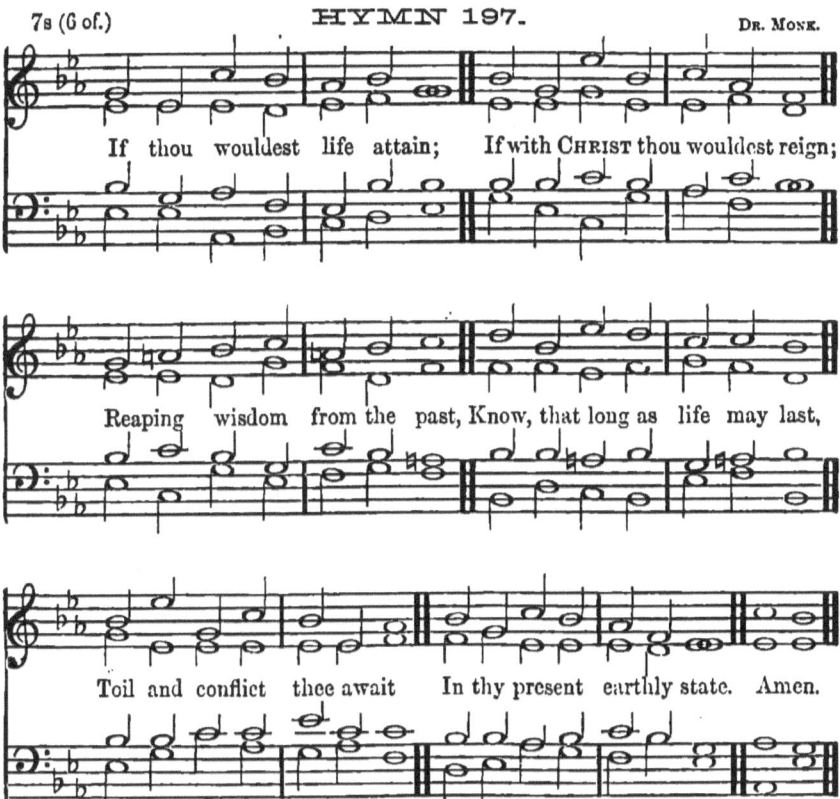

If thou wouldest life attain;
If with CHRIST thou wouldest reign;
Reaping wisdom from the past,
Know, that long as life may last,
Toil and conflict thee await
In thy present earthly state. Amen.

2
Labour, while it yet is day;
Labour, while you labour may;
Labour, for the night is long;
Labour, for the foe is strong;
Labour, for the prize is great;
Labour, for the hour is late.

3
Soon the struggle will be past;
Calm and peace will come at last;
Soon through death's transporting door,
All thy pains and labours o'er,
Thou shalt go to join the Blest
In the realms of Endless Rest.

4
Rest, from toil and anxious care;
Rest, from earthly wear and tear;
Rest, from ever present sin;
Rest without, and rest within;
Rest, which no abatement knows;
Rest, and infinite repose.

5
JESU, Who for me didst die
On the Cross of Calvary,
Not in aught that is my own,
But in Thy true Blood alone
Do I put my trembling trust;
Spare, O spare a worm of dust! Amen.

Sundays after Trinity.

HYMN 198. L. M. R. R. Chope.

Take up thy Cross, the SAVIOUR said, If thou would'st My disciple be; Deny thyself, the world forsake, And humbly follow after Me. Amen.

2
Take up thy Cross; let not its weight
Fill thy weak spirit with alarm;
His Strength shall bear thy spirit up,
And brace thy heart, and nerve thine arm.

3
Take up thy Cross, nor heed the shame;
Nor let thy foolish pride rebel:
Thy LORD for thee the Cross endured,
To save thy soul from death and Hell.

4
Take up thy Cross, then, in His Strength,
And calmly every danger brave;
'Twill guide thee to a better Home,
And lead to victory o'er the grave.

5
Take up thy Cross, and follow CHRIST,
Nor think till death to lay it down;
For only he who bears the Cross
May hope to wear the glorious Crown.

6
To Thee, Great LORD, the ONE IN THREE,
All praise for Evermore ascend;
O grant us in our Home to see
The Heavenly life that knows no end.
Amen.

Sundays after Trinity.

HYMN 199. L.M. R. R. Chope.

A-wake, my soul, and with the sun Thy dai-ly stage of du-ty run; Shake off dull sloth, and ear-ly rise, To pay thy morn-ing sa-cri-fice. A-men.

2
Redeem thy misspent moments past,
And live this day as if thy last;
Thy talents to improve take care;
For the great Day thyself prepare.

3
Wake and lift up thyself, my heart,
And with the Angels bear thy part,
Who all night long unwearied sing
High glory to the Eternal KING.

4
LORD, I my vows to Thee renew:
Disperse my sins as morning dew;
Guard my first springs of thought and will,
And with Thyself my spirit fill.

5
Glory to Thee, Who safe hast kept,
And hast refreshed me whilst I slept;
Grant, LORD, when I from death shall wake,
I may of Endless life partake.

6
Praise GOD, from Whom all blessings flow;
Praise Him, all creatures here below;
Praise Him above, Angelic Host,
Praise FATHER, SON, and HOLY GHOST.
Amen.

2

When first the world sprang forth,
　In majesty arrayed,
And bathed in streams of purest light;—
　What power was there displayed!
　But oh! what love, when CHRIST,
　For our transgressions slain,
Was by the Eternal FATHER raised
　For us to life again!

3

　His new-created world
　The Mighty MAKER viewed,
With thousand lovely tints adorned,
　And straight pronounced it good.
　But oh! much more He joyed
　That self-same world to see,
Washed in the LAMB's All-saving Blood
　From its impurity.

4

　Nature each day renews
　Her beauty evermore;
Whence to GOD's hidden Majesty
　The soul is taught to soar.
　But CHRIST, the Light of all,
　The FATHER's Image Blest,
Gives us to see our GOD Himself
　In Flesh made manifest!

5

　Again the Holy morn
　Calls us to prayer and praise,
Wakening our hearts to gratitude
　With its enlivening rays.
　Blest TRINITY! vouchsafe
　That to Thy Guidance true,
What Thou forbiddest we may shun;
　What Thou commandest, do.　　Amen.

Sundays after Trinity.

HYMN 201. L. M. Freylinghausen, 1704.

Forth in Thy Name, O Lord, we go, Our daily duty to renew; Thee, only Thee, resolved to know, In all we think, or speak, or do. Amen.

2
The task Thy wisdom hath assigned
O may we carefully fulfil;
In all our works Thy Presence find,
And gladly do Thy holy Will.

3
O may we bear Thine easy Yoke;
With patience watch, with fervour pray;
And still to things Eternal look
Through all the duties of the day.

4
Whate'er Thy bounteous Hand hath given,
For Thee, O God, we would employ;
And, looking for our rest in Heaven,
Serve Thee on earth with holy joy.

5
To Thee, Great Lord, the One in Three,
All praise for Evermore ascend;
O grant us in our Home to see
The Heavenly Life that knows no end.
Amen.

Sundays after Trinity.

HYMN 202.

L. M.   R. REDHEAD.

Our limbs refreshed with slum-ber now, And sloth cast off, in prayer we bow; And whilst we sing Thy Prais-es high, O FA-THER, be Thy Pre-sence nigh. A-men.

2
To Thee our earliest morning song,
To Thee our heart's full powers belong;
And Thou, O HOLY ONE, prevent
Each following action and intent.

3
As shades at morning flee away,
And night before the star of day,
So may each error of the night
Be purged by Thee, Celestial Light.

4
Remove, we pray Thee, each offence;
Shut out each sin of thought and sense;
That by our lips, who Thee adore,
Thou may'st be praised for Evermore.

5
O FATHER, what we ask be done,
Through JESUS CHRIST, Thine Only SON;
Who with the HOLY GHOST and Thee,
Shall live and reign Eternally.   Amen.

Sundays after Trinity.

L. M.   HYMN 203.   J. S. Bach, 1750.

O Thou, the FATHER'S Image Blest, Who callest forth the morning ray; O Thou Eternal LIGHT of LIGHT, Whom day and night alike obey. A-men.

2
True SUN! upon our souls arise,
Shining in beauty Evermore,   [beams
And through each heart the quick'ning
Of Thine Eternal SPIRIT pour.

3
Confirm in us each good resolve;
Subdue the wily Tempter's might;
Turn each misfortune to our good;
In all we do direct us right.

4
Be Thou, O CHRIST! our daily food;
Do Thou our daily cup supply,
While from the SPIRIT'S living Well
We drink unfailing strength and joy.

5
To GOD, the Eternal THREE IN ONE,
Be Endless praise and glory given,
Who called us when in darkness lost,
To share the light and life of Heaven.
                         Amen.

Sundays after Trinity.

HYMN 204. L.M. O. GIBBONS. Adapted by R. R. C.

New every morning is the Love, Our wakening and up-rising prove; Through sleep and dark-ness safe-ly brought, Re-stored to life, and power, and thought. A-men.

2
New mercies, each returning day,
Hover around us while we pray;
New perils past, new sins forgiven,
New thoughts of GOD, new hopes of Heaven.

3
If on our daily course our mind
Be set to hallow all we find;
New treasures still, of countless price,
GOD will provide for sacrifice.

4
The trivial round, the common task
Will furnish all we need to ask,
Room to deny ourselves, a road
To bring us daily nearer GOD.

5
Only, O LORD, in Thy dear Love
Fit us for perfect rest above;
And help us, this and every day,
To live more nearly as we pray. Amen.

Sundays after Trinity.

HYMN 205.

L. M. — GERMAN, 1651.

On this the day which saw the Earth From utter darkness first have birth; The day its MAKER rose again, And vanquished death and burst our chain. A-men.

2
Away with sleep and slothful ease!
We raise our hearts and bend our knees,
Our vain and wandering thoughts recall,
And early seek the LORD of all.

3
O FATHER of unclouded Light!
We pray Thee, kneeling in Thy Sight,
From all defilement to be freed,
From every sinful thought and deed.

4
Grant us, O SAVIOUR, what we crave;
Stretch forth Thy strong Right Hand to save;
And give us, of Thy boundless Grace,
The blessings of Thy Heavenly Place;

5
That we thence exiled by our sin,
Hereafter may be welcomed in:
That blessed time awaiting now,
With hymns of glory here we bow.

6
All glory, SAVIOUR LORD, to Thee,
Who over death didst triumph, be;
To Thee be fear and homage given,
By Hell, and Earth, and highest Heaven
Amen.

Sundays after Trinity.

HYMN 206. — C.M. — R. R. Chope.

O Holy Spirit! Lord of Grace, Eternal Source of Love, Inflame, we pray our inmost hearts, With Fire from Heaven above. Amen.

2
As Thou dost join in holiest bond
The FATHER and the SON,
So fill us all with mutual love,
And link our hearts in one.

3
To GOD the FATHER, GOD the SON,
And GOD the HOLY GHOST,
All glory be from saints on earth,
And from the Angel Host.   Amen.

Sundays after Trinity.

HYMN 207.

6s (3 of.) R. R. Chope.

When morning gilds the skies, My heart a-wak-ing cries; May Je-sus Christ be praised. A-men.

2
Alike at work and prayer
To Jesus I repair;
May Jesus Christ be praised!

3
To Thee, my God above,
I cry with glowing love;
May Jesus Christ be praised!

4
When evil thoughts molest,
With this I shield my breast;
May Jesus Christ be praised!

5
Does sadness fill my mind?
A solace here I find;
May Jesus Christ be praised!

6
Be this at meals your grace,
In every time and place;
May Jesus Christ be praised!

7
Be this, when day is past,
Of all your thoughts the last;
May Jesus Christ be praised!

8
In Heaven's Eternal bliss
The loveliest strain is this;
May Jesus Christ be praised!

9
The powers of darkness fear
When this sweet chant they hear;
May Jesus Christ be praised!

10
Be this, while life is mine,
My Canticle Divine;
May Jesus Christ be praised!

11
Be this the Eternal Song,
Through all the ages long;
May Jesus Christ be praised!
            Amen.

Sundays after Trinity.

2
To Thee our morning hymn we raise,
In mingled penitence and praise:
Pardon our sins, O LORD, we pray,
And keep us safely through the day.

3
Thou, LORD! of every human heart
The ONE Omniscient Searcher art;
The Good Physician, making whole
The hidden wounds which kill the souL

4
MOST HOLY! we Thine Aid implore,
Our stricken souls to health restore;
Eternal FATHER, Mighty SON!
And HOLY SPIRIT, THREE IN ONE!
      Amen.

Sundays after Trinity.

HYMN 209.

8, 7s. Dr. Boyce, 1779.

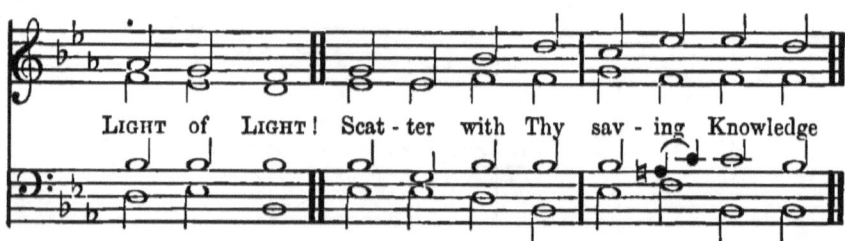
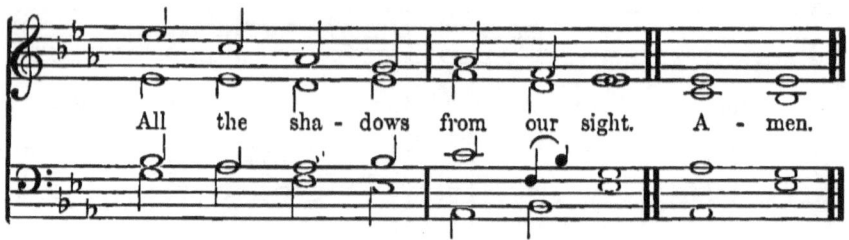

Brightness of the Father's Glory! God of God, and
Light of Light! Scatter with Thy saving Knowledge
All the shadows from our sight. A-men.

2
When our eyes grow dim and weary,
  May our souls on Thee depend,
Who with Thy Right Hand vouchsafest
  All Thy faithful to defend.

3
When the body's feeble nature
  Bows, oppressed by grief and pain,
Help our souls to rise uninjured,
  Soaring up to Thee again.

4
Only Hope of man's salvation!
  Hear us, help us, when we pray;
Those whom Thou by death hast purchased,
  Cast not in Thy Wrath away.

5
Praise and worship to the Father,
  Praise and worship to the Son,
Praise and worship to the Spirit,
  Now and Evermore be done.   Amen.

Sundays after Trinity.

HYMN 210.

L. M. — Ancient. Arranged by J. B. Dykes.

Now that the day-light fills the sky, We lift our hearts to God on High, That He, in all we do or say, Would keep us free from harm to-day. A-men.

2
Would keep our inmost conscience pure,
Our souls from folly would secure;
From all ill sights would turn our eyes,
And close our ears from vanities.

3
So we, when this new day is done,
And night in turn is stealing on,
With conscience by the world unstained,
Shall praise His Name for victory gained.

4
O Father! what we ask be done,
Through Jesus Christ, Thine Only Son;
Who, with the Holy Ghost and Thee,
Shall live and reign Eternally.   Amen.

Sundays after Trinity.

L. M.   HYMN 211.   Ancient.
Arranged by J. B. Dykes.

Be - fore the end - ing of the day, Cre - at - or of the

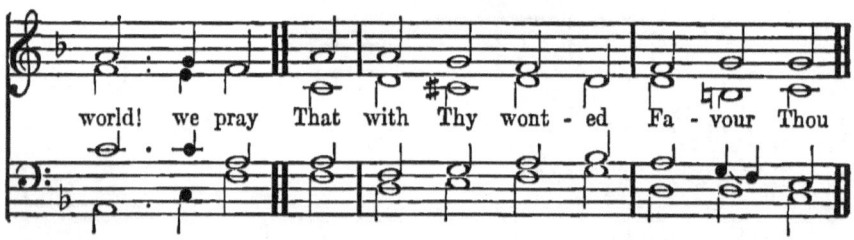

world! we pray That with Thy wont - ed Fa - vour Thou

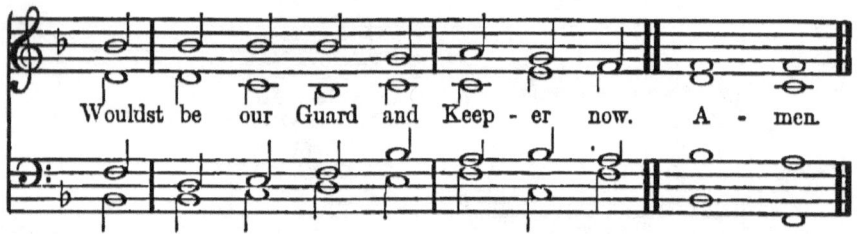

Wouldst be our Guard and Keep - er now. A - men.

2
Uplift us with Thine Arm of Might,
So may our souls rise pure and bright;
With love Divine our hearts inflame,
To praise Thee for Thy glorious Name.

3
Within our spirits ever dwell,
And worldly darkness thence expel;
The faith of old by Saints professed,
Root deep within our inmost breast.

4
Author of all things, Gracious Guide,
In life be ever at our side;
And when the assaults of death impend,
Thy people strengthen and defend.

5
All glory, Saviour Lord, to Thee,
Who over death didst triumph, be;
To Thee be fear and homage given,
By Hell, and earth, and Highest Heaven.
                                     Amen.

Sundays after Trinity.

2
Let mind, and soul, and flesh combine
To herald forth our Creed Divine;
Let love enwrap our mortal frame,
And others catch the living Flame.

3
Thou Ever Blessed THREE IN ONE,
O FATHER and Co-Equal SON,
O HOLY GHOST the COMFORTER,
This grace on Thy Redeemed confer.
       Amen.

Sundays after Trinity.

2

Quench Thou the fires of hate and strife,
The wasting fevers of the heart;
From perils guard our feeble life,
And to our souls Thy Peace impart.

3

FATHER of Mercies! grant our prayer,
And Thou Co-Equal Only SON!
Who with the HOLY SPIRIT art
Through Everlasting ages ONE.   Amen.

Sundays after Trinity.

HYMN 214. Ancient. Arranged by H. S. Irons.

O GOD, of all the Strength and Stay, Who dost Thyself unmoved abide, And all the changing hours of day In their ordained succession guide. Amen.

2

Thy Light upon our evening pour,
So may our life no sunset see;
But death to us an holy door
Of Everlasting glory be.

3

FATHER of Mercies! grant our prayer
And Thou Co-Equal, Only SON!
Who with the HOLY SPIRIT art
Through Everlasting ages ONE.   Amen.

Sundays after Trinity.

HYMN 215. L. M. — S. Webbe, 1816.

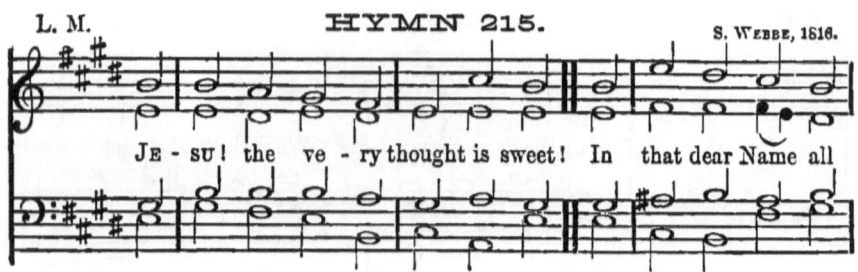
Je-su! the ve-ry thought is sweet! In that dear Name all

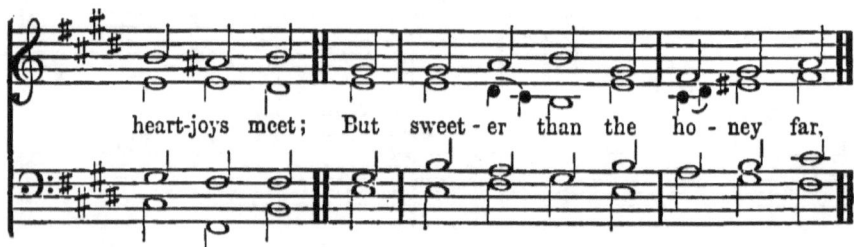
heart-joys meet; But sweet-er than the ho-ney far,

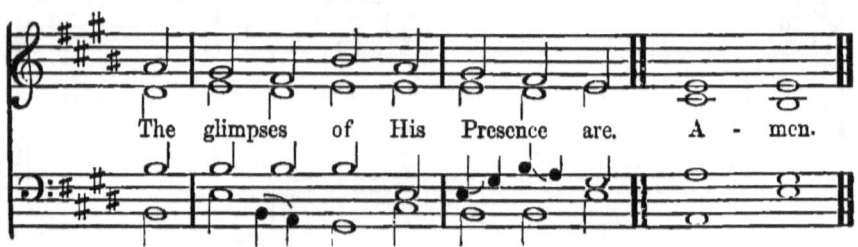
The glimpses of His Presence are. A-men.

2
No word is sung more dear than this,
No name is heard more full of bliss,
No thought brings surer comfort nigh,
Than JESUS, SON of GOD Most High.

3
JESU, the Hope of souls forlorn!
How good to them for sin that mourn!
To them that seek Thee, O how kind!
But what art Thou to them that find?

4
Remain with us, O LORD, to-day,
In every heart Thy Grace display;
That now the shades of night are fled,
On Thee our spirits may be fed.

5
All honour, laud, and glory be,
O JESU, Virgin-born, to Thee;
Praise to the FATHER, and the SON,
And HOLY SPIRIT, THREE IN ONE. Amen.

Sundays after Trinity.

HYMN 216. — 7s. — Arranged by R. F. Smith.

Ere the waning light decay,
God of all, to Thee we pray:
Let Thine Angel guards descend,
Us to succour and defend. Amen.

2
Guard from dreams that may affright,
Guard from terrors of the night;
Guard from foes, without, within,
Outward danger, inward sin.

3
Mindful of our only stay,
Duly thus to Thee we pray:
Duly thus to Thee we raise
Solemn hymns of grateful praise.

4
Hear our prayer, ALMIGHTY KING!
Hear our praises while we sing!
Hymning with the Heavenly Host,
FATHER, SON, and HOLY GHOST. Amen.

Sundays after Trinity.

HYMN 217.

8s (6 of.) — J. S. Bach, 1750.

As every day Thy Mercy spares Will bring its trials and its cares, O Saviour, till my life shall end, Be Thou my Counsellor and Friend! Teach me Thy Precepts all Divine, And be Thy Great Example mine. A-men.

2
When each day's scenes and labours close
And wearied nature seeks repose,
With pardoning mercy richly blest,
Guard me, my Saviour, while I rest;
And as each morning sun shall rise,
Oh! lead me onward to the skies.

3
And at my life's last setting sun,
My conflicts o'er, my labours done,
Jesu, Thy Heavenly Radiance shed,
To cheer and bless my dying bed;
Then from death's gloom my spirit raise,
To see Thy Face and sing Thy Praise.
Amen.

Sundays after Trinity.

2

LORD, on the Cross Thine Arms were stretched
   To draw us to the sky:
O grant us then that Cross to love,
   And in Those Arms to die.

3

To GOD the FATHER, GOD the SON,
   And GOD the HOLY GHOST,
All glory be from Saints on earth,
   And from the Angel Host.   Amen.

Sundays after Trinity.

HYMN 219. L. M. — R. F. Smith.

Sun of my soul, Thou Saviour dear, It is not night if Thou be near; Oh, may no earth-born cloud arise To hide Thee from Thy servant's eyes, A-men.

2
When the soft dews of kindly sleep
My wearied eyelids gently steep,
Be my last thought how sweet to rest,
For ever on my Saviour's Breast.

3
Abide with me from morn till eve,
For without Thee I cannot live;
Abide with me when night is nigh,
For without Thee I dare not die.

4
Come near and bless us when we wake,
Ere through the world our way we take;
Till, in the ocean of Thy Love,
We lose ourselves in Heaven above.

5
Praise God, from Whom all blessings flow;
Praise Him, all creatures here below;
Praise Him above, Angelic Host;
Praise Father, Son, and Holy Ghost.
Amen.

Sundays after Trinity.

HYMN 220.

7s (6 of.) — J. S. BACH, 1750.

FATHER! by Thy Love and Power Comes again the evening hour;
Light has vanished, labours cease, Weary creatures rest in peace:
We to Thee ourselves resign; Let our latest thoughts be Thine. A-men.

2
SAVIOUR! to Thy FATHER bear
This our feeble evening prayer;
Thou hast seen how oft to-day
We like sheep have gone astray;
Blessed SAVIOUR, yet through Thee
Grant that we may pardoned be.

3
HOLY SPIRIT! breathing balm,
Fall on us in evening's calm;
Yet awhile, before we sleep,
We with Thee our vigils keep:
Bend the stubborn heart and will,
Soften, strengthen, comfort still.

4
BLESSED TRINITY! be near
Through the hours of darkness drear:
Watch o'er our defenceless head,
Keep all evil from our bed;
Till the light of morning rays
Wakes us to a song of praise.   Amen.

Sundays after Trinity.

HYMN 221.

8, 7s.   C. J. TAYLOR.

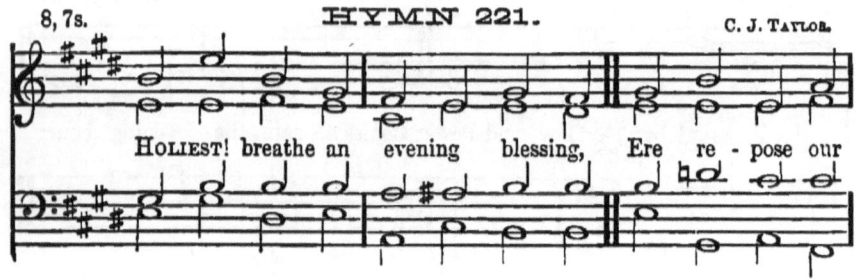

Holiest! breathe an evening blessing, Ere re-pose our spi-rits seal, Sin and want we come con-fess-ing, Thou canst save and Thou canst heal. A-men.

2
Though destruction walk around us,
   Though the arrow past us fly,
Angel Guards from Thee surround us—
   We are safe if Thou art nigh.

3
Though the night be dark and dreary,
   Darkness cannot hide from Thee;
Thou art He, Who, never weary,
   Watchest where Thy people be.

4
Should swift death this night o'ertake us,
   And our couch become our tomb,
May the morn in Bliss awake us,
   Waiting thence our journey Home.
                              Amen.

Sundays after Trinity.

Hymn 222. Arranged by W. H. Havergal. L. M.

Jesu! Who brought'st Redemption nigh, Word of the Father, God Most High: Saviour, to faithless hearts unknown; The sleepless Guardian of Thine Own. Amen.

2
Thy Hand creation made and guides;
Thy Wisdom time from time divides;
O give our wearied bodies rest,
By this world's cares and toils oppressed.

3
That while in scenes of sin and pain
A little longer we remain,
Our flesh may here in such wise sleep
That watch with Thee our souls may keep.

4
Preserve us while we dwell below,
From insults of our ghostly foe,
That he may ne'er victorious be
O'er them who are redeemed by Thee.

5
And when the grave shall claim its prey,
Keep us, O Lord, for Thy Great Day;
And in the vale of death protect
Thy ransomed flock, Thine Own elect.

6
To Thee Who died and now dost live,
Glory and praise Thy people give;
Extolling, with the Heavenly Host,
The Father, Son, and Holy Ghost.
                      Amen.

2

Guard us waking, guard us sleeping;
    And when we die,
May we, in Thy mighty Keeping,
    All peaceful lie;
When the last dread call shall wake us,
Do not Thou, O GOD, forsake us,
But to reign in glory take us,
    With Thee on High.

3

GOD, the FATHER, SON, and SPIRIT,
    Thee now we bless;
Thanks we give, and praise and merit
    To Thee address:
Ever in the new Creation
May we sing of Thy Salvation,
And with joyful adoration
    Thy Love confess.   Amen.

Sundays after Trinity.

HYMN 224.

L. M.   W. HORSLEY, M.B.

Cre-at-or of the light supreme, Who bringest forth the

morn-ing ray. Who, in the in-fan-cy of time,

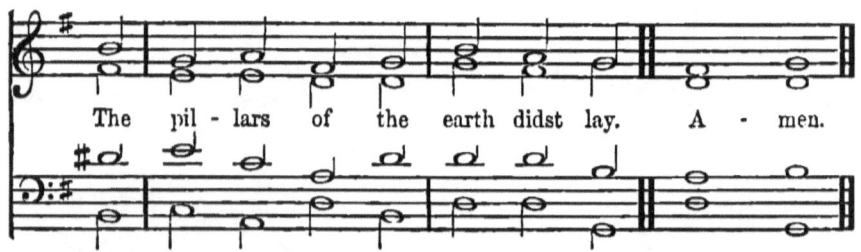

The pil-lars of the earth didst lay. A - men.

2
Who, blending morn with dewy eve,
Didst in Thy Wisdom name them day,—
Now o'er the world dull night descends,
O hearken as to Thee we pray;

3
Lest the sad soul, by guilt o'erwhelmed,
Lose the reward of life Divine,
Eternity fade from our thoughts,
And snares of sin around us twine.

4
O may we knock at Heaven's gate,
The prize of life Eternal win,
Shun every word and work of ill,
And purge our hearts from every sin.

5
These mercies, HOLY FATHER, grant,
And Thou, Co-equal Only SON,
Who, with the HOLY SPIRIT, art
Through Everlasting ages ONE.   Amen.

Sundays after Trinity.

HYMN 225.

L. M. Arranged by R. F. Smith.

Maker of all things, God Most High, Great Rul-er of the star-ry sky, Rob-ing the day in glo-rious light, In sweet re-pose the qui-et night. A-men.

2
We thank Thee for the daylight gone,
We pray Thee as the night comes on;
O help us, as we feebly raise
To Thee our evening hymn of praise.

3
To Thee our lips their tribute bring,
Thee our united voices sing,—
Thee may our chastened souls adore,
To Thee our pure affections soar.

4
Christ! with the Father ever One,
Spirit! of Father and of Son,
God! over all of mighty sway,
Shield us, Blest Trinity! we pray.
Amen.

Sundays after Trinity.

HYMN 226.

8, 7s. R. R. Chope.

2
Save us from the wiles of Satan,
 'Mid the lone and sleepless night,
Sweetly may bright guardian Angels
 Keep us 'neath their watchful sight.

3
Gentle JESUS! look in pity
 From Thy great white Throne above;
All the night Thine Heart is wakeful,
 Ever Thou Thine Own dost love.

4
Shades of even fast are falling,
 Day is fading into gloom;
When the shades of death fall round us,
 Lead Thine exiled children home.

5
Gentle JESUS, hear Thy children
 When they sing their hymns to Thee;
Who, with FATHER and with SPIRIT,
 Art ONE GOD Eternally.   Amen.

Sundays after Trinity.

HYMN 227.

L. M. T. TALLIS, 1585.

Glo-ry to Thee, my God, this night, For all the blessings of the light. Keep me, O keep me, King of kings, Beneath Thine Own Al-might-y Wings. A-men.

2
Forgive me, Lord, for Thy dear Son,
The ill that I this day have done;
That with the world, myself, and Thee,
I, ere I sleep, at peace may be.

3
Teach me to live that I may dread
The grave as little as my bed;
Teach me to die, that so I may
Rise glorious at the awful day.

4
O may my soul on Thee repose,
And may sweet sleep mine eyelids close,
Sleep that shall me more vigorous make
To serve my God when I awake.

5
When in the night I sleepless lie,
My soul with Heavenly thoughts supply;
Let no ill dreams disturb my rest,
No power of darkness me molest.

6
Praise God, from Whom all blessings flow;
Praise Him, all creatures here below;
Praise Him above, Angelic Host;
Praise Father, Son, and Holy Ghost. Amen.

Sundays after Trinity.

HYMN 228. 10s. R. F. Smith.

Abide with me; fast falls the eventide; The darkness deepens; Lord, with me abide: When other helpers fail, and comforts flee, Help of the helpless, O abide with me. Amen.

2
Swift to its close ebbs out life's little day;
Earth's joys grow dim, its glories pass away;
Change and decay in all around I see;
O Thou Who changest not, abide with me.

3
I need Thy Presence every passing hour;
What but Thy Grace can foil the Tempter's power?
Who like Thyself my Guide and Stay can be?
Through cloud and sunshine, Lord, abide with me.

4
I fear no foe with Thee at hand to bless;
Ills have no weight, and tears no bitterness;
Where is death's sting—where, grave, thy victory?
I triumph still, if Thou abide with me.

5
Hold Thou Thy Cross before my closing eyes;
Shine through the gloom, and point me to the skies;
Heaven's morning breaks, and earth's vain shadows flee;
In life, in death, O Lord, abide with me.
Amen.

Sundays after Trinity.

6, 4, 6, 6. HYMN 229. R. R. Chope.

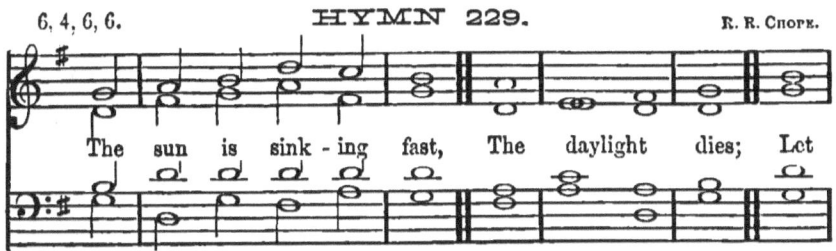

The sun is sink-ing fast, The daylight dies; Let

love awake and pay Her evening sa-cri-fice. Amen.

2
As CHRIST, upon the Cross
  In death reclined,
Into His FATHER's Hands
His parting Soul resigned;

3
So now herself my soul
  Would wholly give
Into His sacred Charge
In Whom all spirits live;

4
So now beneath His Eye
  Would calmly rest,
Without a wish or thought
Abiding in the breast,

5
Save that His Will be done,
  Whate'er betide;
Dead to herself, and dead,
In Him, to all beside.

6
Thus would I live; yet now
  Not I, but He,
With all His Power and Love
Henceforth alive in me!

7
One Sacred TRINITY!
  One LORD Divine!
Myself for ever His!
And He for ever mine! Amen.

2

The day is gone, its hours have run,
And Thou hast taken count of all,—
The scanty triumphs grace hath won,
The broken vow, the frequent fall.
Through life's long day and death's dark night,
O Gentle JESUS! be our Light.

3

Grant us, Dear LORD! from evil ways
True absolution and release;
And bless us more than in past days
With purity and inward peace.
Through life's long day and death's dark night,
O Gentle JESUS! be our Light.

4

Do more than pardon; give us joy,
Sweet fear and sober liberty,
And simple hearts without alloy,
That only long to be like Thee.
Through life's long day and death's dark night,
O Gentle JESUS! be our Light.

5

Labour is sweet, for Thou hast toiled;
And care is light, for Thou hast cared;
Ah! never let our works be soiled
With strife, or by deceit ensnared.
Through life's long day and death's dark night,
O Gentle JESUS! be our Light.

6

For all we love, the poor, the sad,
The sinful, unto Thee we call;
O let Thy Mercy make us glad;
Thou art our JESUS, and our All!
Through life's long day and death's dark night,
O Gentle JESUS! be our Light.

7

Sweet SAVIOUR! bless us; night is come;
O HOLY JESUS! nearer be.
We pray Thee tarry round our home,
For we are one day nearer Thee!
Through life's long day and death's dark night,
O Gentle JESUS! be our Light.   Amen.

Sundays after Trinity.

S. M.   HYMN 231.   Ravenscroft's Psalter, 1621.

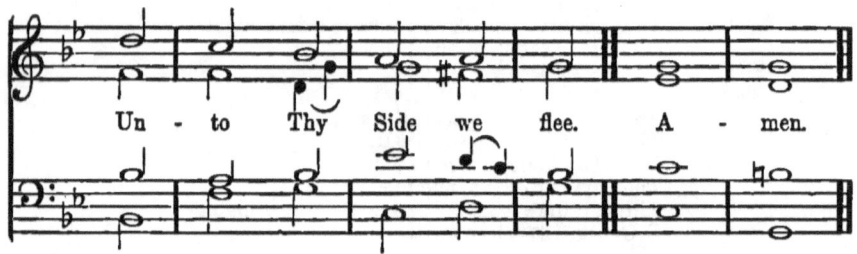

The day is past and gone, Great God, we bow to Thee; A-gain as shades of night steal on, Un-to Thy Side we flee. A-men.

2
O when shall that day come,
Ne'er sinking in the west,
That country and that holy Home,
Where none shall break our rest?

3
Where all things shall be peace,
And pleasure without end,
And golden harps that never cease,
With joyous hymns shall blend?

4
Where we, preserved beneath
The shelter of Thy Wing,
For Evermore Thy Praise shall breathe,
And of Thy Mercy sing?

5
To God the Father praise,
And to the Eternal Son,
And to the Holy Ghost always,
Co-equal Three in One.   Amen.

Sundays after Trinity.

HYMN 232.

2
The joys of day are over:
  We lift our hearts to Thee,
And ask that pure and holy
  The hours of darkness be.
O Jesu! make their darkness light,
And save us through the coming night.

3
The toils of day are over:
  We raise our hymn to Thee,
And ask that free from peril
  The hours of darkness be.
O Jesu! keep us in Thy Sight,
And guard us through the coming night.
                              Amen.

Sundays after Trinity.

C. M.   HYMN 233.   Dr. Turton, Lord Bishop of Ely.

Son of the Highest! deign to cast
On us a pitying eye;
Thou, Who repentant Magdalene,
Didst call to joys on High. A-men.

2
O Jesu! Balm of every wound!
  The sinner's only Stay!
Grant us, like Magdalene, to weep
  In this Thy Mercy's Day.

3
O Thou, Who hast forgiven much,
  Help us to love Thee more!
And teach us how in penitence
  Thy Mercy to implore.

4
O Holy Trinity! to Thee
  Be praise and glory given,
For all the Love which Thou hast shown
  To win lost man to Heaven.   Amen.

Sundays after Trinity.

L. M. — HYMN 234. — W. B. Gilbert.

All ye who seek, in hope and love, For your dear LORD, look up above! Where traced upon the azure sky, Faith may a glorious Form descry. A-men.

2
Lo! on the trembling verge of light,
A Vision all Divinely bright!
Immortal, Infinite, Sublime!
Older than chaos, space, or time!

3
Hail, Thou, the Gentiles' Mighty LORD!
All hail, O Israel's KING adored!
To Abraham sworn in ages past,
And to his seed while earth shall last.

4
To Thee the Prophets witness bear;
Of Thee the FATHER doth declare,
That all, who would His Glory see,
Must hear and must believe in Thee.

5
To JESUS, from the proud concealed,
But Evermore to babes revealed,
All glory with the FATHER be,
And HOLY GHOST Eternally.   Amen.

Sundays after Trinity.

HYMN 235. L. M. Dr. Turton, Lord Bishop of Ely.

Light of the soul, O Saviour Blest! Soon as Thy Presence fills the breast, Darkness and guilt are put to flight, And all is sweetness and de-light. A-men

2

Son of the Father! Lord Most High!
How glad is he who feels Thee nigh!
How sweet in Heaven Thy Beam doth
Denied to eye of flesh below. [glow,

3

O Light of Light Celestial!
O Charity ineffable!
Come in Thy hidden Majesty;
Fill us with love, fill us with Thee.

4

To Jesus, from the proud concealed,
But Evermore to babes revealed,
All glory with the Father be,
And Holy Ghost Eternally.   Amen.

Sundays after Trinity.

HYMN 236.

L. M. — Arranged by J. S. Bach, 1730.

Let every heart ex-ult-ing beat With joy at Jesus'
Name of bliss; With every pure de-light re-plete,
And pass-ing sweet its mu-sic is. A-men.

2
JESUS the comfortless consoles,
JESUS each sinful fever quells;
JESUS the power of Hell controls,
JESUS each deadly foe repels.

3
O speak His Glorious Name abroad!
JESUS let every tongue confess,
Let every heart and voice accord
The Healer of our souls to bless.

4
JESU! the sinner's Friend, abide
With us, and hearken to our prayer;
Thy frail and erring wanderers guide,
And all our dread transgressions spare.

5
O CHRIST! all glory be to Thee,
Effulgent with this Name Divine;
All honour, worship, majesty,
JESU! for Evermore be Thine.   Amen.

Holy Communion.

HYMN 237.

Of that glorious Body broken, O my soul, the Mystery sing! And the Blood all price exceeding, Shed by Him Who came to bring To a fallen world Redemption, CHRIST, our SAVIOUR and our KING. Amen.

2

Of a pure and spotless Virgin
    Born for us, on earth below,
He, as MAN with man conversing,
    Dwelt, the seed of truth to sow;
Till He closed, in solemn order,
    This His Sojourning of woe.

3

On the night of that Last Supper,
    Seated with His chosen band,
He the Paschal victim eating,
    First fulfils the law's command,
Then as Food, to His disciples
    Gives Himself with His Own Hand.

4

By His Word, the Word Incarnate,
    Maketh bread His Flesh to be;
Wine the Blood of CHRIST becometh,
    Though unchanged Its substance be,
But in every guileless spirit
    Faith accepts the Mystery.

5

This great Sacrament ordained
    Let us all revering hail;
Ancient rites are past for ever,
    Newer means of Grace prevail;
Willing faith the lack supplieth,
    Where our earthly senses fail.

6

To the Everlasting FATHER,
    To the Everlasting SON,
To the Co-Eternal SPIRIT,
    Undivided THREE IN ONE,
Honour, praise, salvation, blessing,
    Now and Evermore be done.   Amen.

Holy Communion.

2
O Blest Memorial of our dying LORD,
Who Living Bread to men dost here afford!
O may our souls for ever feed on Thee,
And Thou, O CHRIST, for ever Precious be.

3
Fountain of Goodness! JESU, LORD and GOD!
Cleanse us, unclean, with Thy Most Cleansing Blood.
Increase our faith and love, that we may know
The hope and peace which from Thy Presence flow.

4
O CHRIST! Whom now beneath a veil we see,
May what we thirst for soon our portion be;
To gaze on Thee unveiled, and see Thy Face,
The vision of Thy Glory and Thy Grace.   Amen.

Holy Communion.

C. M.   HYMN 239.   W. B. Gilbert.

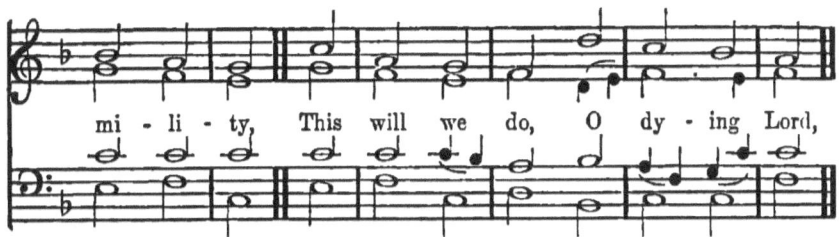

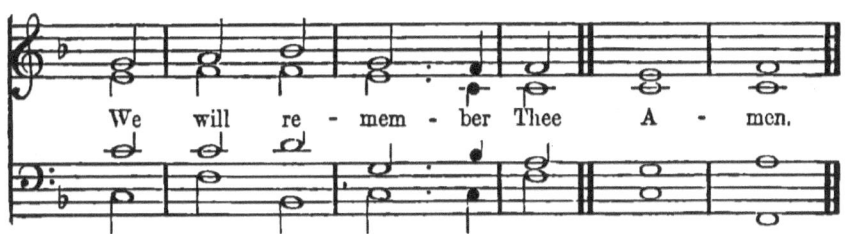

According to Thy gracious Word, In deep humility, This will we do, O dying Lord, We will remember Thee. Amen.

2

Thy Body, broken for our sake,
  Our Bread from Heaven shall be;
The Cup, Thy precious Blood, we take,
  And thus remember Thee.

3

Can we Gethsemane forget?
  Or there Thy Conflict see,
Thine Agony and bloody Sweat,
  And not remember Thee?

4

When to the Cross we turn our eyes,
  And gaze on Calvary,
O Lamb of God, our Sacrifice,
  We must remember Thee.

5

To Thee, O Jesu, Light of Light,
  All praise and glory be;
To God the Father Infinite,
  And Holy Ghost to Thee.   Amen.

Holy Communion.

HYMN 240.

C. M.   A. H. Brown.

O God, un-seen yet e-ver near, Thy Presence

may we feel; And, thus in-spired with ho-ly fear,

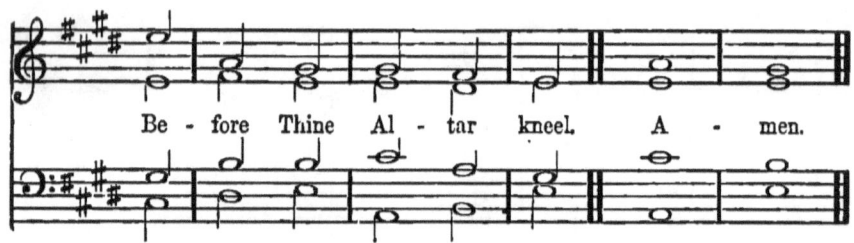

Be-fore Thine Al-tar kneel. A-men.

2
Here may Thy faithful people know
   The blessings of Thy Love,
The streams that through the desert flow,
   The manna from above.

3
We come, obedient to Thy Word,
   To Feast on Heavenly Food;
Our meat, the Body of the Lord,
   Our drink, His precious Blood.

4
Thus may we all Thy Words obey,
   For we, O God, are Thine;
And go rejoicing on our way,
   Renewed with strength Divine.

5
To Father, Son, and Holy Ghost,
   The God Whom we adore,
Be glory, as it was, is now,
   And shall be Evermore.   Amen.

Holy Communion.

HYMN 241.

7s. Dr. Gauntlett.

God of all re-deem-ing Grace, By Thy cleansing Mer-cy healed, Up to Thee our souls we raise, And to Thee our bo-dies yield. A-men.

2
Thou the sacrifice receive
Humbly offered through Thy Son:
May we ever in Thee live,
May Thy Will in us be done.

3
Meet it is, and just and right,
That we should be wholly Thine,
In Thy Holy Word delight,
In Thy Service all combine,

4
O that every deed and word
May proclaim how good Thou art;
Holiness unto the Lord
Still be written on each heart.   Amen.

Holy Communion.

O God of Mer-cy, God of Might, How should frail sinners bear the sight, If, as Thy Power is sure-ly here, Thine o-pen Glo-ry should ap-pear. A-men.

2
For now, Thy people are allowed
To scale the mount and pierce the cloud,
And faith may feed her eager view
With wonders Sinai never knew.

3
Fresh from the atoning sacrifice,
The world's CREATOR bleeding lies,
That man, His foe, by whom He bled,
May take Him for his Daily Bread.

4
O agony of wavering thought,
When sinners first so near are brought!
"It is my MAKER—dare I stay?
My SAVIOUR—dare I turn away?"

5
Sweet, awful hour! the only sound
One gentle footstep gliding round,
Offering by turns, on JESU's Part,
The Cross to every hand and heart.

6
Refresh us, LORD, to hold it fast;
And when Thy Veil is drawn at last,
Let us depart where shadows cease,
With words of blessing and of peace.
Amen.

Holy Communion.

HYMN 243.

L. M.   Arranged by J. B. Dykes.

My God, and is Thy Table spread, And doth Thy Cup with love o'er-flow? Thither be all Thy children led, And let them all Thy Sweetness know. A-men.

2

Hail, Sacred Feast, which Jesus makes,
Rich Banquet of His Flesh and Blood!
Thrice happy he who here partakes
That Sacred Stream, that Heavenly Food.

3

Why are its dainties all in vain
Before unwilling hearts displayed?
Was not for us the Victim slain?
Are we denied the children's bread?

4

O let Thy Table honoured be,
And furnished well with joyful guests;
And may each soul salvation see
That here its sacred pledges tastes.

5

To Father, Son, and Holy Ghost,
The God Whom Heaven and earth adore,
From men and from the Angel Host
Be praise and glory Evermore.   Amen.

Holy Baptism.

HYMN 244.

7s.   Arranged by J. B. Dykes.

Lamb of God! for sinners slain; By Thy Mercy born again, For Thy Guidance still we pray, Lest from grace we fall away. A-men.

2
By the mystic, cleansing Flood,
By the Water and the Blood,
Washed and sanctified to Thee,
Pure and holy let us be.

3
Aid us with Thy daily Grace,
Steadfastly to run our race;
Grant us victory in the strife,
And the prize of Endless life.

4
Laud and praise from all on earth
To the God of our New Birth;
Praise Him, all ye Heavenly Host,
Father, Son, and Holy Ghost.
Amen.

Holy Baptism.

HYMN 245. C.M. — M. Pratorius, 1609.

The Spi-rit on the waters moved, At the Cre-a-tion's morn; And from the wa-ters, by His Power, The Heaven and earth were born. A-men.

2
On the Baptismal Water broods
  Regenerating Love;
And there the soul is born anew,
  Created from above.

3
Baptized in Christ, we died to sin,
  And to New Life were born;
O may we rise, and hail with joy
  The Resurrection morn.

4
Baptized in Christ we put on Christ,
  And then were clothed in Light;
O may we keep that garment pure,
  And ever walk in white.

5
So may we stand with Saints in Bliss,
  That white-robed Company,
Before the Everlasting Throne,
  And render thanks to Thee.

6
O Father, Son, and Holy Ghost,
  One God and Persons Three,
Whose Name we bear, in Whom we live,
  Eternal glory be!   Amen.

School Festivals.

HYMN 246.

6, 8s. J. B. Dykes.

O Je-su! God and Man, For love of children once a Child, O Je-su! God and Man, The Vir-gin-born, the un-de-filed. A-men.

2
O Jesu! God and Man!
 We are all children dear to Thee:
O lead us to Thyself,
 To love Thee for Eternity.

3
O Jesu! Lord and God!
 The Friend of children ever sure,
Thy Blood has washed us clean
 From guilt,—O keep us always pure.

4
O Jesu! Saviour Dear!
 We thank Thee ever for Thy Love,
And pray that to the Faith
 We may all true and faithful prove.

5
O Jesu! Mary's Son!
 On Thee for Grace we children call,
That we each other love,
 But Thee above, and chief of all.

6
O Jesu! bless our work;
 Our sorrows soothe, our sins forgive;
O happy, happy they
 Who in the Love of Jesus live!

7
O God! most Great and Good!
 At work, at play, and day and night
O may we think of Thee,
 Who hast us always in Thy Sight. Amen.

School Festivals.

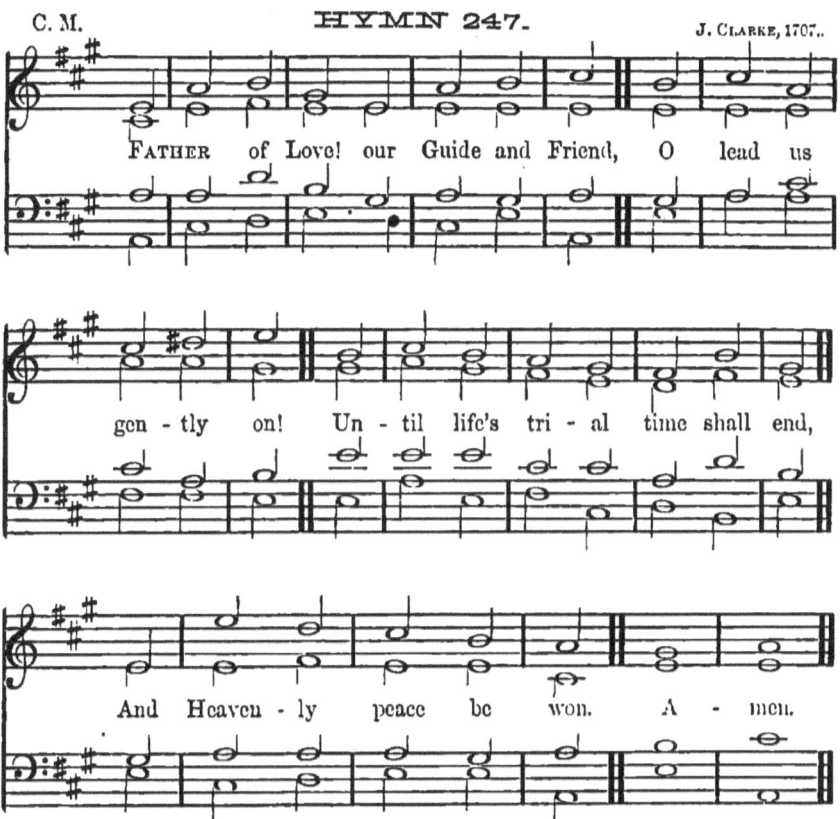

Hymn 247. C. M. J. Clarke, 1707.

Father of Love! our Guide and Friend, O lead us gently on! Until life's trial time shall end, And Heavenly peace be won. Amen.

2
We know not what the path may be,
　As yet by us untrod;
But we can trust our all to Thee,
　Our Father and our God.

3
If called, like Abraham's child, to climb
　The hill of sacrifice,
Some Angel may be there in time—
　Deliverance shall arise.

4
Or if some darker lot be good,
　Oh teach us to endure
The sorrow, pain, or solitude,
　That make the spirit pure!

5
Christ by no flowery pathway came,
　And we, His followers here,
Must do Thy Will, and praise Thy Name,
　In hope, and love, and fear.

6
And till in Heaven we sinless bow,
　And faultless anthems raise;
O Father, Son, and Spirit, now
　Accept our feeble praise.　　Amen.

School Festivals.

HYMN 248.

Blest Voice of Love! O Word Divine! Lord, Thou hast called young children Thine—Of such shall Heaven's bright Kingdom be! On children's heads Thy Hand was laid, And childlike innocence was made Holy, when touched, O Lord, by Thee. Amen.

2

"To Him That loved us!" we would raise,
As sons of God, our earliest praise,
To Him that washed us from our stains;
In Heaven high praise is echoing now,
There Angels and Archangels bow;
For ever their pure joy remains.

3

They rest not, day and night, but cry
Thrice-Holy Lord! the Heavens on high
And all the earth Thy Glory fills!

"They rest not!"—earth's exulting hymn
Is echoed by the Cherubim,
Beyond the Everlasting hills.

4

Yet in that choir what sounds more dear,
More welcome to the Eternal Ear,
Than blameless joy of infant songs?
To Thee, the glorious Lord alone,
Creator, Saviour, Holy One,
Creation's homage all belongs.   Amen.

School Festivals.

HYMN 249. L. M. C. T. Bowen.

Can earthly voic-es fit-ly sing Thy Prais-es, O E-ter-nal King! Yet who, O Lord, should si-lent stand, A-mong the crea-tures of Thy Hand? A-men.

2
Could we by searching find out Thee,
Our hymns might not more worthy be;
At best we only know in part,
Though we can give Thee all our heart.

3
Thy sons of light the song began
When Thou createdst earth and man;
O when shall man, forgetful long,
Reply with one united song!

4
We thank Thee that the wise and great
Are not alone to celebrate
The Everlasting Father's Care,
But all may mingle praise and prayer.

5
Yes, Thou art praised through earth and
Praised by the wisdom of the wise, [skies,
Praised by the humble, pure, and true,
And by the songs of children too.

6
Glory to God! is Heaven's own voice,
Bidding Thy creatures thus rejoice—
Thy creatures all, Thy Church the most—
Praise Father, Son, and Holy Ghost.
Amen.

School Festivals.

HYMN 250.

8s (6 of.) — G. COOPER.

We praise Thee, O our GOD! to Thee, FATHER, our hymns once more as-cend; Thy Mercy's ever new, and we Hail with new song our changeless FRIEND! O may our gratitude now rise, And find ac-cept-ance in the skies! A-men.

2 And, O Thou HOLY, UNDEFILED,
Who once didst condescend to be
Of woman born, a lowly Child,
Receive our infant minstrelsy,
And let it mingle with the song,
Which Angels Evermore prolong!

3 And Thou, the SPIRIT of all Grace,
O, HOLY GHOST, the COMFORTER!
The Church is Thy blest Dwelling-place,
And we would seek Thy Presence here.
Here we have been baptized and blest;
Here by Thy Grace our souls would rest!

4 Thy Face, O LORD, our Angels see
E'en now, yet watch us from above;
So, while our hearts are fixed on Thee,
May we our earthly duties love;
Then, when the things of time depart,
We shall be with Thee, where Thou art!
Amen.

Confirmation.

HYMN 251.

Lord, shall Thy children come to Thee? A boon of Love Divine we seek; Brought to Thine Arms in in-fan-cy, Ere hearts could feel, or tongue could speak; Thy children pray for grace that they May come themselves to Thee to-day. Amen.

2
Lord, may we ever here remain,
Oft as we see Thy Table spread,
And, tokens of Thy dying Pain,
The Wine poured out, the broken Bread;
Bless, bless, O Lord, Thy children's prayer,
That they may come, and find Thee there.

3
Lord, may we come! not thus alone
At holy times, or solemn rite,
But every hour, till life be flown,
Through weal or woe, in gloom or light,
Come to Thy Throne of grace, that we,
In faith, hope, love, confirmed may be.

4
Lord, may we come, come yet again!
Thy children ask one blessing more;
To come, not now alone, but then,
When life, and death, and time are o'er,
Then, then to come, O Lord, and be
Confirmed in Heaven, Confirmed by Thee!
Amen.

Confirmation.

Hymn 252.

C. M.   J. B. Dykes.

Spi-rit of Wisdom! guide Thine Own, Who make Thee now their Choice; That they may ne-ver walk a-lone, But hear Thy Heaven-ly Voice. A-men.

2
Spirit of Understanding! Light
  Shed that the world ne'er saw;
Open their eyes, to see aright
  The wonders of Thy Law.

3
Spirit of Counsel! 'neath the cloud
  Of sorrow and dismay,
Cheer Thou their souls with anguish bowed,
  And chase all doubt away.

4
Spirit of Strength! infuse Thy Might,
  Nerve Thy young soldiers' arms;
Temptation let them put to flight,
  And banish Hell's alarms.

5
Spirit of Knowledge! Whose deep Things
  Are now but darkly shown;
Lead them, on Resurrection wings,
  To know as they are known.

6
Spirit of Godliness! unfold
  The joys of Heavenly Grace;
Give peace on earth, the bliss untold
  Of Saints who see God's Face.

7
Spirit of Holy Fear! inspire
  Dread Reverence of Thy Name;
That we, with the Celestial Choir,
  May praise Thee without blame. Amen.

Confirmation.

Hymn 253. C.M. — J. Turle.

Pour down, O Lord, on this our youth Thy holiest Gifts of Grace, And let the seed of sacred Truth Find in each heart a place. A-men.

2
The Cross that marked their infant brow
In deeper lines impress,
That they may keep the solemn vow
Which now their lips profess.

3
Their Saviour's soldiers may they be,
And tread the path He trod;
From youth to age remember Thee,
And love the Lord their God.

4
Thy sons and daughters may they prove
Adopted and forgiven;
And having here enjoyed Thy Love,
Behold Thy Face in Heaven.

5
To God, Who freely loved us first,
All might, all glory, be;
To Father, Son, and Holy Ghost,
Through all Eternity. Amen.

Confirmation.

HYMN 254.

Soldiers of Christ, arise,
And put your Armour on,
Strong in the strength which God supplies
Through His Eternal Son. Amen.

2
Strong in the Lord of Hosts,
And in His mighty Power!
Who in the Strength of Jesus trusts
Is more than conqueror.

3
Stand then in His great Might,
With all His Strength endued;
And take, to arm you for the fight,
The Panoply of God.

4
From strength to strength go on,
Wrestle, and fight, and pray;
Tread all the powers of darkness down,
And win the well-fought day.

5
That having all things done,
And all your conflicts past,
Ye may obtain, through Christ alone,
A Crown of joy at last.

6
Jesu, Eternal Son,
We praise Thee and adore,
Who art with God the Father One
And Spirit Evermore. Amen.

Holy Matrimony.

HYMN 255.

2 Still in the pure Espousal
  Of Christian man and maid
The HOLY THREE are with us,
  The threefold Grace is said.

3 For dower of blessed children,
  For love and faith's sweet sake,
For high mysterious union,
  Which nought on earth may break,

4 Be present, Awful FATHER,
  To give away this bride,
As Eve Thou gav'st to Adam
  Out of his own pierced side;

5 Be present, SON of Mary,
  To join their loving hands,

As Thou didst bind two Natures
  In Thine Eternal Bands;

6 Be present, Holiest SPIRIT,
  To bless them as they kneel,
As Thou for CHRIST, the Bridegroom,
  The Heavenly Spouse dost seal.

7 O spread Thy pure Wing o'er them,
  Let no ill power find place,
When onward to Thine Altar
  The hallowed path they trace,

8 To cast their crowns before Thee,
  In perfect sacrifice,
Till to the home of gladness
  With CHRIST'S Own Bride they rise.
                              Amen.

Holy Matrimony.

When on Creation's morn The world in beauty shone, The LORD beheld that all was good, But man was left alone. Amen.

2
On Eden's happy bowers
Fresh joy GOD'S Presence shed,
When to the man, flesh of his flesh,
A spouse He blessing led.

3
At Cana's Feast again
His Power was there to bless,
When to create the world anew
He came in Righteousness.

4
Mysterious Bond! that twice
The SON of GOD thus graced.
Yet to Himself, the Church His Bride,
The "Mystery great" is traced!

5
In Eden, Cana, both,
CHRIST'S Presence was the Light;
Without His Presence, all unblest
And vain the Solemn Rite.

6
LORD! at Thine Altar now
Thy Blessing we implore:
In sickness, health, till death these part,
Be with them Evermore. Amen.

Visitation of the Sick.

HYMN 257.

C. M.   Este's Psalter, 1592.

O Saviour of the faithful dead! With Whom Thy servants dwell, Though cold and damp the turf is spread Above their narrow cell,— Amen.

2
No more we cling to mortal clay;
  We doubt and fear no more;
Nor shrink to tread the dreary way
  Which Thou hast trod before.

3
When, soon or late, this feeble breath
  No more to Thee shall pray,
Support me through the vale of death,
  And in the darksome way.

4
When quickened by Thy Power again,
  I wait Thy just Decree,
Judge of the world! remember then,
  That Thou hast died for me!   Amen.

Burial of the Dead.

HYMN 258.

J. B. Dykes.

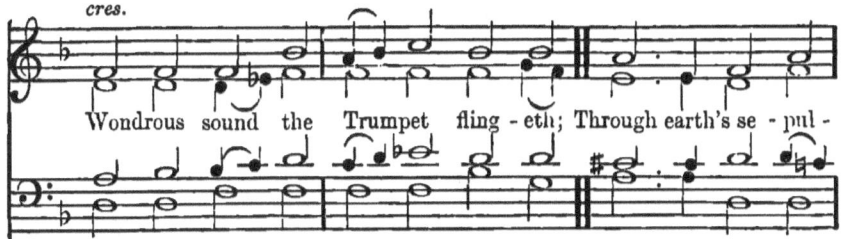

2

Death is struck, and nature quaking,
All Creation is awaking,
To its JUDGE an answer making!

Lo! the Book, exactly worded,
Wherein all hath been recorded!
Thence shall Judgment be awarded.

When the JUDGE His Seat attaineth,
And each hidden deed arraigneth,
Nothing unavenged remaineth.

3

What shall I, frail man, be pleading,
Who for me be interceding,
When the just are mercy needing?

KING of Majesty tremendous!
Who dost free salvation send us,
FOUNT of Pity, then befriend us!

Think, Kind JESU! my salvation
Caused Thy wondrous Incarnation;
Leave me not to reprobation.

4

Faint and weary, Thou hast sought me,
On the Cross of suffering bought me;—
Shall such Grace be vainly brought me?

Righteous JUDGE! for sin's pollution
Grant Thy Gift of Absolution,
Ere that Day of retribution!

Guilty, now I pour my moaning,
All my shame with anguish owning;
Spare, O GOD! Thy suppliant, groaning!

5

Thou the sinful Woman savedst,
Thou the dying Thief forgavest,
And to me a hope vouchsafest.

Worthless are my prayers and sighing,
Yet, Good LORD, in grace complying,
Rescue me from fires undying!

With Thy favoured sheep O place me,
Nor among the goats abase me,
But to Thy Right Hand upraise me.

[TURN OVER.

Ember Days.

HYMN 259.

C. M. W. Wheall, 1745.

Christ is gone up! yet ere He passed From earth in

Heaven to reign, He formed One Ho-ly Church to last

'Till He should come a-gain. A-men.

2
His twelve Apostles first He made
  His Ministers of Grace;
And they their hands on others laid,
  To fill in turn their place.

3
So age by age, and year by year,
  His Grace was handed on;
And still the Holy Church is here,
  Although her Lord is gone

4
Let those find pardon, Lord! from Thee,
  Whose love to her is cold;
Bring wanderers in, and let there be
  One Shepherd and One Fold.

5
To God the Father, God the Son,
  And God the Holy Ghost,
By man on earth be glory done,
  And by the Heavenly Host. Amen.

Ember Days.

HYMN 260. L. M. — R. R. Chope.

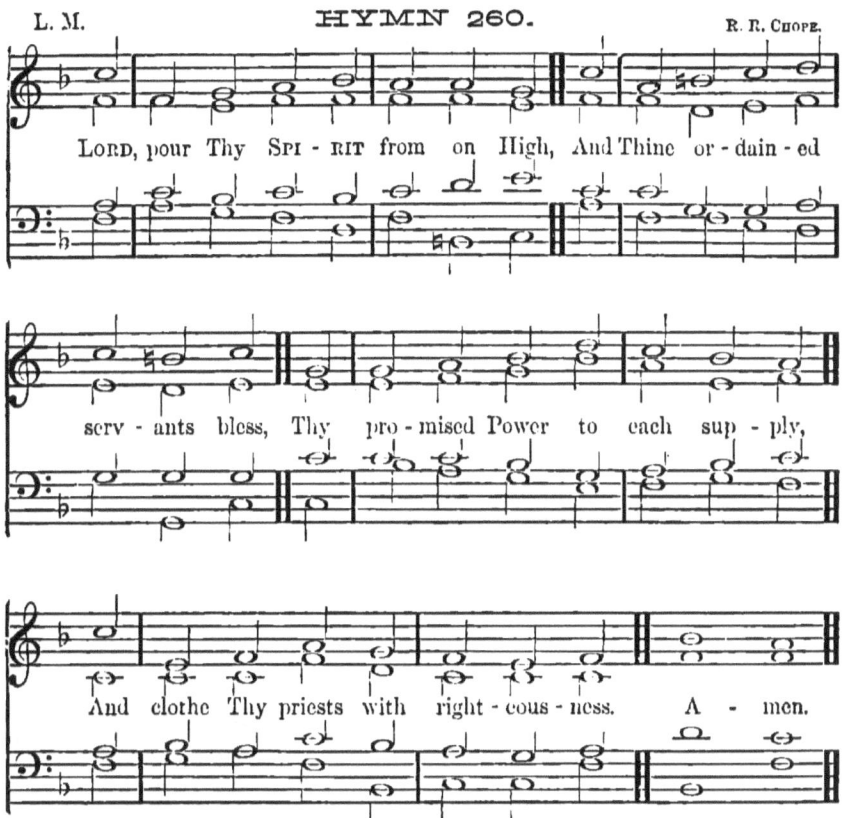

Lord, pour Thy Spirit from on high, And Thine ordained servants bless, Thy promised Power to each supply, And clothe Thy priests with righteousness. Amen.

2
Within Thy Temple when they stand,
To teach the truth as taught by Thee,
Saviour, like stars in Thy Right Hand,
Let all Thy Church's Pastors be.

3
Wisdom, and zeal, and faith impart,
Firmness and meekness from above,
To bear Thy people in their heart,
And love the souls whom Thou dost love;

4
To watch and pray, and never faint,
By day and night their guard to keep,
To warn the sinner, cheer the saint,
Protect Thy lambs, and feed Thy sheep.

5
So, when their work is finished here,
May they in hope their charge resign;
Before Thy Throne with joy appear,
And there with crowns of glory shine.
Amen.

Missions.

HYMN 261.

7, 6 (8 of.) S. Reay.

From Greenland's ic-y mount-ains, From India's co-ral strand,
Where Afric's sun-ny fountains Roll down their golden sand,
From many an ancient ri-ver, From many a palmy plain, They
call us to de-li-ver Their land from error's chain. Amen.

2 What though the spicy breezes
   Blow soft o'er Ceylon's isle,
Though every prospect pleases,
   And only man is vile;
In vain with lavish kindness
   The gifts of GOD are strown,
The heathen in his blindness
   Bows down to wood and stone.

3 Can we whose souls are lighted
   With wisdom from on High,
Can we to men benighted
   The lamp of life deny?
Salvation! Oh, Salvation!
   The joyful sound proclaim,
Till each remotest nation
   Has learnt MESSIAH's Name.

4 Waft, waft, ye winds, His Story,
   And you, ye waters, roll,
Till like a sea of glory
   It spreads from pole to pole;
Till o'er our ransomed nature
   The LAMB for sinners slain,
REDEEMER, KING, CREATOR,
   In bliss returns to reign. Amen.

Missions.

HYMN 262. C.M. — Scotch Psalter, 1635.

Thou, LORD, the Hope of all the earth, Art now gone up on High: Hast paid our ran-som, and hast led Cap-tive cap-tiv-i-ty. A-men.

2
Rich gifts for men hast Thou received,
　Although they did rebel,
Yea, even for Thy foes, that GOD
　'Mongst them may ever dwell.

3
Thou giv'st the word: the preachers rise,
　Their arms not Hell can foil;
Kings with their armies are o'erthrown;
　Thy Church divides the spoil.

4
Thou, LORD, the Mighty GOD, make strong
　In us what Thou hast wrought:
To Thee, for Thy loved Temple's sake,
　By kings shall gifts be brought.

5
To Thee shall Egypt's princes come,
　With their assembled bands,
And Ethiopia to our GOD
　Shall humbly stretch her hands.

6
O all ye kingdoms of the earth,
　Sing praises to our KING!
To FATHER, SON, and HOLY GHOST,
　Loud praises ever sing! Amen.

Missions.

HYMN 263.

8, 7s. E. J. Hopkins.

Lord, a Saviour's Love displaying, Show the heathen

lands Thy Way; Thousands still like sheep are straying

In the dark and cloudy day. A-men.

2
Shades of death are gathering o'er them,
 Lord, they perish from Thy Sight!
Let Thine Angel go before them;
 Bring the Gentiles to Thy Light.

3
Fetch them home from every nation;
 From the Islands of the sea;
By the Word of Thy Salvation
 Call the wanderers back to Thee.

4
Thou their pasture hast provided,
 Grant the blessing long foretold;
Let Thy Sheep, Divinely guided,
 Find at last the one true Fold.

5
Honour, glory, virtue, merit,
 Blest Redeemer! be to Thee,
Who with Father and with Spirit
 Art one God Eternally.   Amen.

Harvest.

HYMN 264.

8s (6 of.) — J. H. Schein, 1645.

Lord of the harvest, once again We thank Thee for the ripened grain; For crops safe carried, sent to cheer Thy servants through another year; For all sweet holy thoughts supplied By seed-time, and by harvest-tide. A-men.

2 The bare dead grain, in Autumn sown,
  Its robe of vernal green puts on;
  Glad from its wintry grave it springs,
  Fresh garnished by the King of kings:
  So, Lord, to those who sleep in Thee
  Shall new and glorious bodies be.

3 Nor vainly of Thy Word we ask
  A lesson from the reaper's task:
  So shall Thine Angels issue forth;
  The tares be burnt; the just of earth,
  To wind and storm exposed no more,
  Be gathered to their Father's Store.

4 Daily, O Lord, our prayers be said,
  As Thou hast taught, for daily bread;
  But not alone our bodies feed,
  Supply our fainting spirits' need:
  O Bread of Life, from day to day
  Be Thou their Comfort, Food, and Stay!
  Amen.

2

What is earth but God's Own Field,
Fruit unto His Praise to yield?
Wheat and tares therein are sown,
Unto joy or sorrow grown;
Ripening with a wondrous power,
Till the final Harvest-Hour:
Grant, O Lord of Life, that we
Holy grain and pure may be.

3

For we know that Thou wilt come,
And wilt take Thy people Home;
From Thy Field wilt purge away
All that doth offend, that day;
And Thine Angels charge at last
In the fire the tares to cast,
But the fruitful ears to store
In Thy Garner Evermore.

4

Come then, Lord of mercy, come,
Bid us sing Thy Harvest-Home!
Let Thy Saints be gathered in,
Free from sorrow, free from sin;
All upon the golden floor
Praising Thee for Evermore:
Come, with thousand Angels, come;
Bid us sing Thy Harvest-Home! Amen.

Harvest.

HYMN 266.

C. M. T. B. Hosken.

Father of Mercies, God of Love, Whose Gifts all

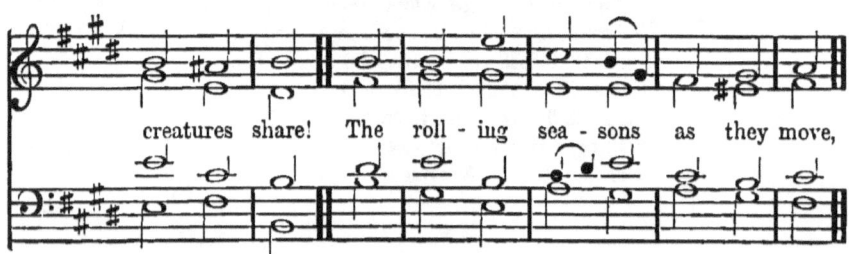

creatures share! The rolling seasons as they move,

Proclaim Thy constant Care. Amen.

2
When in the bosom of the earth
  The sower hid the grain,
Thy Goodness marked its secret birth,
  And sent the early rain.

3
The seasons, Gracious Lord, are Thine!
  The spring-tide knew Thy Call;
Thou mad'st the Summer suns to shine,
  The Summer dews to fall.

4
O ne'er may our forgetful hearts
  O'erlook Thy bounteous Care;
But what our Father's Hand imparts,
  Still own in praise and prayer.

5
So shall our suns more grateful shine,
  Our showers more genial fall,
When all our hearts and lives are Thine,
  And Thou adored in all.   Amen.

In Times of Trouble.

HYMN 267. L. M. R. R. Chope.

God of our life, to Thee we call, Afflicted at Thy Feet we fall: When the great waterfloods prevail, Leave not our trembling hearts to fail. Amen.

2
Friend of the friendless and the faint,
Where shall we pour our sad complaint?
Where but to Thee, Whose open Door
Invites the helpless and the poor?

3
Did ever sinner plead with Thee,
And Thou reject his lowly plea?
Does not Thy Word still pledged remain,
That none shall seek Thy Face in vain?

4
Then hear, O Lord, our humble cry,
And bend on us Thy pitying Eye!
To Thee their prayer Thy people make;
Hear us for our Redeemer's Sake. Amen.

In Times of Trouble.

HYMN 268.

Though clouds obscure the path we tread
Through dreary wastes of woe,
Faith bids us lift our drooping head,
And leave our cares below. Amen.

2
To humble us, to make us wise,
Affliction's hand may come,
To teach us how to sympathize,
Or bring the wanderer home.

3
In God, in Whom all wisdom, power,
And love, unchanged abide,
Christians, in every trying hour,
May undismayed confide.

4
Dark as the unknown plan appears,
Good is the aim and end;
And we may smile through all our tears,
If Jesus be our Friend. Amen.

In Times of Trouble.

HYMN 269.

C. M. — GERMAN.

Lord, in Thy Wrath Thou thinkest yet On mercy to Thy Saints; On Thee our waiting hopes are set; Remember our complaints. Amen.

2
Of old the Flood, with thunders loud,
 Rose, till Thy Wrath was stayed;
But then Thy Bow was in the cloud,
 Thy Promise surely made.

3
Earth, at Thy Word, her treasure yields,
 Summer and Winter come;
Our seed-time and our harvest-fields,
 To cheer our hearth and home.

4
And though the Angel of Thy Wrath
 With Pestilence may smite;
Midway he pauses in his path,
 When prayer is made aright.

5
Lord of all power and might! Who dost
 With goodness all things fill,
Thou Father, Son, and Holy Ghost,
 Refresh Thy people still.   Amen

In Times of Trouble.

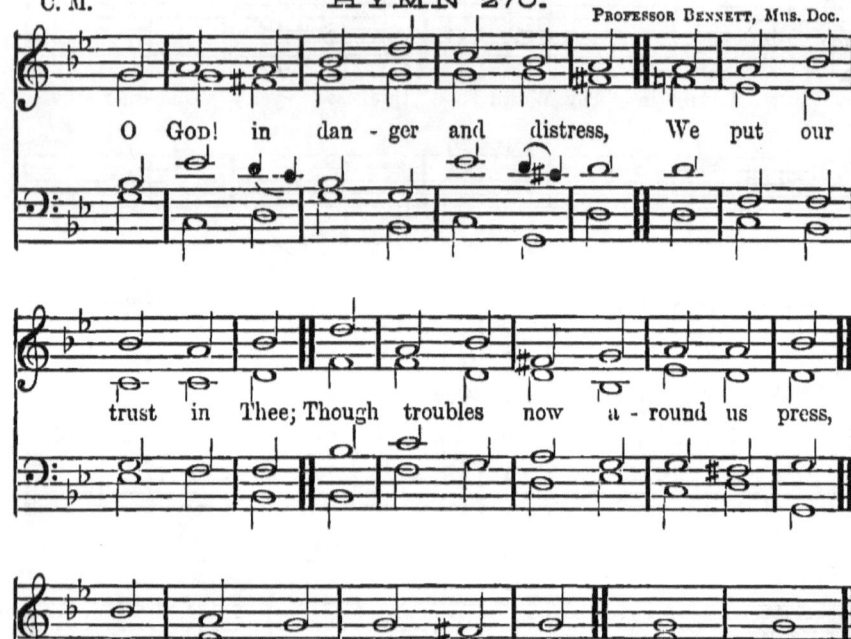

O God! in danger and distress, We put our trust in Thee; Though troubles now around us press, Unto Thy Side we flee. A-men.

2
There hide us, O Thou King of Peace,
    Until the storm is o'er,—
Till wars throughout the world shall cease,
    And troubles be no more.

3
We know the wonders Thou hast wrought
    For all Thy Saints of old;
How for Thy people Thou hast fought,
    And made the fearful bold.

4
Not by themselves that blessed Land
    Could they have hoped to win;
It was Thy Promise and Thy Hand
    That brought them safely in.

5
O God—their God and ours—behold!
    A faithful God art Thou!
Thou didst not fail Thy Saints of old;
    Thou wilt not fail us now.

6
Through Thee the conquest shall be won
    O'er Satan and his host,
O God the Father, God the Son,
    And God the Holy Ghost! Amen.

In Times of Trouble.

HYMN 271. L.M. J. Cooper.

Thou Mighty FATHER, Prince of Peace, Send forth the SPIRIT of Thy Love; Bid wars and angry tumults cease, And earth be calm as Heaven above! Amen.

2
Our sins provoked Thy Judgments, LORD,
And we against Thy Mercy strove;
Oh, be our pardon now restored,
Our hearts be calm as Heaven above!

3
To Thee our sorrows all are known,
And Thou in kindness dost reprove;
Peace is Thy Gift, and Thine alone,
Perfect and calm in Heaven above!

4
Yet send us here some sign of rest,
Thine Olive-branch, Celestial DOVE!
Till, with the TRINITY All-blest,
We know the calm of Heaven above!
                    Amen.

Friendly Societies.

HYMN 272.

L. M. — Ancient. Arranged by J. B. Dykes.

To Thee, O God, our praise belongs, For Heaven and earth their anthems pour; And Angel Hosts with choral songs Circle Thy Throne for Evermore. Amen.

2
And Thou dost not our songs despise,
But, as a father hears his child,
So dost Thou listen from the skies,
O God, our Father reconciled!

3
Without the shining of Thy Face,
How mournful this dark world would be!
With suppliant heart we seek Thy Grace,
Saviour, and Guide, we look to Thee.

4
And as our tongues confess Thy Name,
So may our hearts Thy Statutes prize!
As now Thy Glory we proclaim,
So may we praise Thee in the skies.

5
To Thee, Great Lord, the One in Three,
All praise for Evermore ascend;
O grant us in our Home to see
The Heavenly life that knows no end.
Amen.

Friendly Societies.

HYMN 273. C.M. — Scotch Psalter, 1635.

Lord, as to Thy dear Cross we flee,
And plead to be forgiven,
So let Thy Life our pattern be,
And form our souls for Heaven. Amen.

2
Help us, through good report and ill,
  Our daily Cross to bear;
Like Thee, to do our Father's Will,
  Our brethren's grief to share.

3
Let grace our selfishness expel,
  Our earthliness refine;
And kindness in our bosom dwell,
  Both free and true like Thine.

4
If joy shall at Thy Bidding fly,
  And grief's dark day come on,
We in our turn would meekly cry,
  "Father, Thy Will be done."

5
Kept peaceful in the midst of strife,
  Forgiving and forgiven;
O may we lead the pilgrim's life,
  And follow Thee to Heaven. Amen.

2
He tells the number of the stars,
   And by their names He calls them;—
He breaks His people's prison bars,
   And marks whate'er befalls them.
     O sing unto the LORD,
     Upon the harp give praise
     For benefits outpoured
     On us, His favoured race!
   O give our GOD the glory!

3
He maketh health and joy abound,
   And peace in all our borders;
Since might in Him alone is found
   To rule the world's disorders.
     For not to every land
     His Mercy yet is known;
     Let us before Him stand!
     Praise Him, the THREE IN ONE!
   O give our GOD the glory!   Amen.

Thanksgiving.

HYMN 275.

6, 7, 6, 7, 6, 6, 6, 6. Arranged by H. S. Irons.

Now thank we all our God, With heart, and hands, and voi-ces,
Who wondrous things hath done; In Whom His World re-joic-es;
Who from our mo-ther's arms Hath blessed us on our way
With countless gifts of love, And still is ours to-day. Amen.

2
Oh, may this bounteous God
Through all our life be near us,
With ever joyful hearts
And blessed peace to cheer us;
And keep us in His Grace,
And guide us when perplexed,
And free us from all ills
In this world and the next.

3
All praise and thanks to God,
The Father, now be given,
The Son, and Him Who reigns
With Them in highest Heaven,
The One Eternal God,
Whom earth and Heaven adore,
For thus it was, is now,
And shall be Evermore. Amen.

Thanksgiving.

HYMN 276.

6, 7s. R. R. Chope.

Praise we our GOD with joy, And gladness never ending; Angels and Saints with us Their grateful voices blending. Amen.

2 He is our FATHER dear,
With Parent's Love o'erflowing;
Mercies unsought, unknown,
On wayward hearts bestowing.

3 He is our SHEPHERD true,
With watchful care unsleeping;
On us, His erring sheep,
An Eye of pity keeping.

4 He, with a mighty Arm,
The bonds of sin hath broken;
And to our burdened hearts
In words of peace hath spoken.

5 Bleeding we lay, but He
With soothing bands hath bound us;
Dark was our path, but He
Hath poured His Light around us.

6 Graces in copious stream
From that pure Fount are welling,
Where, in our heart of hearts,
Our GOD hath set His Dwelling.

7 His Word our lantern is,
His Peace our consolation;
His Sweetness all our rest,
Himself our great Salvation.

8 Then live we all to GOD,
On Him in Faith relying;
He be our Guide in life,
Our Joy and Hope in dying. Amen.

Laying the Foundation Stone of a Church.

HYMN 277.

L. M. — Arranged by W. H. Havergal.

O Lord of Hosts, Whose Glo-ry fills The bounds of the E-ter-nal hills, And yet vouchsafes, in Christ-ian lands, To dwell in Tem-ples made with hands; A-men.

2
Grant that all we, who here to-day,
Rejoicing, this Foundation lay,
May be in very deed Thine Own,
Built on the precious Corner-stone.

3
Endue the creatures with Thy Grace,
That shall adorn Thy Dwelling-place;
The beauty of the oak and pine,
The gold and silver, make them Thine.

4
To Thee they all pertain; to Thee
The treasures of the earth and sea;
And when we bring them to Thy Throne,
We but present Thee with Thine Own.

5
The heads that guide endue with skill,
The hands that work preserve from ill,
That we, who these Foundations lay,
May raise the topstone in its day.

6
Both now and ever, Lord, protect
The Temple of Thine Own elect;
Be Thou in them, and they in Thee,
O Ever-Blessed Trinity!   Amen.

Feast of the Dedication of a Church.

HYMN 278. S.M.

O Word of God above! Who fillest all in all, Hallow this House with Thy sure Love, And bless our Festival. Amen.

2
Grace in this Font is stored,
To cleanse each guilty child;
The Spirit's blest Anointing poured
Brightens the once defiled.

3
Here Christ of His Own Blood
Himself the Chalice gives,
And feeds His Own with Angels' Food,
On which the spirit lives.

4
For guilty souls that pine
Sure Mercies here abound;
And healing Grace, with oil and wine,
For every secret wound.

5
Yea, God enthroned on High
Here also dwells to bless;
Here trains the souls that contrite sigh
His Mansions to possess.

6
Against this Holy Home
Dark tempests harmless rain;
And Satan's angels fiercely come
With utmost strength in vain.

7
To God the Father praise,
And to the Eternal Son
And to the Holy Ghost always,
Co-Equal Three in One.   Amen.

Dedication of a Church.

HYMN 279. Ancient. Arranged by R. R. Chope.

Bless-ed Ci-ty, Heavenly Sa-lem, Vi-sion dear of peace and love, Who, of liv-ing stones up-build-ed, Art the joy of Heaven a-bove, And, with An-gel Hosts encircled, As a bride to earth dost move. A-men.

2
From Celestial realms descending,
  Bridal glory round thee shed,
Meet for Him whose Love espoused thee,
  To thy LORD shalt thou be led;
Purest gold thy street; of jasper
  All thy walls are fashionéd.

3
Bright with pearls the portals glitter,
  They are open Evermore,
And by virtue of His Merits
  Thither faithful souls may soar,
Who for CHRIST's dear Name, in this
  Pain and tribulation bore.   [world

4
Many a blow and biting sculpture
  Polished well those stones elect,
In their places now compacted
  By the Heavenly Architect,
Who therewith hath willed for ever
  That His Palace should be decked.

5
CHRIST is made the sure Foundation,
  And the Precious Corner-stone,
Who, the two-fold walls uniting,
  Binds them closely into one;
Holy Sion's Help for Ever,
  And her Confidence alone.

6
All that dedicated City,
  Dearly loved of GOD on High,
In exultant jubilation
  Pours perpetual melody;
GOD the ONE IN THREE adoring
  In glad hymns Eternally.

7
To this Temple, where we call Thee,
  Come, O LORD of Hosts, to-day;
With Thy wonted Loving-kindness,
  Hear Thy servants as they pray;
And Thy fullest Benediction
  Shed within its walls alway.

8
Here vouchsafe to all Thy servants
  What they ask of Thee to gain,
What they gain from Thee for ever
  With the Blessed to retain,
And hereafter in Thy Glory
  Evermore with Thee to reign.

9
Praise and honour to the FATHER,
  Praise and honour to the SON,
Praise and honour to the SPIRIT,
  Ever THREE, and ever ONE,
ONE in might, and ONE in glory,
  While Eternal ages run.   Amen.

This long Hymn will be found useful for Collections. On ordinary occasions, the first four, or last five verses, will be found sufficient.

Feast of the Dedication of a Church.

HYMN 280.

From high-est Heaven the Father's Son Descending like a mystic stone, Cut from a mountain without hands, Came down below and filled all lands, Uniting midway in the sky His

House on earth, and House on High. A - men.

2

That House on High,—it ever rings
With praises of the KING of kings;
For ever there, on harps Divine,
They hymn the Eternal ONE and TRINE;
We, here below, the strain prolong,
And faintly echo Zion's song.

3

O LORD of lords invisible!
With Thy pure Light this Temple fill;
Hither, oft as invoked, descend;
Here to Thy people's prayer attend;
Here, through all hearts, for Evermore,
Thy SPIRIT's quickening Graces pour.

4

Here may the faithful, day by day,
In kneeling adoration pray;
And here receive from Thy dear Love
The blessings of that Home above;
Till, loosen'd from this mortal chain,
Its Everlasting joys they gain.

5

To GOD the FATHER, glory due
Be paid by all the Heavenly Host;
And to His Only SON Most True;
With Thee, O Mighty HOLY GHOST!
To Whom praise, power, and blessing be,
Through ages of Eternity.   Amen.

S. Andrew.

HYMN 281.

C. M. J. L. Summers.

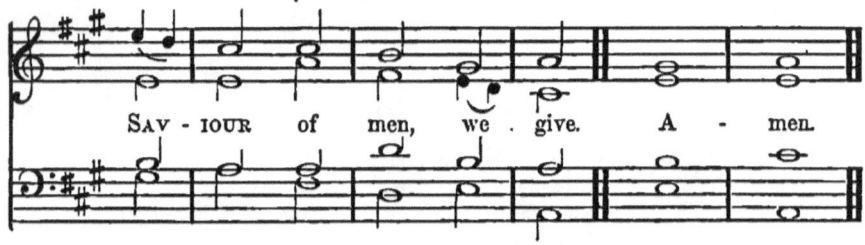

2
All glory for Thy chosen band,
  To whom the charge was given,
From land to land to publish peace,
  And point the way to Heaven.

3
All glory for Saint Andrew's faith,
  Who sought Thy low abode,
And, warmed by love, his brother led
  To Thee, the LAMB of GOD.

4
For him we bless and praise Thy Name,
  And humbly pray that we,
Strong in Thy Faith, may follow him,
  As he, LORD, followed Thee.

5
To Thee, O FATHER; SON, to Thee,
  To Thee, O SPIRIT Blest,
Through Endless ages glory be
  By all Thy Church addrest.   Amen.

S. Thomas.

HYMN 282. C. M. — Este's Psalter, 1592.

O Thou, Who did'st, with love un-told, Thy doubting

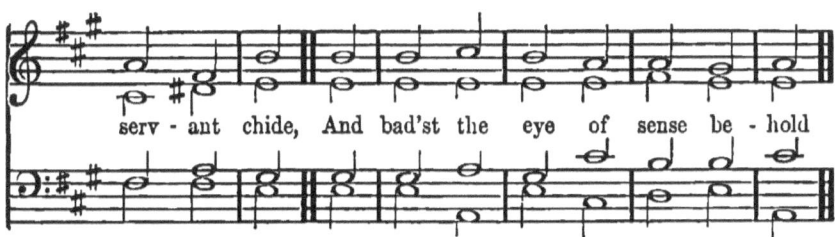

serv-ant chide, And bad'st the eye of sense be-hold

Thy wound-ed Hands and Side, A-men.

2
Grant us, like him, with heartfelt awe,
  To own Thee GOD and LORD,
And from his hour of darkness draw
  A fuller faith's reward.

3
And while that wondrous record now
  Of unbelief we hear,
Oh! let us only lowlier bow
  In self-distrusting fear;

4
And pray that we may never dare
  Thy SPIRIT so to grieve;
But at the last their blessing share
  Who see not, yet believe!

5
Our LORD and GOD, Eternal SON,
  To Thee all glory be,
With FATHER, SPIRIT, THREE IN ONE,
  Through all Eternity.   Amen.

Conversion of S. Paul.

2
Or see we drawing near
The dreadful Day of Doom,
When Thou the Avenger shalt appear,
The guilty to consume?

3
On milder vengeance bent,
Thou camest from above,
To bid the hardened heart relent,
And slaughter change to love.

4
The Spoiler fallen lies
Before Thy Glorious Ray,
A shepherd of the flock to rise,—
The flock he sought to slay.

5
From all the Heavenly Host,
And all on earth below,
To Father, Son, and Holy Ghost,
Let Endless praises flow. Amen.

Conversion of S. Paul.

HYMN 284.

8, 7, 8, 7, 4, 7.   JOHN HULLAH.

'Gainst what foeman art thou rushing, Saul, what madness drives thee on? In-no-cents in fu-ry crushing, Children of the Sin-less ONE; O how short-ly Shall He make His Vengeance known! A-men.

2
See the LORD, from Heaven descending,
　Smites him, blinds him, lays him low;
See the persecutor bending
　Humbly, meekly to the blow:
　　See him rising,
　Friend to CHRIST, no longer foe.

3
Breathing slaughter, chains preparing,
　O, how fierce his anger burned!
Trembling now, and lost his daring,
　Meek obedience he has learned:
　　The destroyer
　Now into a lamb is turned.

4
CHRIST, Thy Power is man's salvation,
　Hardest hearts Thou mak'st Thine Own;
He who wrought such desolation
　That Thy Name might be o'erthrown,
　　Now converted,　　　[known.
　Through the world that Name makes

5
Praise the FATHER, GOD of Heaven,
　Him Who reigns supreme on High!
Praise the SON, for sinners given
　Both to suffer and to die!
　　Praise the SPIRIT,
　Guiding us most lovingly.　　Amen.

Presentation of Christ in the Temple,

COMMONLY CALLED

THE PURIFICATION OF S. MARY THE VIRGIN.

HYMN 285.

Zi-on, ope Thy hallowed gates, Christ before His Temple waits; Types and shadows disappear, Priest and Victim, Christ is here. A-men.

2
Flocks and herds shall bleed no more,
Altars smoke not as before,
Now the Everlasting Son
Comes as Man for man to atone.

3
Simeon's aged eyes behold;
Anna hails the Hope foretold;
Awe and joy around are spread,
By that Heavenly Presence dread.

4
Silent kneels the Mother blest,
Pondering all things in her breast;
Solemn thoughts by man unheard,
Fitly greet the silent Word.

5
Glory to the Father, Son,
And Blest Spirit, Three in One;
Holy Trinity, we raise
Unto Thee our ceaseless praise. Amen.

Annunciation of the Blessed Virgin Mary.

Praise we the Lord this day, This day so long fore-told; Whose Promise shone with cheering ray On waiting Saints of old. A-men.

2
The Prophet gave the sign
For faithful men to read;
A Virgin, born of David's line,
Shall bear the promised Seed.

3
Ask not how this should be,
But worship and adore
Like her, whom Heaven's High Majesty
Came down to shadow o'er.

4
Meekly she bow'd her head
To hear the gracious Word;
Mary, the pure and lowly maid,
The favoured of the Lord.

5
Blessed shall be her name
In all the Church on earth,
Through whom that wondrous mercy came,
The Incarnate Saviour's Birth.

6
To God the Father, Son,
And God the Holy Ghost,
By Saints below be honour done,
And by the Angel Host. Amen.

2

Your God e'en now doth stand
At Heaven's opening door;
His fan is in His Hand,
And He will purge His Floor.
 The wheat He claims
 And with Him stows;
 The chaff He throws
 To deathless flames.

3

Ye haughty mountains, bow
Your heads that seek the sky;
Ye valleys, hiding low,
Lift up yourselves on high;
 Make His Way plain
 Your KING before;
 For Evermore
 He comes to reign.

4

O may thy voice around,
Thou harbinger of light,
On our dull ears still sound,
Lest here we sleep in night
 Till Judgment come,
 And on our path
 Shall burst the wrath
 And Endless doom.

5

To GOD the FATHER, SON,
And SPIRIT ever Blest,
Eternal THREE IN ONE,
All worship be addressed.
 As heretofore
 It was, is now,
 And shall be so
 For Evermore. Amen.

S. Peter.

2
Who from the labours of the deep
Didst set Thine Own Apostle free;
To feed on earth Thy chosen sheep,
And build a Glorious Church to Thee:

3
Grant us, devoid of worldly care,
And leaning on Thy bounteous Hand,
To seek Thy Help in humble prayer,
And on that Sacred Rock to stand;

4
And when, our livelong toil to crown,
Thy Call shall set the spirit free;
To cast with joy our burden down,
And rise, O LORD, and follow Thee.
    Amen.

S. Bartholomew.

C.M. HYMN 289. Arranged by J. B. Dykes.

How blest are they whose hearts are pure, From guile their spi-rits free; To them shall GOD Himself re-veal, His Glo-ry they shall see. A-men.

2
Their simple souls upon His Word,
In fullest light of love,
Place all their trust, and ask no more
Than guidance from above.

3
They who in faith, unmixed with doubt,
The engrafted Word receive,
Whom the first sign of Heavenly Power
Persuades, and they believe,—

4
They, as they walk this painful world,
See hidden glories rise;
Our God the sunshine of His Love
Unfolds before their eyes.

5
For them far greater things than these
Does CHRIST the LORD prepare,
Whose bliss no heart of man can reach,
No human voice declare.

6
To FATHER, SON, and HOLY GHOST,
The GOD Whom we adore,
Be glory, as it was, is now,
And shall be Evermore. Amen.

S. Matthew.

2
With earnest zeal 'twas Thy Delight
  To do Thy FATHER's Will:
Oh, may such zeal our souls excite,
  His Precepts to fulfil!

3
If in some dark affliction's day
  Our path through sorrow run,
May we, like Thee, have grace to say,
  "Thy Will, O LORD, be done."

4
In Thee a sacred burning Love
  In all Thy Course did shine;
Oh, may such love within us prove
  That we, O LORD, are Thine!

5
Supported by Almighty Grace,
  We'll tread Thy Heavenly Road,
And carefully Thy Footsteps trace,
  Which lead to Thine Abode.

6
All glory to the FATHER be,
  All glory to the SON,
All glory, HOLY GHOST, to Thee,
  While Endless ages run.   Amen.

S. Michael and all Angels.

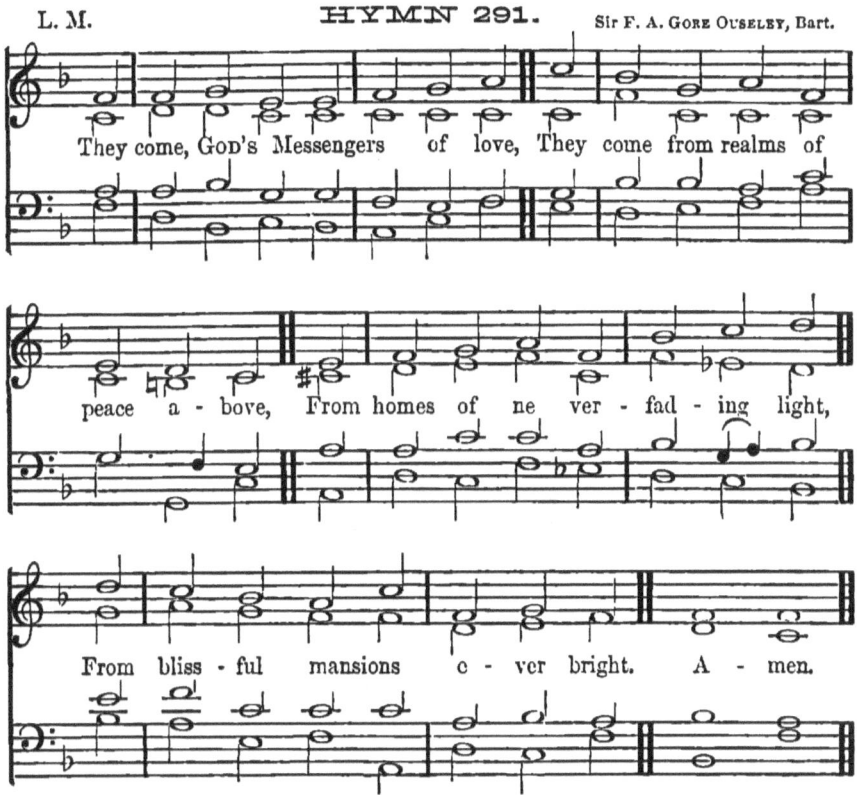

HYMN 291. L. M. Sir F. A. Gore Ouseley, Bart.

They come, God's Messengers of love, They come from realms of peace above, From homes of never-fading light, From blissful mansions e'er bright. Amen.

2
They come to watch around us here,
To soothe our sorrow, calm our fear:
Ye Heavenly Guides, speed not away
God willeth you with us to stay.

3
But chiefly at its journey's end
'Tis yours the spirit to befriend,
And whisper to the willing heart,
"O Christian soul, in peace depart."

4
Blest Jesu, Thou Whose Groans and Tears
Have sanctified frail nature's fears,
To earth in bitter sorrows weighed,
Thou didst not scorn Thine Angels' aid;

5
An Angel guard to us supply
When on the bed of death we lie;
And by Thine Own Almighty Power
O shield us in the last dread hour.

6
To God the Father, God the Son,
And God the Spirit, Three in One,
From all above and all below
Let joyful praise unceasing flow. Amen.

S. Michael and all Angels.

2
Thousand times ten thousand, bending
  At Thy Throne, their homage pay;
Flames of fire in strength excelling,
  Swift Thy Pleasure to obey.

3
Fashioned in a wondrous order,
  Thee they serve, their LORD and KING;
Grant that in our cares and danger,
  They to us may succour bring.

4
Praise to Thee! Who hast created
  Earth and Heaven, with all their Host,—
Praise to Thee, O GOD! Most Mighty,
  FATHER, SON, and HOLY GHOST.
            Amen.

S. Luke.

HYMN 293.

L.M. — W. James.

Be-hold, and see Christ's chosen Saint In triumph wear his Christ-like chain; No fear lest he should swerve or faint; "His life is Christ, his death is gain." A-men.

2

Two converts, watching by His side,
Alike his love and greetings share;
Luke the beloved, the sick soul's guide,
And Demas, named in faltering prayer.

3

Pass a few years,—look yet once more,—
The Saint is in his bonds again;
Save that his hopes more boldly soar,
He and his lot unchanged remain.

4

But only Luke is with Him now,—
Alas! but let us muse awhile,
Nor deem our shelter here below
All safe e'en in the Church's aisle.

5

Ah! dearest Mother, since too oft
The world yet wins some Demas frail
E'en from thine arms, so kind and soft,
May thy tried comforts never fail!

6

When faithless ones forsake thy wing,
Be it vouchsafed thee still to see
Thy true, fond nurslings closer cling,
Cling closer to their Lord and Thee.
      Amen.

All Saints.

Hymn 294. C.M. — Dr. Gauntlett. Inserted by permission of the proprietors of the Church Hymn and Tune Book.

Those whom one Glory crowns above, One day re-

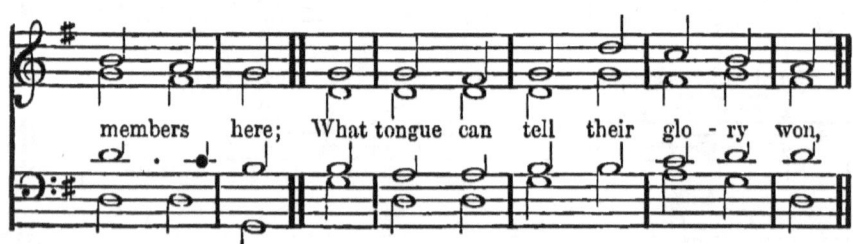

members here; What tongue can tell their glory won,

In peril, toil, and fear. A-men.

2
A countless Host in bright array,
  Around the Throne they stand,
With robes made white in Jesu's Blood,
  And palms in every hand.

3
They rest not day and night, but still
  The voice of praise prolong;
Like mighty waters sounds afar
  The thunder of their song.

4
Hunger and thirst are felt no more,
  Nor sun with scorching ray:
God is their Sun, the Lamb their Light,
  In that Eternal Day.

5
Glory to God, the Father, Son,
  And Spirit, Ever Blest;
Who for His Faithful hath prepared
  That Everlasting Rest. Amen.

All Saints.

HYMN 295.

For all Thy Saints, O Lord, Who strove in Thee to live, Who followed Thee, obeyed, adored, Our grateful hymn receive. Amen.

2
For all Thy Saints, O Lord,
Accept our thankful cry,
Who counted Thee their great Reward,
And strove in Thee to die.

3
They all, in life and death,
With Thee, their Lord, in view,
Learned from Thy Holy Spirit's Breath
To suffer and to do.

4
For this Thy Name we bless,
And humbly pray that we
May follow them in holiness,
And live and die in Thee!

5
All might, all praise be Thine,
Father, Co-Equal Son,
And Spirit, Bond of Love Divine,
While Endless ages run. Amen.

Apostles.

HYMN 296. S. M.

The E-ter-nal Spirit's Gifts, The A-pos-tles' glo-rious praise, Their vic-to-ries and high re-ward, Of these our song we raise. A-men.

2
Princes of Israel they,
Triumphant chiefs of war,
Brave soldiers of the Heavenly Court,
True lights beheld afar.

3
Theirs was the shield of faith,
And quenchless zeal's pure glow;
And theirs the Spirit's Sword, which laid
The power of this world low.

4
In them the Father shone,
In them the Son o'ercame,
In them the Holy Spirit wrought,
And filled their hearts with flame.

5
Then to the Father, Son,
And Spirit, glory be;
As was, and is, and shall be so
Through all Eternity.   Amen.

Evangelists.

HYMN 297. C. M. — J. S. Bach, 1750.

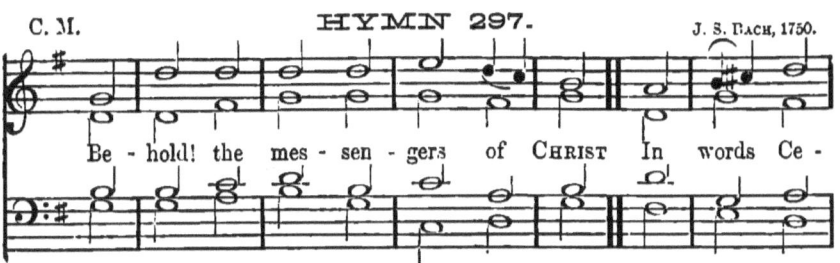

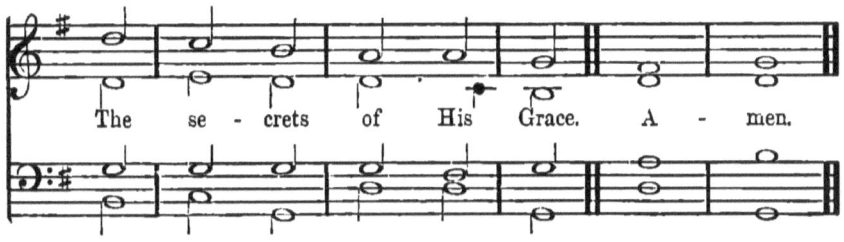

Behold! the messengers of Christ In words Celestial trace The hidden Mysteries of God, The secrets of His Grace. Amen.

2
The things through mists and shadows [dim,
By elder prophets seen,
In the full light of day they saw,
With not a cloud between.

3
One Holy Spirit rules them all,
For He to each was near;
To us by them That Spirit speaks,
His Voice in them we hear.

4
O Holy Spirit! Who to man
Those Words of truth didst give,
Thy Truth incite us to receive,
And by its rules to live. Amen.

Martyrs.

L. M.   HYMN 298.   J. B. Dykes.

O! who are they so pure and bright, Before the Throne arrayed in white? They stand serene, and calmly fair, As conscious of high welcome there. Amen.

2
See from afar a lengthening band
Of lowly penitents, that stand
With Angels gladdening their abode;
But who are these so near to God?

3
That starry crown around their brow,
It tells their sacred glory now;
Blest virgin souls who, faultless, come
From Font of Grace, or Martyrdom!

4
These, these are they, the undefiled,
The child-like Saint,—the Saint-like child,
Marked with Christ's Cross, or earth's dark frown,
But wearing there that starry crown.

5
O help us, Saviour, by Thy Grace,
Near Thee to win that Heavenly place,
Now following where Thy Footsteps trod;
Blameless and harmless sons of God!
                Amen.

Martyrs.

Hymn 299. L. M. Arranged by W. H. Havergal.

Ye servants of a martyred Lord, His Martyrs' toils and praise record, The palms and crowns that never fade, Which God in store for them hath laid. A-men.

2
Long tossed upon the stormy tide,
With Christ their Leader and their Guide,
Baptized in Blood, they homeward passed,
And in still waters rest at last.

3
O Saviour, may our portion be
With those who gave themselves to Thee,
Throughout Eternity to sing
High praise to Thee, the martyrs' King.

4
As soldiers, Lord, of Thy dear Cross,
Prepare our souls for pain and loss;
On Thy Right Arm make us confide,
And gladly die for Him Who died.

5
Praise to the Father, and the Son,
And Holy Spirit, Three in One;
Eternal praise to Each be given
By all on earth and all in Heaven. Amen.

Cross be-low, He fol-lows in His Train. A-men.

2

The martyr first, whose eagle eye
  Could pierce beyond the grave,
Who saw his Master in the sky,
  And called on Him to save.
Like Him, with pardon on his tongue
  In midst of mortal pain,
He prayed for them that did the wrong;
  Who follows in his train?

3

A glorious band, the chosen few
  On whom the SPIRIT came,
Twelve valiant Saints, their hope they knew,
  And mocked the Cross and flame.
They met the tyrant's brandished steel,
  The lion's gory mane,
They bowed their necks, the death to feel;
  Who follows in their train?

4

A noble army, men and boys,
  The matron and the maid,
Around the SAVIOUR's Throne rejoice,
  In robes of light arrayed.
They climbed the steep ascent of Heaven,
  Through peril, toil, and pain;
O GOD, to us may grace be given
  To follow in their train!   Amen.

Index of First Lines.

The Tunes marked * were composed for this Work, or are now printed for the first time. Most of the arrangements also, of the Tunes, and many of the Hymns are copyright.

R. R. C.

FIRST LINE.	HYMN.	NAME OF TUNE.	AUTHOR, ETC.	METRE.
Abide with me; fast falls the eventide	228	* S. Saviour	R. F. Smith	10s.
Above the starry spheres	128	* S. Perpetua	S. Gee	S.M.
According to Thy gracious Word	239	Renfrew	W. B. Gilbert	C.M.
Again the Holy morn	200	Ayr	Scotch Psalter	S.M.D.
Alike in happiness and woe	290	* S. Mildred	R. R. Chope	C.M.
Alleluia! best and sweetest	52	Alleluia, dulce carmen	M. Haydn	8, 7s (6 of.)
All hail the power of Jesu's Name	38	* Laud	J. B. Dykes	C.M.
All is o'er, the pain, the sorrow	98	* S. Wulstan	J. B. Dykes	8, 7, 8, 7, 7, 7.
All people that on earth do dwell	151	Old Hundredth		L.M.
All ye who seek a calm relief	61	* S. Timothy	R. R. Chope	C.M.
All ye who seek, in hope and love	234	* Arne	W. B. Gilbert	L.M.
Angels, from the realms of glory	15	* S. Osmund	H. S. Irons	8, 7, 8, 7, 4, 7.
Arise, O Lord, and shine	43	* Sherborne	R. R. Chope	6, 6, 6, 6, 8, 8.
Around the Throne of God a band	177	S. Blasius	Dr. Gauntlett	L.M.
As every day Thy Mercy spares	217	Aylsham	J. S. Bach	8s (6 of.)
As now the sun's declining rays	218	S. Fulbert	Dr. Gauntlett	C.M.
At the Lamb's high Feast we sing	105	Hartford	B. Milgrove	7s.
Awake, my soul, and with the sun	199	* S. Augustine	R. R. Chope	L.M.
Before the ending of the day	211	S. Dunstan	Ancient	L.M.
Behold, and see Christ's chosen Saint	293	* S. Lawrence	W. James	L.M.
Behold the glories of the Lamb	114	Winchester	Este's Psalter	C.M.
Behold the messengers of Christ,	297	S. Nicomede	J. S. Bach	C.M.
Behold the Saviour of mankind	86	Dundee	Ravenscroft's Psalter	C.M.
Be present, ye faithful	17	Adeste fideles	Proper Tune	P.M.
Bethlehem! earth's noblest cities	41	Tranby	S. M. Barkworth	8, 7s.
Blessed city, Heavenly Salem	279	* Urbs Beata	Ancient	8, 7s (6 of.)
Blest Voice of Love, O Word Divine	248	* S. Cuthbert	W. Horsley	8s (6 of.)
Brief life is here our portion	148	S. Alphege	Dr. Gauntlett	7, 6s.
Brightest and best of the sons of the morning	50	* Epiphany	E. J. Hopkins	11, 10s.
Brightness of the Father's Glory	209	Thirsk	Dr. Boyce	8, 7s.
Bright was the guiding star that led	41	* Glasgow		C.M.
By the Cross, sad vigil keeping	88	Stabat Mater	Ancient	8, 8, 7, 8, 8, 7.

INDEX OF FIRST LINES.

FIRST LINE.	HYMN.	NAME OF TUNE.	AUTHOR, ETC.	METRE.
Can earthly voices fitly sing	249	* S. Matthias	C. T. Bowen	L.M.
CHRIST, above all glory seated	121	Thurgau	Genevan Psalter	8, 7s.
CHRIST, from Whom all blessings flow	110	* Tintern	A. H. Brown	7s (6 of.)
CHRIST is become our Paschal LAMB	107	Coventry	Dr. Howard	C.M.
CHRIST is gone up, yet ere He passed	259	Bedford	W. Wheall	C.M.
CHRIST, Whose Glory fills the skies	48	Ratisbon	Werner	7s (6 of.)
Christians, awake! salute the happy morn	23	Stockport	Dr. Wainwright	10s (6 of.)
Come, HOLY GHOST, our souls inspire	125	* Veni Creator	R. Stuart	L.M.P.
Come, HOLY GHOST, Who ever ONE	212	* S. Philip	Ancient	L.M.
Come! ye Heavenly choirs descending	100	S. Ignatius	Italian	8, 7s.
Come, ye thankful people, come	265	S. George	Dr. G. J. Elvey	7s (8 of.)
CREATOR of mankind	173	S. Bride	Dr. Howard	S.M.
CREATOR of the light supreme	224	S. Gregory	W. Horsley, M.B.	L.M.
CREATOR of the rolling flood	288	S. Margaret	Dr. Gauntlett	L.M.
CREATOR of the stars of night	4	Conditor Alme	Ancient	L.M.
CREATOR! SPIRIT! LORD of Grace	131	* S. Barnabas	J. B. Dykes	L.M.
Day of Wrath, O Day of mourning	258	* Dies Iræ	J. B. Dykes	8s (9 of.)
Day of Wrath! that awful Day	1	* S. Fabian	Chiefly Felton	7s (3 of.)
Days and moments quickly flying	34	* S. Sylvester	J. B. Dykes	P.M.
Ere the waning light decay	216	H. Innocents	R. F. Smith	7s.
Eternal GOD, we look to Thee	172	* Bede	W. B. Gilbert	C.M.
Exiled afar from their blest home	147	S. Crispin	R. F. Smith	L.M.
FATHER, by Thy Love and Power	220	Salzburg	J. S. Bach	7s (6 of.)
FATHER of all, to Thee we raise	133	Te Deum Patrem	Dr. Rogers	L.M.
FATHER of Heaven, Whose Love profound	136	Bavaria	German	L.M.
FATHER of Love, our Guide and Friend	247	S. Magnus	J. Clark	C.M.
FATHER of Mercies, GOD of Love	266	* S. Hilary	T. B. Hosken	C.M.
Fierce raged the tempest o'er the deep	187	* S. Aelred	J. B. Dykes	8, 8, 8, 3.
For all Thy Saints, O LORD	295	Erin		S.M.
For thee, O dear, dear Country	149	* Chope	English	7, 6s. D.
Forth goes the Standard of our KING	81	Vexilla Regis	Ancient	L.M.
Forth in Thy Name, O LORD, we go	201	S. Jerome	Freylinghausen	L.M.
For Thy Mercy and Thy Grace	33	* S. Basil	R. R. Chope	7s.
From Greenland's icy mountains	261	* Ceylon	S. Reay	7, 6s. D.
From Heaven to earth glad tidings I unfold	39	* S. Joseph	J. B. Dykes	10, 10, 10, 4.
From highest heaven the FATHER'S SON	280	* Dedication	R. R. Chope	8s (6 of.)
'Gainst what foeman art thou rushing	284	* Berwick	J. Hullah	8, 7, 8, 7, 4, 7.
Glorious things of thee are spoken	176	Alla Trinita Beata	Laudi Spirituali	8, 7s. D.
Glory and praise to Thee, REDEEMER Blest	83	Basle	Goudimel	10s.
Glory be to JESUS	73	* S. Agnes	R. R. Chope	6, 5s.
Glory to Thee, my GOD, this night	227	Tallis	Tallis	L.M.
Glory to Thee, O LORD	32	Franconia	German	S.M.
GOD from on High hath heard	20	* S. Blaise	T. B. Hosken	6s. D.

INDEX OF FIRST LINES.

FIRST LINE.	HYMN.	NAME OF TUNE.	AUTHOR, ETC.	METRE.
God of all redeeming Grace	241	Redhead, No. 48	Dr. Gauntlett	7s.
God of Mercy, God of Grace	47	* S. Boniface	Chiefly Gibbons	7s (6 of.)
God of our life, to Thee we call	267	* S. Felix	R. R. Chope	L.M.
God, That madest earth and Heaven	223	* S. Richard	R. R. Chope	8, 4, 8, 4, 8, 8, 8, 4.
Go forward in your course	26	* S. Martin	R. R. Chope	6s.
Go to dark Gethsemane	94	* Cawnpore	W. Horsley	7s (6 of.)
Great God! what do I see and hear	8	Advent	Luther	8, 7, 8, 7, 8, 8, 7.
Great Mover of all hearts, Whose Hand	60	S. Cyril	Sir F. A. G. Ouseley	8, 8, 6, 8, 8, 6.
Hail the day that sees Him rise	118	* Ascension	S. Reay	7s.
Hark! a thrilling voice is sounding	3	Winter	Winter	8, 7s.
Hark! the Herald Angels sing	18	S. Vincent	Mendelssohn	7s (10 of.)
Hark! what mean those holy voices	16	* Ovington	R. R. Chope	8, 7s.
Have mercy, Lord, on me	68	Aylesbury	J. Chetham	S.M.
Have mercy on us, God Most High	137	Wishaw New	Scotch Psalter	C.M.
Hear Thy children, Gentle Jesus	226	* S. Palladius	R. R. Chope	8, 7s.
He is risen, He is risen	109	* Kensington	W. Meadows	8, 7, 8, 7, 7, 7.
He Whom the Father from above	184	Linz	Rihel	C.M.
High let us swell our tuneful notes	22	Nativity	H. Lahee	C.M.
Holiest! breathe an evening blessing	221	* Tonbridge	C. J. Taylor	8, 7s
Holy, Holy, Holy! Lord God Almighty	132	* Southwell	R. F. Smith	P.M.
Holy Spirit, Lord of Light	126	* Bury	S. Reay	7s (6 of.)
Hosanna to the Living Lord	159	* S. Constantine	J. B. Dykes	8, 8, 8, 8, 7.
How blest are they whose hearts are pure	289	* Manchester	Ravenscroft's Psalter	C.M.
How blest were they who walked in love	58	* S. Thomas	R. B. Wall	L.M.
How sweet the Name of Jesus sounds	195	S. Anne	Denby	C.M.
If thou wouldest life attain	197	* S. Swithun	Dr. Monk	7s (6 of.)
In our Lord's atoning Grief	82	Oldenburg	T. B. Hosken	7s.
In stature grows the Heavenly Child	46	* S. Bartholomew	R. R. Chope	C.M.
In the hour of trial	78	* Magdalene	J. B. Dykes	6, 5s. D.
In vain doth Herod rage and fear	40	Hostis Herodes	Ancient	L.M.
Jerusalem, blest city	145	S. Omer	Dr. Gauntlett	7, 6s.
Jerusalem, my happy Home	174	* S. Oswin	J. B. Dykes	C.M.
Jerusalem, the golden	150	* Jerusalem	J. B. Dykes	7, 6s.
Jesu, Lord, we kneel before Thee	77	* S. Giles	E. J. Hopkins	8, 7, 8, 7, 4, 7.
Jesu, Lover of my soul	154	* S. Austin	J. A. Lloyd	7s, D.
Jesu, Meek and Gentle	188	* S. Lambert	R. R. Chope	6, 5s.
Jesu, Redeemer of the world	21	* Finchale	J. B. Dykes	L.M.
Jesu, the very thought is sweet	215	Melcombe	S. Webbe	L.M.
Jesu, the very thought of Thee	51	S. Bernard	. . . .	C.M.
Jesu, Who brought'st Redemption nigh	222	Cannons	G. F. Handel	L.M.
Jesus! all hail, Who for my sin	79	* Purleigh	A. H. Brown	8, 8, 6, 8, 8, 6.
Jesus calls us o'er the tumult	169	Turnau	Gnadau's Choralbuch	8, 7s.
Jesus came, the Heavens adoring	155	* Alford	E. J. Hopkins	8, 7s (6 of.)
Jesus Christ is risen to-day	101	Easter	Worgan	7s.
Jesus is God! The glorious bands	175	S. Mark	Dr. Croft	C.M.D.

INDEX OF FIRST LINES.

FIRST LINE.	HYMN.	NAME OF TUNE.	AUTHOR, ETC.	METRE.
Jesus lives!.	103	Lindisfarne	J. B. Dykes	7, 8, 7, 8, 4.
Jesus, Name of wondrous love . .	170	* S. Bees	J. B. Dykes	7s.
Lamb of God, for sinners slain . .	244	S. Columba	. . . .	7s.
Lamb of God, That in the Bosom .	192	Stutgard	German	8, 7s.
Let every heart exulting beat . .	236	Elgin	German	L.M.
Let us with a gladsome mind . .	191	* Milton	R. F. Smith	7s.
Lift up your heads, Eternal gates .	119	* Abridge	Isaac Smith	C.M.
Light of the soul, O Saviour Blest .	235	S. Edward	Bishop of Ely	L.M.
Lo! from the desert homes . .	287	Croft's 148th	Dr. Croft	6, 6, 6, 6, 4, 4, 4, 4.
Lo! He comes with clouds descending	11	* S. Andrew	J. B. Dykes	8, 7, 8, 7, 4, 7.
Lord, a Saviour's Love displaying .	263	* S. Ebbe	E. J. Hopkins	8, 7s.
Lord, as to Thy dear Cross we flee .	273	Caithness	Scotch Psalter	C.M.
Lord, have mercy, and remove us .	65	* Arundel	J. B. Dykes	8, 7s.
Lord, have mercy, when we strive .	164	* S. Paul	R. R. Chope	7,7,7,7,7,7,7,6.
Lord, I beseech Thee, on this day .	69	Uxbridge	Ravenscroft's Psalter	C.M.D.
Lord, in the desert bleak and bare .	71	* S. Enurchus	Bishop of Ely	C.M.
Lord, in this Thy Mercy's Day .	60	* Convent	T. B. Hosken	7s (3 of.)
Lord, in Thy Name Thy servants plead	116	Chester	Este's Psalter	C.M.
Lord, in Thy Wrath Thou thinkest yet	269	Cologne	German	C.M.
Lord Jesu! when we stand afar .	194	* S. Sepulchre	G. Cooper	L.M.
Lord of Mercy and of Might . .	161	* Maidstone	W. B. Gilbert	7, 7, 7, 5.
Lord of Power, and Lord of Might .	183	* S. Ninian	Dr. Monk	7s (6 of.)
Lord of the harvest, once again .	264	Milan	J. H. Schein	8s (6 of.)
Lord of the worlds above . . .	57	* S. Godric	J. B. Dykes	6, 6, 6, 6, 4, 4, 4, 4.
Lord, pour Thy Spirit from on High	280	* S. Adamnan	R. R. Chope	L.M.
Lord, shall Thy children come to Thee	251	* S. Werburg	J. B. Dykes	8s (6 of.)
Lord, Thy Word abideth . . .	59	* S. Cyprian	R. R. Chope	6s.
Lord, we raise our cry to Thee . .	56	* Milman	J. B. Dykes	7, 7, 7, 7, 8, 8.
Maker of all things, God Most High	225	S. Ambrose	Ancient	L.M.
Maker of earth, to Thee alone . .	53	Farrant	R. Farrant	C.M.
My God, and is Thy Table spread .	243	Winchester New	Crasselius	L.M.
My God, how wonderful Thou art .	160	Chichester	Ravenscroft's Psalter	C.M.
My God, my Father, while I stray .	166	* Herbert	R. R. Chope	8, 8, 8, 4.
My God, the Spring of all my joys .	113	Gibbons	Gibbons	C.M.
Nearer, my God, to Thee . . .	153	* Stapleton	R. R. Chope	6, 4, 6, 4, 6, 6, 4.
New every morning is the love . .	204	Angel's Hymn	Gibbons	L.M.
Now morning lifts her dewy veil .	111	S. Peter	A. R. Reinagle	C.M.
Now thank we all our God . .	275	Nun danket	German	6, 7, 6, 7, 6, 6, 6, 6.
Now that the daylight fills the sky .	210	S. Patrick	Ancient	L.M.
O blessed day, when first was poured	37	Norfolk	Dr. Howard	L.M.
O Christ, our Hope, our heart's Desire	144	Salisbury	Ravenscroft's Psalter	C.M.
O Christ, the Light of Heavenly Day	167	* Coleford	Bishop of Ely	L.M.
O Christ, Who dost prepare a place	171	* Upminster	Bishop of Ely	L.M.
O come, and mourn with me awhile .	91	S. Cross	J. B. Dykes	L.M.
O come, and with the early morn .	104	Gloucester	Ravenscroft's Psalter	C.M.
O come, come Thou, Emmanuel .	5	Darmstadt	J. Schop	8s (6 of.)

INDEX OF FIRST LINES.

FIRST LINE.	HYMN.	NAME OF TUNE.	AUTHOR, ETC.	METRE.
O Death, thou art no more	157	* Liverpool	W. T. Best	6, 6, 6, 4.
O'erwhelmed in depths of woe	90	* Waterbrook	J. B. Dykes	8.M.
Of that glorious Body broken	237	Pange lingua	Ancient	8, 7s (6 of.)
Oft in danger, oft in woe	180	Vienna	German	7s.
O GOD, in danger and distress	270	Boulcote	Dr. Bennett	C.M.
O GOD of all the Strength and Stay	214	* Iconium	Ancient	L.M.
O GOD of Hosts, the mighty LORD	143	* Charlton	German	C.M.
O GOD of life, Whose Power benign	134	* Cilicia	J. B. Dykes	8s (3 of.)
O GOD of Mercy, GOD of Might	242	* Shropshire	E. J. Hopkins	L.M.
O GOD, our Help in ages past	158	* Thetford	Bishop of Ely	C.M.
O GOD, the LORD of place and time	213	* S. Theodore	Ancient	L.M.
O GOD, Thy Soldiers' Crown and Guard	27	S. Polycarp	. . .	L.M.
O GOD, unseen, yet ever near	240	Barnstaple	A. H. Brown	C.M.
O Gracious FATHER, bend Thine Ear	63	Saxony	Old Chorale	L.M.
O Heavenly WORD, Eternal LIGHT	7	Breslau	Mendelssohn	L.M.
O help us, LORD, each hour of need	76	Wimborne	German	C.M.
O HOLY SPIRIT, LORD of Grace	206	* Hartland	R. R. Chope	C.M.
O JESU, GOD and Man	246	* S. Helen	J. B. Dykes	6, 8s.
O JESU, LORD of Heavenly Grace	106	* Charmouth	E. B. Fripp	L.M.
O JESU, Source of holiness	281	* Lea	J. L. Summers	C.M.
O KING Eternal, LORD of Grace	208	S. Eligius	Dr. Gauntlett	L.M.
O KING of Angels, LORD of Grace	95	S. Lucian	Ancient	L.M.
O LORD of Hosts, Whose Glory fills	277	Commandments	Old melody	L.M.
O LORD, turn not Thy Face from us	70	Damascus	Playford's Psalter	C.M.
Once more the solemn season calls	62	Northampton	Dr. Croft	C.M.
On Jordan's bank, the Baptist's cry	12	S. Agatha	. . .	L.M.
On this the day which saw the earth	205	S. Elizabeth	Layriz	L.M.
O perfect GOD, and perfect MAN	75	Bethlehem	. . .	C.M.
O Sacred Head, surrounded	89	Passion Chorale	J. S. Bach	7, 6s, D.
O SAVIOUR, now at GOD's Right Hand	117	Bristol	Ravenscroft's Psalter	C.M.
O SAVIOUR of the faithful dead	257	Old Common	Este's Psalter	C.M.
O SAVIOUR of the world forlorn	24	S. Amandus	Dr. Gauntlett	L.M.
O SAVIOUR, Whom this Holy morn	25	* Dr. Tye	Tye	C.M.
O Thou Almighty Source of Love	179	S. Adalgitha	M. Vulpius	C.M.
O Thou Eternal KING Most High	120	Doncaster	Dr. Monk	C.M.
O Thou, from Whom all goodness flows	168	French	Scotch Psalter	C.M.
O Thou, the FATHER's Image Blest	203	S. Gilbert	J. S. Bach	L.M.
O Thou, Who art gone up, on High	142	S. James	R. Courteville	C.M.
O Thou, Who by a star didst guide	45	York	Scotch Psalter	C.M.
O Thou, Who didst with love untold	282	S. Faith	Este's Psalter	C.M.
O Thou, Who gav'st Thy servant grace	30	Whitehall	H. Lawes	L.M.
Our Blest REDEEMER, ere He breathed	140	Olmutz	German	8, 6, 8, 4.
Our limbs refreshed with slumber now	202	Redhead, No. 4	R. Redhead	L.M.
O who are they so pure and bright	298	* S. Oswald	J. B. Dykes	L.M.
O WORD of GOD above	278	S. Alban	. . .	S.M.
O worship the KING	196	Old 104th	Ravenscroft's Psalter	5, 5, 5, 5, 6, 5, 6, 5.
Pour down, O LORD, on this our youth	253	* Abbey	J. Turle	C.M.
Praise GOD, Who sent His guiding star	42	Erfurt	Luther	L.M.
Praise the LORD, ye Heavens adore Him	115	* Scudamore	R. R. Chope	8, 7s.
Praise we our GOD with joy	276	* S. Lucy	R. R. Chope	6, 7s.

INDEX OF FIRST LINES.

FIRST LINE.	HYMN.	NAME OF TUNE.	AUTHOR, ETC.	METRE.
Praise we the LORD this day	286	* S. Nicolas	S. Gee	S.M.
Resting from His Work to-day	99	Redhead, No. 76	R. Redhead	7s (6 of.)
Ride on! Ride on! in majesty	84	* S. Drostane	J. B. Dykes	L.M.
ROCK of Ages! cleft for me	156	* Gethsemane	J. B. Dykes	7s (6 of.)
RULER of the Hosts of light	124	* S. Chad	J. B. Dykes	7s.
SAVIOUR, abide with us	112	* Emmaus	R. R. Chope	S.M.
SAVIOUR, when in dust to Thee	72	* Lent	J. B. Dykes	7s (8 of.)
See the destined day arise	87	Redhead No. 47	R. Redhead	7s.
Shadows are fled, a brighter ray	35	S. David	Ravenscroft's Psalter	C.M.
Soldiers of CHRIST, arise	254	* S. Edmund	E. T. Billings	S.M.
Songs of praise the Angels sang	189	Culbach	German	7s.
SON of the HIGHEST, deign to cast	233	* Peterborough	Bishop of Ely	C.M.
Sons of men, behold from far	49	* Wigan	T. Graham	7s.
So rest, my REST	97	Minden	Ch. Peter	4, 4, 7, 7, 6.
Source of Light and Life Divine	55	* S. Matthew	R. R. Chope	7s.
SPIRIT of GOD, That moved of old	129	* S. Machutus	R. B. Wall	L.M.
SPIRIT of mercy, truth, and love	130	* Bloomsbury	T. Graham	L.M.
SPIRIT of Wisdom, guide Thine Own	252	* Elvet	J. B. Dykes	C.M.
SUN of my soul, Thou SAVIOUR dear	219	* S. Catharine	R. F. Smith	L.M.
Sweet SAVIOUR, bless us ere we go	230	* Faber	R. R. Chope	8s (6 of.)
Sweet the moments, rich in blessing	74	Sychar	J. B. Dykes	8, 7s.
Take up thy Cross, the SAVIOUR said	193	* S. Prisca	R. R. Chope	L.M.
Thanks be to God! for meet and right	274	Worms	German	8,7,8,7,6,6,6,7.
The Advent of our GOD	2	Narenza	German	S.M.
The day is past and gone	231	Canterbury	Ravenscroft's Psalter	S.M.
The day is past and over	232	* S. Anatolius	J. B. Dykes	7, 6, 7, 6, 8, 8.
The Eternal SPIRIT'S Gifts	296	S. Petrock		S.M.
Thee we adore, O hidden SAVIOUR, Thee	238	* S. Britius	Ancient	10s.
The happy morn is come	108	* Lansdowne	R. R. Chope	6, 6, 6, 6, 8, 8.
The Head that once was crowned with thorns	185	* Brentwood	A. H. Brown	C.M.
The hymn for infant martyrs raise	31	S. Chrysostom	. . . .	8s (6 of.)
The Life which GOD'S Incarnate WORD	28	* S. Remigius	J. A. Lloyd	C.M.
The LORD will come, the earth shall quake	10	Spires	The Psalter	L.M.
The loved disciple of the LORD	29	S. Stephen	W. Jones	C.M.
There is a Fountain filled with Blood	80	* S. Hugh	E. J. Hopkins	C.M.
The Saints on earth and those above	190	* Horwood	S. Reay	C.M.
The SON of GOD goes forth to war	300	Thornton	Ravenscroft's Psalter	C.M.D.
The SPIRIT on the waters moved	245	Manheim	M. Prätorius	C.M.
The Strain upraise of Joy and Praise	163	* Dykes	J. B. Dykes	P.M.
The sun is sinking fast	229	* Caswall	R. R. Chope	6, 4, 6, 6.
The Voice that breathed o'er Eden	255	* S. Cecilia	R. R. Chope	7, 6s.
They come, GOD'S Messengers of Love	291	Woolmer	Sir F. A. G. Ouseley	L.M.
The year begins with Thee	36	Leipsic	Mendelssohn	S.M.
This day the Light, of Heavenly birth	138	* S. Denys	S. Reay	L.M.
Those whom one glory crowns above	294	Rochester	Dr. Gauntlett	C.M.

INDEX OF FIRST LINES.

FIRST LINE.	HYMN.	NAME OF TUNE.	AUTHOR, ETC.	METRE.
Thou art the Way, by Thee alone	165	Lincoln	Ravenscroft's Psalter	C.M.
Though clouds obscure the path we tread	268	Culross	Scotch Psalter	C.M.
Thou, LORD, the Hope of all the earth	262	London New	Scotch Psalter	C.M.
Thou Mighty Father, Prince of Peace	271	* Johnstone	G. Cooper	L.M.
Thou, O CHRIST, Thy Work hast done	122	* S. Colman	R. R. Chope	7s.
Thou Who camest from above	182	* Guisborough	C. T. Bowen	7s.
Thou, Who didst leave Thy FATHER'S Breast	6	* S. Benedict	T. G. Parry	C.M.
THREE IN ONE, and ONE IN THREE	135	Capetown	German Chorale	7, 7, 7, 5.
Thrice HOLY GOD, of wondrous might	139	S. Serf	H. Lahee	L.M.D.
'Tis for conquering kings to gain	152	Durham	Dr. Gauntlett	7s D.
To CHRIST, the Prince of Peace	141	* S. Etheldreda	Dr. Monk	S.M.
To Thee, O God, our praise belongs	272	. . .	Ancient	L.M.
Watch now, ye Christians, watch and pray	9	* S. Luke	Meyerbeer	8, 7s.
We praise Thee, O our GOD to Thee	250	* Brompton	G. Cooper	8s (6 of.)
We saw Thee not, when Thou didst come	146	Bremen	J. S. Bach	8s (6 of.)
We sing the praise of Him Who died	85	S. Simon	J. Milton	L.M.
When CHRIST, the LORD would come on earth	13	S. Jude	H. Müller	L.M.
When GOD of old came down from Heaven	127	Sinai	M. Hussey	C.M.
When I look back on all my sins	186	Cyprus	Bishop of Ely	L.M.
When I survey the wondrous Cross	96	* Calvary	Chiefly Eaton	L.M.
When morning gilds the skies	207	* S. Ode	R. R. Chope	6, 6, 6.
When on Creation's morn	256	* Croxdale	J. B. Dykes	S.M.
When our heads are bowed with woe	67	* Butterby	J. B. Dykes	7s.
When shades of night around us close	14	* S. Leonard	J. A. Lloyd	L.M.
Where Angelic Hosts adore Thee	202	* Pittington	J. B. Dykes	8, 7s.
Wherefore so heavy, O my soul	193	Carlisle	W. T. Best	C.M.
Where high the Heavenly Temple stands	123	* Monmouth	R. B. Wall	L.M.
While now with shades of night opprest	64	* Nathan	S. Gee	L.M.
While shepherds watched their flocks by night	19	Attalia	T. Tallis	C.M.
Whilst on the Cross Thy latest Breath	92	Babylon Streams	Scotch Psalter	L.M.
Why art thou weary, O my soul	181	S. Valentine	German	8, 7, 8, 7, 8, 8, 7.
Why SAVIOUR, dost Thou come	283	S. Michael	Psalter	S.M.
With CHRIST we share a mystic grave	162	Deptford	J. Selby	C.M.
Ye boundless realms of joy	54	Waterstock	J. Goss	6, 6, 6, 6, 4, 4, 4, 4.
Ye holy Angels bright	178	* Bickleigh	S. Reay	6, 6, 6, 6, 4, 4, 4, 4.
Ye servants of a martyred LORD	299	Goldel	Goldel	L.M.
Ye sons and daughters of the LORD	102	* Temple	E. J. Hopkins	8, 8, 8, 4.
Ye that pass by, behold the MAN	93	* Witham	R. R. Chope	L.M.
Zion, ope thy hallowed gates	285	* S. Clement	R. R. Chope	7s.

Hymns for the Sundays throughout the Year.

	MORNING. Hymn.		AFTERNOON. Hymn.		EVENING. Hymn.	
		*		*		*
SUNDAYS IN ADVENT:						
1	1	2	3	4	2	5
2	7	59	6	1	14	8
3	11	12	9	3	10	13
4	5	3	10	8	11	258
SUNDAYS AFTER CHRISTMAS:						
1	18	155	16	19	20	22
2	15	189	20	22	175	276
SUNDAYS AFTER EPIPHANY:						
1	39	46	41	42	44	43
2	40	45	46	47	49	48
3	208	50	40	51	45	51 p. 2
4	51 p. 3	187	49	48	39	228
5	207	41	47	43	48	51
6	47	52	51	167	147	52
SEPTUAGESIMA	53	54	57	60	197	55
SEXAGESIMA	173	59	53	54	57	61
QUINQUAGESIMA	58	56	173	55	61	60
SUNDAYS IN LENT:						
1	62	71	63	65	72	64
2	67	70	71	69	68	66
3	74	67	75	73	64	72
4 (Midlent)	76	77	156	79	80	78
5 (Passion)	82	81	80	173	95	96
6 (Palm)	84	83	81	82	85	156
EASTER DAY	100	101	103	109	102	101
SUNDAYS AFTER EASTER:						
1 (Low)	104	108	106	107	110	112
2	111	105	141	152	114	115
3	113	144	103	176	106	182
4	110	107	115	51	113	114
5 (Rogation)	111	105	106	110	103	107
SUNDAY AFTER ASCENSION DAY	117	121	120	142	123	124
WHIT SUNDAY	125	128	126	127	129	131
TRINITY SUNDAY	133	132	134	135	136	137
SUNDAYS AFTER TRINITY						
1	138	139	140	141	142	143
2	144	145	146	147	148	149
3	150	151	152	155	157	153
4	158	159	161	162	160	154

* The Hymn appointed in the second column is that, if any, which specially relates to the subject of the day.

HYMNS FOR THE SUNDAYS THROUGHOUT THE YEAR.—(CONTINUED.)

	MORNING. Hymn.		AFTERNOON. Hymn.		EVENING. Hymn.	
SUNDAYS AFTER TRINITY:		*		*		*
5	164	165	168	169	166	156
6	167	179	170	171	172	163
7	173	183	174	177	175	176
8	178	179	182	183	181	180
9	184	185	186	189	187	188
10	190	191	192	214	220	219
11	199	193	194	195	222	221
12	200	196	197	216	223	224
13	201	198	51	137	225	226
14	202	136	156	217	148	227
15	203	144	150	148	149	228
16	204	139	152	51 p. 2	150	229
17	205	140	153	218	231	230
18	206	137	154	140	152	232
19	207	148	214	144	51 p. 3	219
20	208	113	156	153	229	230
21	209	151	216	166	139	227
22	210	150	165	154	144	231
23	211	153	139	156	232	230
24	212	114	217	153	140	219
25	213	154	166	177	149	229
26	215	156	218	188	153	189

Hymns for Holy Days.

	Morning. Hymn.					Evening. Hymn.				
S. Andrew	296				281	184				281
S. Thomas	184				282	296				282
Christmas Eve	12				15	13				16
Christmas Day	18	19	17		23	20	21	22	24	25
S. Stephen	300				26	22				27
S. John	30				29	28				29
Holy Innocents	21				31	22				32
Circumcision	35				36	37				38
Epiphany	40				39	41				42
Conversion of S. Paul	147				283	283				284
Purification	174				285	289				285
S. Matthias	184				296	295				184
Annunciation	289				286	174				286
Ash Wednesday	63				62	66				68
HOLY WEEK. Monday before Easter	82				81	83				84
Tuesday " "	80				85	156				86
Wednesday " "	74				88	87				73
Thursday " "	89				237	95				90
Good Friday	92				91	93				94
Easter Eve	96				97	98				99
Monday in Easter Week	111				102	103				112
Tuesday in Easter Week	109				108	107				106
S. Mark	150				297	298				297
S. Philip and S. James	296				165	184				165
ROGATION. Monday before Ascension	113				116	188				77
Tuesday " "	170				164	146				116
Wednesday " "	67				116	169				228
Ascension Day (Holy Thursday)	117				118	119				122
Monday in Whitsun Week	125				130	126				127
Tuesday in Whitsun Week	129				131	142				185
S. Mary Magdalene, 22d July	186				233	194				233
Transfiguration, 6th August	175				234	155				235
Holy Name of JESUS, 7th August	170				38	195				236
S. Barnabas	298				296	185				296
S. John Baptist	12				287	12				287
S. Peter	299				288	184				288
S. James	184				296	298				300
S. Bartholomew	184				289	296				289
S. Matthew	297				290	298				290
S. Michael and All Angels	292				291	291				292
S. Luke	297				293	297				293
S. Simon and S. Jude	298				296	296				184
All Saints	190				294	190				295

Hymns for Certain Days and Occasions.

		Morning. Hymn.	Afternoon. Hymn.	Evening. Hymn.
WEEKLY.	Monday	199　201	209	218　225
	Tuesday	202　204	214	219　226
	Wednesday	203　206	216	220　227
	Thursday	201　208	211	221　228
	Friday	207　210	222	223　229
	Saturday	215　213	217	224　230

DAILY, Ps. cxix. 164.	Before six o'clock, A.M.,	202
	At six " "	207
	" nine " "	212
	" twelve " noon	213
	" three " P.M.	214
	" six " "	228
	" nine " "	232

At Midnight (Ps. cxix. 62.) . . . 223, 220, 231.

Holy Communion	237, 238, 239, 240, 241, 242, 243.
Holy Baptism	244, 245, 162.
School Festivals	246, 247, 248, 249, 250.
Confirmation	251, 252, 253, 254, 180, 125, 131.
Holy Matrimony	255, 256.
Visitation of the Sick	257, 198, 186, 181, 171, 162, 157, 148.
Burial of the Dead	258, 158, 157, 67, 1.

Ember Days	259, 260, 125, 131.
Missions	261, 262, 263.
Harvest	264, 265, 266.
" Deficiency of Crops	269.
In Times of Trouble	267, 268.
" " Famine	269.
" " War	270, 271.
" " Pestilence	269.
Friendly Societies	272, 273.
Thanksgiving	274, 275, 276, 191, 151.
Foundation Stone of a Church	277.
Dedication of a Church	278, 279, 280.
New Year's Eve	33, 34.
New Year's Day	33, 34, 35, 36, 37, 38.

THE PRAYER BOOK, NOTED

AND

POINTED

THROUGHOUT ALL ITS SERVICES,

With Numerous Chants and Accompanying Harmonies.

BY THE

REV. R. R. CHOPE, B.A.,

ASSISTED BY

REV. R. F. SMITH, M.A., SOUTHWELL; AND J. TURLE, ESQ., ORGANIST OF WESTMINSTER ABBEY.

READY.

The VERSICLES, CANTICLES, LITANY, ATHANASIAN CREED, EASTER ANTHEMS, and PSALTER, Noted and Pointed, with HARMONIES, in Cloth, lettered.

VERSICLES, CANTICLES, LITANY, ATHANASIAN CREED, and EASTER ANTHEMS.
   Ditto,   ditto,   ditto,   bound in Cloth, gilt lettered.

CANTICLES and EASTER ANTHEMS, Pointed and Noted.

LITANY (in full) and EASTER ANTHEMS, Pointed, with HARMONIES.

PRECES and ATHANASIAN CREED, Pointed, with HARMONIES.

PSALTER, Noted and Pointed, bound in Cloth.

ACCOMPANYING HARMONIES, to the GREGORIAN TONES, Cloth, gilt lettered.

IN THE PRESS.

COMMUNION SERVICE.

CONFIRMATION, BURIAL SERVICES, &c., &c.

ACCOMPANYING HARMONIES to the whole PRAYER BOOK, Noted.

The PRAYER BOOK, Noted and Pointed throughout, with all the PRAYERS, RUBRICS, HARMONIES, &c., in full.

* LARGE SIZE of Ditto, for Altar, Desk, and Organ Use.

    * 25 Copies of this Edition will be printed on Vellum for Illumination.

"In the books hitherto pointed for Gregorian Chants, many of the Psalms and Canticles are badly set; the harmonies are faulty; very many of the melodies are *not* pure; further change of chant is impossible, though they have far too little change of tune or key for either the Psalms or Canticles; many of the best Gregorian Mediations and Endings have been omitted; the syllabic notation is too much, or is wrongly insisted on; and the whole plan of using the antique square note and unintelligible stave of four lines, with notes, nevertheless, in modern character for the harmonies, is needlessly perplexing.

"The design of the present Work is to *remedy* these defects."—*Preface*.

LONDON: WILLIAM MACKENZIE, 22 PATERNOSTER ROW;
SIMPKIN, MARSHALL, & CO., STATIONERS' HALL COURT.

NOW READY,

THE CONGREGATIONAL HYMN AND TUNE BOOK,

CONTAINING

Three Hundred different Four-Part Tunes, with their Hymns, from Ancient and Modern Sources.

BY THE

REV. R. R. CHOPE, B.A.,

ASSISTED BY

REV. J. B. DYKES, M.A., Mus. Doc., and late Precentor of Durham Cathedral;

W. T. BEST, Esq., Organist of St. George's Hall, Liverpool;

G. COOPER, Esq., Organist of Her Majesty's Chapels Royal;

REV. R. F. SMITH, M.A., Southwell;

E. J. HOPKINS, Esq., Organist of the Temple Church, London;

DR. MONK, Organist of York Cathedral;

J. TURLE, Esq., Organist of Westminster Abbey;

AND OTHERS.

PRICES.

		s.	d.		s.	d.
Imperial 16mo.—Cloth boards, gilt lettered, red edges, fine tinted paper,		5	6	to the Clergy	4	6
Ditto	Cloth boards, gilt lettered, without red edges,	5	0	......	4	0
Ditto	Limp Cloth, turned in, on second paper, without the Preface,	3	6	......	3	0
Ditto	Limp Cloth, cut flush, ditto, ditto,	2	6	......	2	2
S. Royal 18mo.—Cloth boards, gilt lettered, red edges, fine tinted paper,		2	6	......	2	2
Ditto	Limp Cloth,	1	6	......	1	2

THE HYMNAL.

		s.	d.		s.	d.
Royal 32mo.—Cloth boards, gilt lettered, red edges, fine tinted paper,		0	10	to the Clergy	0	9
Ditto	Limp Cloth, cut flush, on second paper,	0	6	......	0	5
Demy 32mo.—Glazed Cloth, on second paper,		0	4	......	0	3

IN THE PRESS.—Hymns with Treble Part; Hymns, in large type, for the Drawing-room; ditto, ditto for the Cottage; and an Edition with the Tunes only.

FIRST EDITION OF THE ABOVE.

CONTAINING ONE HUNDRED AND SIX HYMNS AND TUNES.

		s.	d.
PRICES.—In Cloth, gilt lettered, red edges,		1	6
Paper,		0	10
THE HYMNAL, in Cloth, red edges,		0	4
Ditto	Paper,	0	2
Ditto	Large Type,	0	6

Ditto, to the Clergy, for the Poor, through Rev. R. R. CHOPE (9 Ovington Square, Brompton, S.W.):—
PRICES:—In Cloth, 1s.; Paper, 6d.; THE HYMNAL, in Cloth, 3d.; Paper, 1d.; Large Type, 4d.

"Pre-eminently *the* Hymnal for the People."—*Church of the People.*

LONDON: WILLIAM MACKENZIE, 22 PATERNOSTER ROW;
SIMPKIN, MARSHALL, & CO., STATIONERS' HALL COURT.

www.ingramcontent.com/pod-product-compliance
Lightning Source LLC
Chambersburg PA
CBHW030253240426
43673CB00040B/962